LONGEING THE RIDER FOR A PERFECT SEAT

A HOW-TO GUIDE
FOR RIDERS, INSTRUCTORS, AND LONGEURS

LINDA BENEDIK

TRAFALGAR SQUARE
NORTH POMFRET, VERMONT

First published in 2007 by
Trafalgar Square Books
North Pomfret, Vermont 05053

Printed in China

Disclaimer of Liability
The author and publisher shall have neither liability nor responsibility to any person or entity with respect to any loss or damage caused or alleged to be caused directly or indirectly by the information contained in this book. While the book is as accurate as the author can make it, there may be errors, omissions, and inaccuracies.

Library of Congress Cataloging-in-Publication Data

Benedik, Linda.
Longeing the rider for a perfect seat : a how-to guide for riders, instructors, and longeurs / Linda Benedik.
p. cm.
Includes bibliographical references and index.
ISBN 978-1-57076-384-7 (alk. paper)
1. Horsemanship--Study and teaching. I. Title.
SF310.5.B46 2007
798.2'3--dc22
2007030483

Photo credits: Megan Draheim (pp. 5 *top*, 5 *bottom*, 16, 21 *left*, 21 *right*, 28, 37, 50 *top & middle*, 51, 54, 56, 66, 71, 77, 81, 87, 89, 90, 92 *top*, 97 *right*, 101, 103, 105, 106, 107, 108, 110, 111 *right*, 112, 114, 116, 119 *top left & right*, 121 *left*, 123, 125, 126, 129, 130, 131, 132, 166, 177, 191, 195, 197, 199, 207); Kathy Andrle (pp. i, 1, 3, 7, 8, 11, 12, 14, 15 *top*, 18, 21 *middle*, 22, 23, 24, 29, 33, 36, 38, 40, 44, 48, 57 *bottom*, 61, 68, 70, 73, 75, 84, 85, 86, 91, 92 *bottom*, 93, 94, 96, 97 *left*, 99, 104, 109, 111 *left & middle*, 115, 117, 119 *bottom*, 120, 121 *middle & right*, 128, 133, 136, 145, 147, 154 *bottom left*, 159, 160, 164, 165, 168, 169 *right*, 171, 185, 189, 202, 203, 210, 214, 218, 219 *top left & right*, 220); Linda Benedik (pp. 5 *bottom*, 17, 19, 20, 30, 41, 42 *top*, 49, 57 *top*, 64 *top*, 65, 88, 113, 127, 140, 169 *left*, 201, 209, 211, 212 *left*, 213, 214, 215 *top & middle*, 216, 217, 218, 219 *bottom left*); Deirdre Lewis (pp. 35, 54, 55, 64 *bottom*); Holiday Reinhorn (39, 42 *middle left & right*, 50, 52); Valley View Vaulting (pp. 212 *right*, 215 *bottom*, 219 *bottom right*); Janine Pizano (p. 43 *middle & bottom*); Julia Bruns (pp. 42 *bottom*, 43 *top*); Gregory Helm (p. 219 *middle left*); Roy Elderkin (p. 224)

Illustration credits: Greg Mondin (pp. 45, 47, 48, 96, 103, 104, 126, 129, 131, 137, 151, 194); Rebecca Burke (pp. 4, 6, 12, 13, 23, 25, 27, 38, 59, 91, 172); Linda Benedik (pp. 90, 174, 176, 180, 183, 186, 188); David Kaufman (pp. 175, 182, 187)

Book and cover design by Carrie Fradkin
Typeface: Stone Sans

10 9 8 7 6 5 4 3 2 1

Dedication

To the equine teachers that helped present this program—Radar, Grandly, Amadeus, Gustavo—and to lesson horses everywhere for their contribution to rider education.

Contents

Introduction

"Perfection" is a concept that all riders aspire to, whether conscious of it or not—perfect equitation, the elusive perfect ten in a dressage test, a perfectly flawless jumping round, or simply a blissful moment of perfect communication with their horse.

Because this equestrian ambition is universal, perfection motivates riders of any discipline, ability, and experience to want to succeed on horseback. To help riders more clearly and patiently work toward this common equestrian goal, this book, aptly entitled *Longeing the Rider for a Perfect Seat*, presents my Riding Without Reins longeing program to guide you from wherever you are in your development, to a more "perfect" riding seat and position.

Certainly, achieving a "perfect seat" is a fantasy—as we all know, our riding performance can never really be completely perfect. Each rider, regardless of age or experience, is a work in progress, and each rider's idea of "perfect" is something a little different: the dressage rider strives for a deeper, more influential seat, the hunter/jumper rider a lighter and more agile seat, the rider of a cutting horse a more responsive, adaptable seat, and so on. However, with participation in my Riding Without Reins longeing program, *every* rider can be assured of taking the necessary strides toward these related, but variable aspects of seat "perfection." Remember, success in any riding endeavor is, in short, *all about the seat*!

A long-established practice, longeing is vital to both horse and rider training. But while there are several excellent books and videos available that teach you how to longe horses properly, or incorporate longeing in your horse training program, the specifics on how to longe a rider were traditionally passed down orally, and a full program of detailed instructions has not been available in book form—until now.

Longeing benefits every rider by enhancing safety and enjoyment, and is the ideal venue for honing rider basics. In learning to ride, you come to realize that your body is a symphony of parts, and becoming proficient with your "instruments" is necessary before orchestrating them together to effectively communicate with the horse. Because you can more rapidly refine *self-control* without your reins, longeing is an indispensable opportunity to master your instruments while learning to adapt synchronously to the horse's movement. By progressing through the natural stages of seat development while on the longe line—transitioning from passenger to follower, then to leader—riders acquire the prerequisite skills to secure their seat independently of the limbs, and thus earn the right to pick up the reins and pursue their chosen competitive or recreational activity on horseback.

Since longeing is often perceived as a beginner practice, a fateful consequence for those not blessed with a good seat, or a dreary excursion into monotony, you may wonder what new light I could possibly shed on the practice of repetitiously riding on a circle. In truth, there is a wealth of personal insights that riders at any level can acquire on the longe. And in our never-ending quest for riding mastery, riders today should understand this—history has proven that longeing doesn't just promise, it *guarantees* more direct skill advancement.

For beginners, longeing enables a correct basic seat from the start. For seasoned riders, it promotes refinement. Although developing an independent, influential seat is a learned process, longeing is *dedicated* to that mission and provides ongoing opportunities for maintaining and improving skills. Longeing *maximizes* learning—shaving off months, possibly years of struggle and frustration—developing the sensitivities of the rider while preserving those of the horse, and promoting safety and enjoyment regardless of the reasons we ride.

Riding will always be complex, but the learning process *can* be easier and more direct, and with this book I will show you how. For nearly four decades my career has been dedicated to upholding the equestrian traditions passed down to me through teachers, academic study, and apprenticeships. As an educator, I have applied the classical principles in a practical, holistic manner when training innumerable riders to cultivate a balanced, supple, correct position on horseback.

Over time, I devised ways to streamline the equestrian learning process by blending complementary mind-body techniques—such as yoga and other tools for "skilled relaxation"—with traditional riding instruction to facilitate the acquisition of basic riding skills, sculpt the rider's position, and promote his or her confidence and balance in motion.

Now, in the pages that follow, I will share my methods and explain how riding on the longe line can develop the balanced position you long for and the independent aids you know you need—indeed, if there ever was a direct route to riding mastery, longeing is it! And with its deep-rooted history, consistently positive results, and promise to better every rider while offering a safe learning environment, as a teaching aid longeing is to me, in fact, pretty close to "perfection."

Note to the Reader

This book was not written with only riders in mind—it is designed as a resource for *riders, instructors,* and *longeurs*. While riders will discover a practical system that will help them develop self-control and an independent balanced seat, instructors and longeurs will find how-to guidelines for effectively, safely, and constructively longeing students, fellow instructors, and riding friends. Handy sidebars throughout illustrate specific hands-on bodywork to do with riders on the longe, and I've highlighted important notes and tips instructors and longeurs should specifically keep in mind as they work.

The lessons provided in this book are easily modified and applied to riders of all levels of experience and styles of riding. Although the pictures throughout show horses and riders outfitted in English-style tack and riding clothes, my program is just as applicable to Western riders of all abilities and ages. As in English disciplines, Western riding sports require a seat that is quiet, balanced, and secure and hands that do not interfere with the horse's ability to do his job. The exercises in this book blend longeing traditions with my unique approach to equestrian education and can provide riders the basic seat they need in order to progress from just "holding on" to truly riding with awareness, proficiency, and *feel*.

In addition, many equestrians may have recently become aware of the increasingly popular sport of *equestrian vaulting*—a kind of gymnastics on horseback—when American Megan Benjamin won the individual gold medal and the Women's World Vaulting Championship title, and Team USA won the silver medal, at the 2006 World Equestrian Games in Aachen, Germany. This competitive sport is not only growing in the United States, but vaulting basics (such as dismounting safely from a moving horse) are now offered to riders of all levels as a way to increase security and confidence on horseback and develop the seat. Because of the value I feel this kind of training offers riders of any age, style, or discipline (again on a longe line and without reins), I've included a discussion of "vaulting for riders" in the Appendix, p. 209.

For those who may wonder where the art of rider longeing developed as equitation evolved in various parts of the world, and for those who are curious as to what role it will play in the future of riding instruction and rider seat development, a brief section touching upon these areas follows the vaulting chapter on p. 223.

Finally, throughout the book horses are referred to as "he" and riders, instructors, and longeurs as both "he" and "she," unless a specific horse or person is named in a photograph or example. This is not intended to be sexist or to misrepresent the majority of horses, riders, and instructors, but is only a device used to keep the book as clear and simple as possible for the reader.

PART I

FOUNDATION FOR RIDER LONGEING

Winning the horse's trust and relaxation takes the greatest patience and self-discipline, a lesson that riders can learn only if they are made aware of the necessity of learning it.

WALTER ZETTL

CHAPTER 1

About Riding without Reins

Once the rider obtains the feeling of riding in harmony, he can never again accept anything less. You may ask how we achieve such harmony. Is this the realm of a few "naturally born" horsemen and horses, a state with doors barred against all but the anointed? In fact, it is an achievable goal for those who choose to study, work and care…if you love horses, then riding in harmony is the only way to proceed.

WALTER ZETTL

In my work as an instructor, I've met people participating in all levels of riding, performing in many different disciplines, who are still seeking help with their seat. They ask me "I know what I *should* be doing, but how do I get there from here?" And, I've met beginners who have the impression that learning to ride is a straightforward process—an assumption that results perhaps from our technological slant on life, or watching Hollywood films and accomplished show riders make it look easy! However, as soon as the challenges are revealed and students become aware of the multiple tasks they must manage simultaneously—grappling with countless "things to do" on the horse—they too ask me questions: "Which tasks are most important" How do I prioritize? Where do I begin?

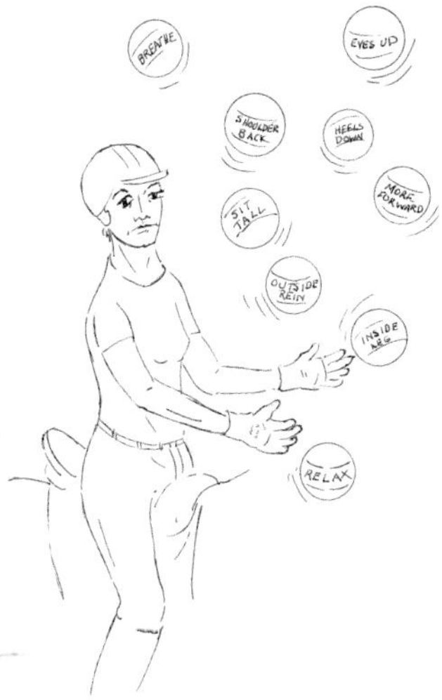

Fig. 1.1 *Learning to ride correctly can seem overwhelming—for many, it represents "multi-tasking at its finest"! Because being longed temporarily reduces your responsibilities, it enables you to ease into the rider's role by concentrating only on balance and self-control. This helps you become organized and learn to juggle an increasing number of mounted tasks simultaneously.*

The answers and solution can be found in my program Riding Without Reins, which is the subject of this book, *Longeing the Rider for a Perfect Seat*. Being longed temporarily takes away your reins, and you are relieved of such tasks as managing the horse's speed, direction, balance and alignment. It reduces your long list of riding responsibilities.

A long-established practice, rider longeing is vital to both rider and horse training. The Spanish Riding School in Vienna, Austria, provides an enduring example of its value. There, longeing the rider is the tried and true method of training riders, who initially spend an average of six months on the longe, and nothing else. For the next three years or more, daily longeing is accompanied by regular riding lessons. As a result, pupils are revered worldwide for their exemplary seats and impeccable equitation.

What Rider Longeing Can Do for You

For beginners, longeing promptly secures confidence and safety, and is a good introduction to rider basics. The sequential skill building offered in this program also ensures that horses are ridden correctly (fig. 1.2).

For more well-seasoned riders, being longed helps to refine their seat, polish skills, assess strengths and weaknesses, and fill in gaps (fig. 1.3). It is a way to maximize time, effort, and resources dedicated to seat development, and sets riders on the path to "self-control" over their body and mind and reaching the ultimate goal, which is *an independent seat* (see p. 14).

Being longed allows you to focus first on acquiring a *feel* of the horse before attempting to control him. All riders will benefit from learning *feel*, a quality many trainers consider very difficult to teach. However, a rider's *feel* can be developed by being longed, which:

- keeps the learning environment safe and controlled

- slows down the pace initially, and then brings it up to tempo
- teaches the rider to work with gravity, not fight against it
- prompts the rider to synchronize breathing and movement by counting

What Rider Longeing Can Do for the Horse

And now, maybe even more important, riding without reins benefits the horse who suffers most from an uneducated seat and an unskilled rider who relies on reins for balance. Riding without reins preserves the horse's sensitive mouth, preventing any unconscious misuse of hands that could cause him pain or discomfort. Though, our hands may be the most adept, trainable body parts we possess, they are what we rely on *instinctively* for steadying ourselves when unstable. For that very reason, the reins are temporary withheld when you are being longed until you learn independence and can use the reins for communication, not for balance.

The courtesy you extend to the horse by developing your seat benefits you as well, since any equine resistance that unskilled hands inadvertently trigger puts you at risk. By eliminating the possibility of "hand riding," and relying on the person longeing for *horse control* until you have acquired sufficient *self-control* to take over, you promote your own safety and enjoyment of riding.

Fig. 1.2 *Being longed on a seasoned horse by an experienced instructor offers a safe, controlled learning environment that enables a beginner to more readily relax and develop a feel for the gaits.*

Fig. 1.3 *Since Gerardo, a more experienced rider, has by now developed an independent control of his seat and limbs, adding the use of the reins on the longe line reinforces his basic skills and enables him to contribute to the horse's training.*

Tension and Relaxation

Due to hurried lifestyles and an overabundance of stress, modern riders typically face "obstacles"—thoughts and behaviors blocking the ability to connect with horses. Our greatest enemy, by far, is *tension*—disturbing us physically, mentally, emotionally, and manifesting in the horse. As a clinician, I have become concerned with the degree of tension I see in riders today. Students frequently describe the difficulty they have relaxing on horseback, and the disappointment that instructors are not teaching them *how*. I sympathize with riders, and realize that most riding instructors today have never received the specific tools to guide human beings on horseback into a relaxed, receptive state of mind-body. Generally speaking, *skilled rider relaxation* is not a subject typically addressed by conventional equestrian lesson plans.

Fig. 1.4 *Stress is an unavoidable by-product of living in our world today. Bursting into the horse's quietude is inconsiderate—we must make an honest effort to leave worries behind and de-stress beforehand.*

The familiar directive "*Relax*!" shouted at a tense rider rarely triggers the appropriate response. Rather, it usually compounds the inability to relax. My strategy for inspiring relaxation in Riding Without Reins starts by addressing obstacles such as tension, fear, and poor posture, and providing optimum conditions for safe learning in a controlled environment—on the longe—where relaxation can be developed as purposefully as posting the trot.

Breathing

After years of evaluating the connection between rider breathing and performance, I've observed common obstacles related to shallow, irregular breathing and holding the breath. These unconscious habits are detrimental to performance, yet perpetuated in every riding discipline. Instruction that calls for an occasional deep breath or delivers well-intended reminders to "*Breathe*!" is benign, and does not result in the rider adapting more productive breathing habits. However, with conscious breath work, riders can learn to dissolve tension, create stability, and regulate rhythm with breath control.

Taking the unconscious act of breathing and making it conscious *while in motion on the horse* is a powerful skill that can lead to observable transformations in rider and horse *often within minutes*. As described in my previous book *Yoga for Equestrians*, it is advantageous to learn conscious breathing in an unmounted setting first, then on horseback. The exercises in Riding Without Reins include prompts to promote breath awareness and control, which can lend a greater sense of ease and calm to everything you do on horseback.

Yoga

Another discipline that harnesses the power of breath is yoga: a 5,000-year-old practice that, literally translated, means "union." Hatha, the most popular

Fig. 1.5 *Blending hatha yoga bodywork and breath work with traditional mounted exercises renews energy and enthusiasm for rider longeing.*

yoga today, helps connect your physical, mental, emotional, and spiritual aspects through postures (asana) and breath control exercises (pranayama). Personal experiences in yoga have expanded my repertoire, and provided supplementary tools for fostering mind-body riding skills in my students and myself. Integrating yoga increases a rider's opportunity for self-discovery; it complements equestrian learning by relieving stress and developing self-discipline. Asana (Sanskrit for "a seat") and pranayama can be practiced both on and off the longe, facilitating your ability to interpret the classical blueprint for a balanced seat and position. By securing your foundation with longeing, you can achieve the artful "flow-experience" of union on horseback, often described as transcendent—moving you beyond mundane mechanics to feeling united with the spirit of the horse (fig. 1.5).

The Most Basic Riding Requirement: Self-Control

With everything riding entails, this is one particular assignment that should represent your most fundamental task. It is aptly described by Alois Podhajsky, former Director of the Spanish Riding School in Vienna and author of several books including *The Complete Training of Horse and Rider in the Principles of Classical Horsemanship* (and a riding master who has had a huge influence on my career as a rider and instructor): "Absolute self-control is the basic requirement for every rider. He must not only be able to control his body but also his temperament." Rider self-control develops in stages, from elementary to sophisticated. The level *you* require is directly proportionate to your goals. For occasional trail riding on a bombproof horse, a low level of self-control may suffice. For international-level competition, a much greater level is required. No matter how serious or casual your riding—how classical, contemporary, recreational, or competitive—you owe it to yourself and the horse to develop the appropriate degree of physical, mental, and emotional self-discipline for your chosen mounted activities. Self-control prevents riders from inadvertently disturbing the horse, thereby encouraging his cooperation and desire to participate with his rider.

Achieving this basic requirement is not merely a theoretical aspect of riding—it is indeed a safety measure. In the absence of discomfort, pain, or confusion, trust grows and a horse demonstrates his willingness. When connected with his rider, he affords insights into rhythm, balance, and movement that only a confident equine imparts. The more refined our self-control, the more trust we inspire, the more a horse will teach. Modern master Charles de Kunffy affirms, "Good riding... is grounded in self-discipline. Without self-discipline, a rider cannot gain the horse's confidence, and so the guide will fail to guide him" (fig. 1.6). When you reflect on self-control being your most "basic" requirement, really contemplate what that means within the context of your own riding; you'll more clearly see your priorities as a rider.

Fig. 1.6 *Christa is well on her way, through self-discipline, to achieving a balanced, independent seat.*

What's in Store

Riding Without Reins takes a *holistic* approach to rider longeing, which not only addresses physical posture and performance but also guides riders to focus wandering thoughts and neutralize emotions. By combining traditional mounted exercises with yoga, conscious breath work, and hands-on bodywork, it demonstrates how a rider can create a personal balance that leads to a deeper self-understanding and connection with the horse. While this program focuses on developing a *basic seat* (see p. 14), it also includes exercises in the *forward* or *two-point* seat (see p. 16) to enhance balance and strength.

Even if the exercises seem simplistic or you've done them many times before, don't rush through them—I've included prompts for when to inhale and exhale, so each exercise can help you become more aware of your breath while riding. Since conscious breathing on the horse may be a new practice for you, it is a good reason to start this program from the beginning and apply conscious breathing to everything you do on horseback, even mounting. As you practice, strive to keep your body animated with breath and in sync with the horse while remaining open to new insights.

The accompanying photographs depict students demonstrating longe-line exercises on lesson horses. They are not experts, but "works-in-progress." Please use the photos as guides; your personal experiences will be unique.

I'll continue here in Part I, by discussing how to establish and develop a good seat. In Part II, I then address the rider being longed, as well as the instructor or "longeur" and what they all need to know. I describe a suitable longeing arena, footing, and circle size; necessary tack, equipment and attire. How to longe a horse, structure a rider longing session, and how to be safe are important chapters. Part III introduces the Riding Without Reins longeing program starting with suppling exercises to be learned first at the halt. Each exercise is laid out with benefits, steps, tips, notes to the instructor, and points to remember. Part IV presents seat work in motion on the horse, guiding you to follow the horse initially in slow gaits, then to lead him actively with your seat, leg, and weight as you work toward riding on the longe in rhythm with an independent seat at all three gaits. The goal of Riding Without Reins is realized as your seat is secured, you become ready to take your reins, and further advance into horse training, if you so desire.

Summary

The Riding Without Reins program is the ideal training method for achieving a solid foundation at any level. The longeur takes responsibility for horse control while, freed from this task, the rider can focus on acquiring "basics" such as *awareness*, *relaxation*, and *alignment*, while eliminating "obstacles" such as *tension*, *gripping*, and *incoordination.* Consequently, the rider can more readily develop the balanced seat and mind-body skills that are so necessary for effective communication with the horse. Being longed provides riders with the opportunity to *participate* in the horse's movement, and gain a more rapid *feel* of the gaits. When skills and feel are confirmed at a basic level, riders may be content with this achievement or opt to pursue more advanced riding, equestrian sports, or horse training. As these involve a greater sophistication of skills, periodic longeing is a great way for advanced riders to reinforce their basic training, and to promote good riding habits while refining self-control.

CHAPTER 2

How to Develop a Correct Seat

It took thousands of years to craft the vocabulary with which we could convey our wishes to the horse, and it took equally long to listen to his messages in silent meditation. Riders have a duty and an obligation to their equine teachers to make sure that these seamless, secret languages—that allow the flow of thought from man to horse and the flow of energy from horse to man—will continue to be passed on to others.

CHARLES DE KUNFFY

What is Equitation?

If we want to communicate with our horses we must first acknowledge that, to them, every expression of our body has content and meaning. Every movement becomes a word, a sentence, a paragraph: information.

KLAUS FERDINAND HEMPFLING

Equitation is the rider's method of communicating with the horse through body language. Well-rounded riders develop equitation on the flat and over fences. They are as competent riding through varied terrain as in an arena. Some riders choose to specialize—in dressage or hunt seat equitation, for example. While it is not the intention of this book to serve as an equitation manual, it promotes a general understanding and the process by which it is most logically learned.

Fig. 2.1 *Equitation is the rider's body language. Learning to communicate nonverbally requires mastery of our most basic requirement: self-control.*

Equitation involves conversing with the horse through our sense of touch and weight distribution, while conveying specific messages to generate the desired reactions (fig. 2.1). The clarity of your exchange relies on many factors—the horse's training, your training, and in particular, your ability to balance talking with listening as in any productive conversation. With this ability you can perform riding maneuvers, in or out of an arena, layering more technical skills upon the basics as you progress.

What is required before you can "speak" in this specialized language is a foundation in these rider basics, including familiarity with the horse's movements and your own. Being longed helps every rider cultivate these skills much more easily than just riding alone. Accomplishing your objectives in all three gaits on the longe line helps you *know how the horse's movements feel* before attempting to direct them yourself. Readiness for using reins and taking the leadership role is determined by your self-control on horseback. Once you can isolate arms, legs, and maintain balance without excessive grip, you are ready to learn equitation.

Active and Passive Aids

"Natural aids" are the physical messages used to help the horse understand. We "talk" with body parts in isolation or in concert with one another by applying a specific touch or pressure—the *active* aids. We "listen" by releasing pressure so the horse can respond as we yield to his movement—the *passive* aids. Once we ask something, we must then allow it. This represents the proverbial balance of "give and take" or "reward and punishment" that riders often hear of, but don't always learn how to implement.

Active Aids

It is the propensity of riders, often guided by well-meaning instructors, to focus on "doing something" to the horse from Day One, "talking" vigorously by kicking, pulling, squeezing hard, and bracing. In addition, excess activity often consists of unconscious muscle clenching—isometric contractions that do not cause an arm or leg to move, just tighten—making it difficult to detect by rider or instructor. An overabundance of physical activity can become an ingrained habit. The more riders use their aids to "shout" or pester the horse, the harder it is to modify this behavior.

Passive Aids

"Doing nothing" or *deactivating* specific muscle groups or body parts defines the passive aids, which are essentially the absence of active aids. A "deficit" in passivity (i.e. an inability to do nothing) is a mainstream "learning gap," which must be addressed in order to be able implement aids correctly.

Being longed "cultivates" passivity. When a rider develops passive aids *first*, it becomes easier for him to integrate the *active aids* into his riding afterward. However, if a rider has been overly "active" for some time, becoming passive is a challenge and involves revamping established riding behavior.

For example, when applying lower legs to *drive* the horse, a rider may unknowingly tighten thighs and knees, which *restricts* the horse. The upper legs aren't likely to change position, but their clenching can cause problems often blamed on the horse that is trying to decipher simultaneous pushing *and* restraining aids. What usually results is the horse lacks impulsion, regularity, or frequently falls out of gaits. Since his behavior is more distinguishable, it's easier to point out his faults: he is *"not through,"* or he *"must go forward,"* while the rider's contribution to this conflict tends to remain unidentified. Until the rider's upper legs yield and allow the horse to respond correctly, he may incur the rider's "wrath" through even more forceful driving aids, and the horse eventually goes numb (fig. 2.3).

Particularly from a rider's point of view, we ought to understand that in music the silences are as important as the notes. So it is in riding that the times of introspective passivity in harmony with the horse's action are as important as the times giving the aids.

CHARLES DE KUNFFY

Fig. 2.3 *An inappropriate combination of pushing and restraining aids is like "driving with the brake on," and blocks the forward energy a rider may struggle to create. Legs that command "stop" and "go" simultaneously are all too often accompanied by overly active hands in an attempt to get the horse "on the bit."*

Such an aiding system is called "independent" because the seat is adhesive enough to follow the horse's movements, allowing the rider's limbs, as well as his torso to be utilized at will for purposeful communication.

CHARLES DE KUNFFY

Independent Aids

The rider's goal is to attain an *independent seat*—one that performs without disrupting the horse. This is an important quality and until is solidly confirmed, you will not have an *influential* seat, that is, one trained to direct the horse and subsequently improve his performance.

An excellent example of an independent seat is seen in vaulting, where coordinated physical control develops without any intention to influence the horse. (I discuss vaulting in some detail, along with photos, on p. 209). In contrast, riders today (especially those taking dressage lessons) often attempt to influence horses before acquiring sufficient independence of seat. Before expecting to exert a positive influence on the horse, and before dressage or any horse training is attempted, riders must be in control of their own body.

Fig. 2.4 *Here I'm helping Jenny cultivate isolated control of her arms and hands, one of the requirements absolutely necessary in order to gain an independent seat.*

Isolated control of arms, legs, torso, and seat is essential, as you fulfill a multitude of physical tasks while riding. This is a huge challenge as your legs are not going to mirror the action of your hands, nor will they always mirror each other. Likewise, hands may or may not act in unison on the horse (fig. 2.4). Relative to the horse's bend, your inside and outside aids take on specific roles. Even the left and right halves of your pelvis must function independently, to deliver weight aids and follow the gaits. Riding situations at any time may require the application of aids in isolation or various combinations, and it is the independence in your seat and aids that enables you to do this.

While this sounds complex and technical, it is more easily understood once we have established a tactile relationship and *feel* of the horse's movement. Toward that end, longeing is indispensable. The key to achieving independence—and overcoming many rider challenges—is *releasing the resistance to movement* that manifests as physical tension and unconscious grip. "Release" is facilitated by many exercises in this book. Your ability to sit passively with arms and legs hanging freely, letting your limbs be jostled, lifted, and dropped by the horse, leads to an independent physical control before influencing is even required.

The Basic Seat

In his book, *Dancing with Horses,* Klaus Ferdinand Hempfling writes: "Sitting a horse seems to be one of the most complicated parts of riding—at least that is the impression given by riding schools and riding students. I maintain that a person with a body of normal mobility can learn to sit a horse in one to three hours on the lunge line, especially if he is an absolute beginner at riding. It is important though that the biomechanics of the horse in all gaits have first been made understandable to the rider...and that he can, with closed eyes, feel the movement and find his way into it."

The riding seat is an instrument of communication—a natural aid—and direct receptor of the horse. It provides a base for contact and anchors us in movement (fig. 2.5). We both *talk* and *listen* through the seat—it is our most valuable asset. Educating the seat involves getting to know a part of our body we may not think about, much less use for communication. Fortunately, there is a way our seat can be trained to move *rhythmically* and with *feel* through a course of rider basics on the longe line, which I present to students at any level in my Riding Without Reins program.

Riding Without Reins teaches the *basic seat*, which is also known as the *balanced seat, full seat, three-point, classical*, or *dressage seat.* It is the prescribed position for English and Western equitation on the flat, and a logical prerequisite for learning other positions, such as the *forward seat*, also called *two-point* (see p. 16).

You do not sit a horse as you sit in most other settings. In fact, the rider's basic seat is a learned posture that has more in common with the way you *stand*—properly aligned spine, head balanced on neck, shoulders over hips, hips over heels (fig. 2.6).

As I said above, the *basic seat* is called the "three-point seat," as it balances on a triangular base of support formed by our

Fig. 2.5 *Anatomically, the rider's seat is comprised of the region from waist to mid-thigh.*

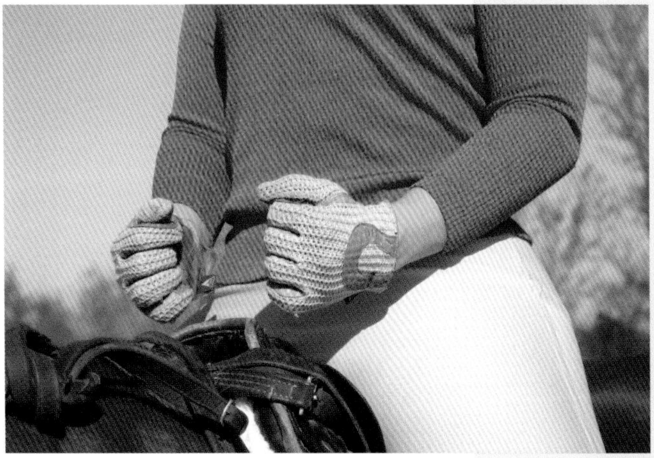

Fig. 2.6 *The basic seat is built upon a symmetrically balanced pelvis that enables an upright sitting posture. Ideally, head and feet should be aligned vertically through your base of support, shoulders and hips horizontally level, and limbs dangling freely from joints.*

The dressage seat, also known as the basic seat, forms the basis for all other types of seat.

GERMAN NATIONAL EQUESTRIAN FEDERATION (FN)

Both seat bones resting in the saddle together with the coccyx, which does not touch the saddle, form the "triangle of the seat" mentioned in many old books about riding.

ALOIS PODHAJSKY

pelvic anatomy (see fig. 2.8). While both seat bones inarguably make up two points, the third is debatable. Some say it is the lower portion of the pubic bone (crotch) in front of the seat bones—the *forward* triangle. Others believe it is the coccyx (tailbone)—the *rearward* triangle.

However, both bases of support can be used and are generally determined by the horse's conformation, his level of training, and the nature of the work he is doing. Balancing on the forward triangle may be ideal when easing weight off a horse's back and when working more compact or collected horses. On a larger, long-backed horse the rearward triangle offers stability in many training situations, such as when you are developing his "carrying" posture and asking him to work from "back to front." And, because riders commonly overarch their lower back or lean too far forward, using your tailbone can afford more stability during your seat development.

Fig. 2.7 *The forward seat is a balanced posture that redistributes weight from the seat bones into the legs, with increased flexion in leg joints, and the appropriate forward angle of the torso.*

The three-point seat may only remain theoretical until a *feel* of it develops through direct experience, particularly when riding off the longe. However, there is a concept that I outline on p. 17 involving getting to know the "four corners" of your seat, which helps to center your pelvis when learning seat balance while being longed on the circle.

Forward (Two-Point) Seat

Also known as the *two-point, light seat, hunt seat*, and the *jumping* or *galloping* position—the forward seat, evolved from the basic seat, has many variations. It involves little to no contact with the seat bones and is adapted for fast-paced activities where the horse's center of gravity is more forward, such as jumping, cross-country, endurance, and foxhunting. Because learning the forward seat improves a rider's versatility, this program features longe exercises in two-point position (fig. 2.7).

Hunt seat riding is a popular English discipline that appeals to those eager to jump. However, when a rider's seat is lightened before a basic seat is acquired, students learn to ride *above* (as opposed to *on* or *in*) the horse's back. This often leads to unrelenting grip and the inability to absorb the horse while sitting, plaguing many riders today.

Although a strong forward seat enables riders to clear jumps and adhere to a fast-moving horse, many fall short in their flat work. When jumping or riding out, instructors may demand inner thigh grip for increased security. Unfortunately, they don't always call for its release on the flat. Because grip pushes riders *away* and prevents absorption of the horse's movement, many long-timers have difficulty sitting the gaits despite years in the saddle. Any ingrained habit can be difficult to break, but this one makes it tough to transition from forward seat to basic seat—to pursue an interest in dressage, for example.

Confirming a basic seat first, *then* segueing into forward seat riding is more sequential. If a rider has secure basics and the ability to balance without excessive grip, transitioning to forward seat riding essentially requires the additional strength necessary to balance *above* the horse in shorter stirrups. And to encourage a *feel* of the horse, a rider's strength should evolve after suppling and the release of tension has been addressed.

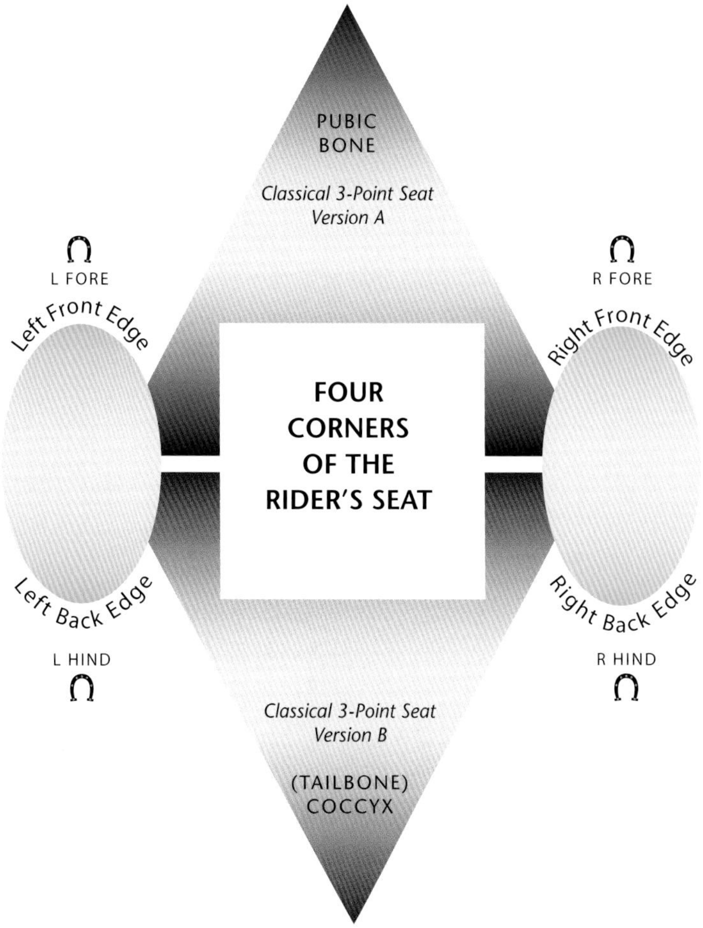

Fig. 2.8 *When learning to use your weight to influence the horse, imagine your seat has "four corners" corresponding to each of the horse's legs.*

Weight Distribution

The ability to distribute weight toward the back, front, left, or right of your seat is fundamental to balanced riding and key to developing the seat's communicative properties. Learning this on a horse standing still is preferable before attempting it in motion, as balancing on the circle involves a specific weight shift (see p. 18).

When mounted at the halt, imagine that you're sitting in the middle of a table with four legs. Also, that your seat has "four corners" corresponding to each of the horse's legs. This idea will help you understand how your seat can directly influence the horse by the way you distribute weight (fig. 2.8).

To become familiar with the four corners, experiment by shifting weight. When you slightly flatten the lower back it shifts weight to the back edges of your seat bones—toward the horse's haunches. Arching the lower back shifts weight to both front edges—toward the forehand. Rocking *back to front* helps you find the middle position and achieve *longitudinal* balance. Shifting from *left to right* helps you sit evenly on both sides of the horse's spine, achieving *lateral* balance. Combining these subtle maneuvers leads you to acquire a centered pelvis, and the ability to shift weight toward the forehand, hindquarters, or any specific "corner" of your seat, or leg of the horse.

Horses respond to weight shift better than signals from a pricking spur or a convulsively tightened calf, or pulling on the bit.

PAUL BELASIK

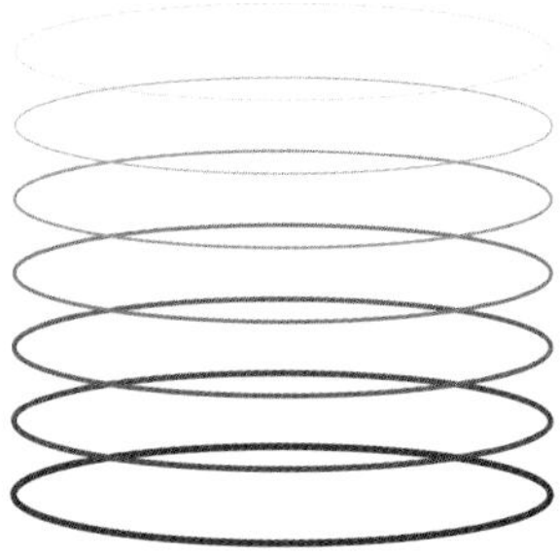

Fig. 2.11 *The Rider's Circular Path: In developing rider basics, the route taken is the archetypal circle—a path infinite in its scope. As the first layer is established, our learning path can spiral to higher levels based on aspirations. A firm foundation is the key to riding success, and even the most advanced riders continue to use the same basic skills, which grow more refined, subtle, and sophisticated over time.*

Absolute self-control is the basic requirement for every rider. He must not only be able to control his body, but also his temperament.

ALOIS PODHAJSKY

self-control and foundation skills are acquired. Then, if desired, your circular path can spiral higher, fueled by aspirations for advanced riding or horse training (fig. 2.11). From novice to competitor, it is vital to realize that equestrian learning is ongoing, even for those at the top levels, and that riding advancements revolve around our ability to sharpen *the same basic skills*.

The Eight Objectives of Self-Control

Tackling a "basic" requirement as multifaceted as self-control is best accomplished by breaking it into steps. The Basic Circle's Eight Objectives (or Rider Basics), can be used as a template of steps and applied to any equestrian activity—mounted or unmounted. Focusing on these Objectives helps you build a solid foundation and provides a framework to support your growth as a rider (see fig. 2.10).

It's best to apply the Objectives in halt exercises first, then in slow gaits, before working in faster paces. Listen to your body. Linger or return to any particular Objective for reinforcement—the more thorough you are, the more secure your basics will be. If at any time you feel "off-track," return to the first Objective: *Awareness*. Then relax, breathe, and continue. (On p. 156 in chapter 8 see the sidebar, What Are the Eight Objectives? This contains information regarding the practical application of the Objectives in rider longeing.)

Awareness

Learn to pay attention and be open to receive information. Are you tense or relaxed, alert or distracted, breathing consistently, irregularly, or holding your breath? Before changing anything, simply notice what is there. See yourself without judgment; become an observer (fig. 2.12).

Honing awareness allows the gathering of information from body and horse. This enables us to establish a baseline and monitor progress, noting where we began, and acknowledging each accomplishment. By cultivating receptivity we tune into what works, what doesn't, and can more wisely decide how to proceed. Self-assessment helps us see riding not as a mechanized activity, but a moment-by-moment sensory experience—an opportunity to become conscious of our own behavior and evaluate its appropriateness in any equestrian activity.

Relaxation

Learn to relax at will. It is unreasonable to expect positive training results without relaxation. Compelling a tight, nervous body to posture and perform creates resistance, making it tighter, whether equine or human. With relaxation "work," we learn to identify and eliminate ineffective mind-body activity and develop the tools to release tension (fig. 2.13).

Cultivating skilled relaxation involves "letting go" of extraneous muscular clenching and self-defeating thoughts. Relaxation allows us to balance muscular activity

Fig. 2.12 *Longeing enables us to become more aware of our thoughts, feelings, actions, and nonactions, which contributes to the self-control needed to communicate clearly through body language.*

Fig. 2.13 *Skilled relaxation techniques involve "letting go" of muscular clenching and self-defeating thoughts. This allows us to "surrender" to the horse's movement.*

Fig. 2.14 *Breathing is a natural process that can become a conscious skill. In breath control exercises, we access an internal mechanism that every rider is equipped with, and learn to use it for improved balance, focus, and rhythmical skills. Combining your own hands-on bodywork, as illustrated, intensifies the power of breath, which can also be used to improve posture and eliminate tension.*

with passivity, to "surrender" to the horse's movement, which heightens awareness and often produces rapid transformations in riding. Monitoring tension and remaining calm is critical to riding performance and the ability to *not disturb* the horse. Riders frequently circle back to this objective, which is paramount to all equestrian activities—to proceed without it is futile.

Breathing

Learn to control your breath. Taking the unconscious act of breathing and making it conscious is an invaluable rider tool. Breath control increases awareness, alignment, stability, and cultivates relaxation and calm in any mounted or unmounted activity (fig. 2.14).

When riding, inhale through your nose to warm and filter the air. Exhale through your mouth for a greater release of tension, and to encourage the relaxation of face, jaw, and throat. Using imagination, an inhalation can be directed into tight areas of your body delivering the energy needed to dissolve physical tension. Focusing on the sound of your breath while moving your body helps bring a focused,

Fig. 2.15 *The strategic touch of an instructor's hand can encourage a relaxed, balanced alignment in halt, as mine is doing here. Remembering this touch helps you sustain your position while in motion on the horse.*

meditative quality to riding or any physical activity.

Contracting the abdominal muscles assists with exhalation (see chapter 5) and helps improve posture by strengthening the core muscles needed for balancing on a moving horse. Even in halt, conscious breathing cultivates rhythmic skills. Controlling the rhythm and depth of the breath is so influential that any equestrian activity can become more centered, balanced, and synchronous when applied.

Alignment

Learn to arrange your body and balance. As I said earlier, the basic seat relies on a correctly positioned skeleton with head over feet and is more akin to standing than sitting. Balanced riding relies on a vertically aligned torso, horizontally parallel hips and shoulders, and the appropriate lateral rotation of the spine when bending the horse (fig. 2.15).

To learn any mounted posture, it is ideally sculpted first in halt, and then adapted to slow gaits before attempting it in faster-paced activities. Correct alignment should never be forced, but allowed to evolve by centering, suppling, and relaxing into the position.

Maintaining balance on a moving horse greatly depends on muscular "texture." Hard, clenched muscles that brace against the horse will disconnect the rider. *Softening* back and seat muscles (while contracting abdominals) preserves alignment and deepens the horse-rider connection. Combining abdominal strength with *appropriate* inner-thigh grip helps maintain alignment in working gaits and beyond. But if a rider's alignment relies on *excessive* grip, to eliminate this undesirable habit, more time should be spent cultivating *Awareness, Breathing,* and *Relaxation* in preparation for achieving the *Suppleness* Objective.

Suppleness

Learn to loosen before strengthening. Suppling encourages flexibility, elasticity, and connection with the horse. Although greatly enhanced by groundwork, mounted suppling can be more challenging, as riders may possess unconscious, fear-based obstacles to overcome before they are able to develop ease of movement on horseback (fig. 2.16).

Rider suppling involves eliminating the excessive muscle power often used to maintain seat and position. Undue gripping with arms and legs is an inappropriate use of strength, usually triggered by an instinctual urge to "hold on," coupled with an inability to "let go." The appropriate strength needed to develop a riding foundation is more a by-product of skill development and the *correct use* of the body, than a basic objective. Except in rare cases where a rider may be *too* loose and in need of a quick course in postural stability, many today exert an overabundance of strength, and exhibit a rigid seat and position in desperate need of suppling.

The suppling exercises in chapters 6 and 7 encourage pliable muscles and moveable joints.

Fig. 2.16 *Christa stretches to encourage suppleness, elasticity, and good posture.*

Rhythm

Learn to embody rhythm. If you believe you have no rhythm, developing breath control will prove otherwise. By matching the length of inhalation with the length of exhalation you can learn to establish rhythm, even in halt. Then, by practicing exercises that involve arm movements, you can learn to blend rhythmical movement with breath in all three gaits. Breath control helps regulate heart rate and contributes to a calm mind-body. This enables you to focus more attention on maintaining rhythm in all mounted activities (fig. 2.17).

To synchronize with the horse's rhythms, your movements can be identified with a unique four-beat cadence in every gait—not by counting hoof beats, but the rhythmical movements of your *seat bones*. Memorizing the rhythmic feel of each gait leads to an embodiment of rhythm and the ability to *keep time with your seat.*

Fig. 2.17 *By studying equine movement and becoming aware of your own, you can follow the horse's lead as though dancing, and learn the "steps" that allow you to rhythmically participate in the gaits.*

Fig. 2.18 *Being able to use your limbs in isolation while separately maintaining seat balance and rhythm in the gaits improves rider coordination, which leads to a kinesthetic feel of the horse.*

Coordination

Learn to develop whole-body dexterity. Coordination involves the *isolation* of muscle groups and body parts, coupled with the ability to engage these physical "tools" simultaneously, in various combinations. Picture a marionette—each part individually controlled by a string. As a rider, you must learn to "pull your own strings" to achieve a sufficient level of self-control to meet the demands of your chosen riding activity (fig. 2.18).

The root of coordination on horseback is the control of your own movements. Through skill-building exercises on the longe, you can assess and improve dexterity, refining your performance over time. As skills evolve, you'll learn to adjust seat and position accurately on demand, and become not only ambidextrous but able to control all four limbs equally well, and in rhythm.

When you take the reins, your coordination ultimately involves the ability to organize self *and* horse, appropriately blending activity with passivity for the desired result. Developing coordination on the longe facilitates the much-anticipated *feel* of the horse, which can occur in progressively higher degrees at each level of your circular path.

Feel

Learn to connect with the horse. In your ongoing efforts to gather knowledge and experience, you'll eventually learn to perceive exactly *when* you are synchronized in motion with the horse. By focusing attention, breathing consciously, memorizing the rhythm of the gaits, you become integrated. Your riding takes on a new dimension—instead of thinking so much about what you are doing, you really start to *feel* it.

This recognition may be a brief "lightbulb moment," or you may become aware of something before your instructor can get the words out—it is a sense of *knowing*. And no matter how fleeting, when the moment arrives, you'll strive to recreate it over and over until you "own" it.

Tapping into *feel*—what many call indescribable, unteachable, or elusive, is easier to achieve than you may have heard. *Feel* is a predictable outcome of a rider longeing program and evolves naturally when the Basic Circle's Eight Objectives are applied to your riding activities (see fig. 2.10).

What blocks the ability to feel are unchecked obstacles, holes in your foundation—virtually a lack of *anything* that could have been addressed by the Objectives preceding this one. If you prepare and remain open to receive information, *feel* on the longe line inevitably occurs. Then, just as *feel* relies on awareness, it also elevates awareness...and your circular path continues.

The Movement Paradox

Effective riding relies on your ability to adhere to a moving horse. While an educated seat gives the impression it is *unmoving*, a rider is in constant motion on the horse and only *appears* still when in sync with his movement. In contrast, an uneducated seat is characterized by stiffness and a lack of movement. Obstacles like tension and inflexibility have many sources, including *trying too hard* to maintain position. Rigidity can be seen in beginners and long-timers both and leads to *bouncing,* which gives the impression that a rider is moving *too much*! But bouncing actually reveals a rider who is *blocking* the horse and resisting the movement.

It is not enough to align in the correct position, you must "relax into it" by learning to move *with* the horse rather than *against* him. Bracing, battling, gripping—these separate you from the horse and increase risks, and your resulting disconnection becomes observable. When you release resistance, horses often breathe a sigh of relief and move forward with enthusiasm and willingness. Increased freedom in the gaits can generate longer strides with more ground cover and buoyancy. As long as your joints remain moveable and you blend the appropriate muscular effort and passivity, you can connect to bigger movement... yet appear unmoving.

A universal rider goal is to *unite* with the horse—to move harmoniously, at the same speed with centers aligned—not one partner lagging behind or dashing in front of the other. This goal can be met only once you learn the horse's fundamental lesson: *"absorb the movement!"* (fig. 2.19). It is the key to appearing "motionless" and not bringing attention to your seat. When you "sit still" in the saddle all eyes gravitate toward the horse's performance, which is enabled by your flexible, moveable seat.

Fig. 2.19 *There is no secret to connecting with a horse in movement—simply put, you must learn to absorb the gaits as he lifts, drops, and bounces your body!*

The Four Phases of Seat Development

Enabling riders of any level to better absorb the horse's movement with the seat is a primary goal of rider longeing. By offering a more direct route to developing this skill, longeing is as essential for beginners as it is for long-time riders, particularly those who may have moved forward too quickly in their training, and as a result, feel disconnected or frustrated. The ability to move with the horse and adhere the seat without bracing or bouncing is a *learned* skill that occurs in stages. To emphasize the *progressive* nature of seat training for riders I have outlined "The Four Phases of Seat Development," identified as:

- ***Phase One:*** *The Untrained Seat—Rider as Passenger*
- ***Phase Two:*** *The "Following" Seat—Horse "Leads," Rider Follows*
- ***Phase Three:*** *The Active Seat—Rider "Leads," Horse Follows*
- ***Phase Four:*** *The Educated Seat—Rider as Trainer*

Riding Without Reins can help you progress through the phases and I encourage you to explore this program from the beginning, with the assurance that you will readily move out of Phase One and into Phase Two.

In fact, longeing the rider is probably best known for its contribution to Phase Two, as it offers the ideal means to develop a "following" seat. In Phase Two, advancement occurs at your own pace as you train your seat sequentially, gait by gait. For example, you are likely to progress more quickly in walk, and then with ongoing seat work in slow trot and canter, eventually learn to participate in all three gaits equally well, over time.

To advance further, you can circle back again through Phase Two while learning to follow the working, medium, and collected gaits depending on the experience of your longe horse. At some point in Phase Two, you will probably segue (without realizing it) into Phase Three—first in walk, and then in slow gaits.

With confirmed Phase Two skills (the ability to follow and participate) and Phase Three skills (the ability to communicate in all gaits), you demonstrate a readiness to take the reins and do so correctly, without relying on them for balance. From there, you might continue refining your equitation skills off the longe line, or choose to advance into Phase Four for continuing seat education to become a *dresseur* or horse trainer.

Phase One: The Untrained Seat—Rider as Passenger

In the beginning, we are passengers—the horse essentially transports us and we have little to no control. Unaccustomed to his movements, even the view from his back is unfamiliar. Learning a new sitting posture, you become aware perhaps for the first time in your life, how you align and how asymmetrical you might be. You may be nervous and unconsciously reacting to the movement, while relying on an instructor and experienced horse for guidance and safekeeping. Reliable teachers understand your initial awkwardness and give you time to shape basic skills.

Riding *with* reins during this phase may feel like driving an all-terrain vehicle with a mind of its own (fig. 2.20). Passengers are sometimes terrified of not being in control, which compounds muscular tension. It is unreasonable to expect a beginner to ride well right off the bat, as humans do not *consciously* communicate physically and usually have no instincts to draw from other than the fight or flight response, which can trigger tension in the horse, increasing risks. To allay fears and give a rider a safe start, being longed is ideal for developing skills and confidence.

Fig. 2.20 *When a passenger sits in the "driver's seat" and attempts horse-control prematurely, incoherent aids and instinctive human reactions can turn a recreational ride into a terrifying experience.*

To the horse, taking the reins signifies you are taking control. However, by no means does it actually give you control—that is something you earn. Loss of control is one of the primary factors in riding accidents and injury[1] and can be frightening for anyone, especially beginners. With reins in hand and insufficient seat skills, beginners are often "over-horsed," as equine behavior may be more dynamic than a person is equipped to handle. It takes many, many hours in the saddle to fully comprehend a rider's role, and until a student develops the skills to fulfill that role, riding without reins on the longe is the safest, most productive learning environment.

My program with suppling exercises to establish a *basic seat* begins with bodywork at the halt divided into three parts—midsection, lower body, and upper body—to help you gain independent control of your seat and limbs (see chapters 5, 6, and 7). This bodywork is intended for all riders as it provides prerequisite information. Long-time riders can use these exercises to fill in learning gaps and new riders will find they help build a solid foundation. In both cases though, Phase One is not a place to linger. You can move directly into Phase Two and learn to follow the horse from day one, but you will need, as all riders do, to go back regularly to these exercises to reinforce your seat work with the basic skills you learn on the longe.

Phase Two: The "Following" Seat—Horse "Leads," Rider Follows

In this phase, you learn to move with the horse, but are not yet his leader. The *following seat* cultivates *passivity* and the ability to absorb movement as the horse leads you rhythmically, like a dance partner. Being

1 AVA, URL: http://www.americanvaulting.org/safety/threepoints.html

Fig. 2.21 *With the help of an experienced longeing team, you can postpone taking charge of horse-control and ride without reins, allowing you to transition safely and more easily from passenger to participant.*

longed allows you to identify and release resistance. As you learn how *not* to disturb the horse, you start to transition from passenger to *follower* (fig. 2.21).

Longeing for a following seat is not limited to beginners—experienced riders with lingering mind-body obstacles still struggling to connect with the horse benefit greatly by working on their following seat. Learning to follow the horse requires flexibility and relaxation; yielding is a matter of trust. And when eliminating habitual obstacles like excessive grip, a rider may feel weak, out of control, or fight to hang onto familiar ingrained behaviors out of habit, despite the fact they inhibit progress.

Often, when a tense rider starts to let go and allows the horse to lift, drop, and swing her body, anxiety escalates due to the perception of more movement. Without obstructions, the rider *does* move more, and the horse exhibits more freedom of movement, as well. However, some are unconvinced that this increased movement in their body is correct, and they think they have become loose and sloppy; some are even embarrassed by it. This undoubtedly stems from the common misconception that to ride well, a rider does not move. In actuality, to *blend* with the horse, you must move as much as he does.

When you release resistance and allow the horse to move you, you move *with* him, not against. As a result, he may feel lighter, more engaged, and rounder when no longer blocked. These desirable changes replace the shortened strides, lumbering gaits, lack of impulsion, "*horse not through*," and the disconnection you may have previously felt. Once you learn to follow without interfering, you are ready to begin riding in the next phase of seat development.

My discussion of how to develop your following seat while longeing on a moving horse begins in chapters 8 and 9. A lot of this work consists of the suppling exercises learned in Phase One, but performed now in walk, trot and canter. Doing these "with conscious breath" in motion on the horse requires preparation and mind-body coordination.

Phase Three: The Active Seat—Rider "Leads," Horse Follows

This phase cultivates leadership and the authoritative qualities of your seat. Rider "authority" does not equate to dominating the horse forcibly. Rather it combines sensitivity and firmness with your growing ability to ride. Due to herd hierarchy, most horses are familiar with being led. However, some test our attempts and will try taking on this role themselves, while others fall apart without a leader. Challenges like these are better left until you have confirmed your active seat and can fulfill your role competently. Most trained horses accept a rider's leadership, and their compliance helps you develop the skills you need to lead the dance.

With an active seat, you regulate the now familiar movements of the gaits by taking on the role of "rhythm-keeper," providing a metronome-like pulse that imparts consistency and cadence in the horse. Requesting tempo changes, engaging the hindquarters, sustaining rhythm, and executing transitions with seat, leg, and weight aids are all tasks that can be accomplished on the longe line without reins (fig. 2.22). In this phase you can overcome fluctuating tempos, irregular gaits, and start feeling the horse respond to both the activity and passivity in your seat.

A seat that enables a fluid performance in the horse often goes unnoticed but undoubtedly belongs to a rider *leading* with authority. Misconceptions about riding may raise the assumption that a rider must simply "take charge" of his or her horse. However, forceful attempts at control can trigger a battle of wills, struggle, and increase risks. An ongoing display of disharmony usually reveals insufficient seat development and a lack of true leadership. Through longeing and progressive seat development, riders can learn to direct using subtler means. An appropriate demonstration of leadership is invisible and overshadowed by the horse's performance.

Fig. 2.22 *To achieve an active seat, continue to absorb the horse and participate in the movement, but also start to assume responsibility for regulating the gaits using a more refined sense of rhythm, coordination, and feel.*

Fig. 2.23 *Once you are able to "lead" the gaits, if you desire further advancement, the next step is to segue into the "educated seat," cultivating your ability to not only influence the horse, but improve him.*

While growing into your active leading role, you'll become more independent and influential and are soon ready to take the reins with confidence. In time, you may find yourself at the threshold of the next phase of seat development, which introduces many levels yet to climb, and helps you transition from rider to trainer.

See chapter 10 for information and exercises to promote the active seat.

Phase Four: The Educated Seat—Rider as Trainer

Spiraling higher on your circular path, aspirations for training and developing the athletic potential of horses may arise. These tasks require a trainer's seat, which not only demonstrates the correct riding position, but advanced levels of functionality as well (fig. 2.23). Prerequisites include all prior phases of seat development wherein a rider becomes an effective trainer capable of inspiring focus and cooperation in the horse. Built upon a foundation of basics and equitation, developing an educated seat will refine seat, leg, weight, and rein skills, leading to your ability to manifest the correct carrying posture in the horse.

In this phase, you exhibit both independence and influence with which to balance and engage the horse, access his current level of training and, commensurate with your advancing skill levels, develop and refine *his* basic skills as defined by the classical training scale: rhythm, relaxation, contact, impulsion, straightness, collection.[2] From here, yet another circular path may begin, as you become a *dresseur* (trainer) of horses and advance up the dressage levels (see chapter 11). This leaves us with the realization that a quest for equestrian training is ongoing, without a final destination.

2 United States Dressage Federation, *Lungeing Manual*

PART II

PREPARATION FOR RIDING WITHOUT REINS

A rider cannot acquire and develop a correct seat and apply the aids without being longed. Even an accomplished rider needs to develop his seat and aids by frequent review sessions on the longe.

CHARLES DE KUNFFY

CHAPTER 3

Setting Up: Longeing Guidelines

Correct longeing is an art.
It does not just mean making the horse run round in a circle.

ALOIS PODHJASKY

The Longeing "Team"

It is ideal if the person who longes you (the "longeur") is also a riding teacher who focuses on seat development. Even more advantageous, would be someone who can also guide you to *relax* through breath work and bodywork. Finding one person to *longe, improve your seat, teach you "feel,"* and *relax* you is a tall order. If you are working with a person like this, you are fortunate, but more likely you will have trouble finding all this guidance, so you need to be creative when building a longeing team.

Fig. 3.1 *When you begin a longeing program you will need an experienced "longeur." This can be a trainer, instructor, experienced rider, or horse handler who knows how to longe a horse properly. You may or may not require an additional teacher for help with your technique and bodywork.*

The Instructor or "Longeur"

The person who longes has a crucial role: to control the horse from the ground and help keep the session safe (fig. 3.1). He or she must be familiar with the proper use of equipment and the application of ground-based aids using his voice, body language, longe rein, and whip. He "describes" the circle by establishing a position in the center, or, in order to stay closer to the rider, he may walk a smaller circle parallel to the horse. He executes transitions, regulates gaits, maintains contact with the bit, and keeps the horse on track. An experienced longeur has the ability to "read" the horse—seeing when the horse's cooperation starts to diminish, for example. Or, by "reading" the rider, he prevents a session from going on too long, thus avoiding fatigue and related injury.

A student should not assume that all equestrian professionals are experienced longeurs, or that longe horses are available everywhere. Discuss your goals with a potential instructor and specify your desire to be longed on an experienced horse. If you own such a horse yourself, ask your current trainer to longe you, or ask an experienced rider and suggest you can trade off longeing each other.

Some longeurs are also instructors who can manage rider and horse equally well. But a hands-on-type instructor may prefer assigning the horse to a longeur so he can focus on his student. Or, a longeur capable of handling the horse but unqualified to coach or teach, may advise you to arrange for an instructor as well.

Assistant to the "Longeur"

Because the longeur's primary responsibility is controlling the horse, and if, as is possible in some cases, he is not an instructor, you may need someone to focus on improving your seat and teaching you riding. At times you'll need to enlist an assistant to read the longeing exercises aloud, or you may need additional help with nontraditional riding exercises like conscious breathing. Vaulting clubs provide both a longeur and a coach to work with riders in private lessons. Or as explained earlier, you can create your own team.

Most vaulting clubs offer private lessons on experienced longe horses to improve seat and foundation skills (rider basics)—see the Appendix for the chapter on vaulting, p. 209. If there are no such clubs nearby, search for a riding instructor who gives longe lessons. Check the stables, riding schools, and freelance professionals in your area and make your interests known. If you desire longeing opportunities on an experienced horse to improve *seat, foundation skills,* and *feel*—you will probably have to look to more than one person.

A "Relaxation" Teacher

Until you find a longeur or instructor who integrates relaxation work with riding lessons, you can "cross-train" with *mind-body practices* that impart complementary skills. For example, try gentle or restorative *yoga* classes for relaxation, or the *Alexander Technique* for improved posture in daily life (fig. 3.2). To address chronic tension and inflexibility try *massage, acupressure,* or other healing methods. For peace of mind and to improve focus, try guided *visualization* and *meditation*—techniques also used when mounted (see Appendix, p. 227).

Fig. 3.2 *You can help yourself relax on horseback by "cross-training" and implementing various mind-body techniques in your practice—for example, thinking of riding as a specialized form of yoga where relaxation, balance, flexibility, and focus are blended with gaits and transitions helps Samantha release tension and focus on her lesson ahead.*

NOTE TO INSTRUCTORS

To be able to provide instruction in mounted relaxation techniques, cross-train yourself: try yoga, Alexander Technique, massage, acupressure or other healing practices to learn how to relax on demand so you can impart this skill to your students. See a list of such resources in the Appendix, p. 227. Being able to recognize and eliminate tension in riders while encouraging relaxation is a necessity for instructors today. Commanding students to "Breathe!" or "Relax!" is ineffective. It's easy to assume everyone has these innate abilities, but on horseback, conscious breathing and relaxing are challenged by fear. When relaxed, students will more readily hear, understand, and apply your instruction and become better riders.

Most importantly, when you achieve a relaxation response off the horse, *bring it with you to the saddle!*

Fig. 3.3 *Part of the longeur or instructor's job is to place his or her hands on the rider's leg to increase awareness and improve position. In this photo, my hand ensures the knee is not gripping, while the other is checking for ankle flexibility.*

Hands-on Bodywork for Posture Adjustment

This can be done by yourself on your body parts within reach, and for others hard to get to, your instructor can help you make postural adjustments using simple touches (fig. 3.3). The only prior experience needed is a working knowledge of the basic seat and the human body. I will be including photos and instructions throughout this book that show these techniques. Although it's possible for a person on the ground to move alongside the horse in walk to help adjust your position, you can't expect him to run and adjust you as you're trotting—believe me, I've tried! By retaining a body memory of the touches performed in halt and walk, you can stimulate the same response to help adjust your position in faster motion.

The Longe Horse

While some believe circle work carries a potential for stress to equine limbs, when correctly applied, longeing is far less risky than other equestrian activities entered into with great enthusiasm, such as advanced collected work, stadium and cross-country jumping, sliding stops, spins, racing, endurance, etc. As for the notion that circle work isn't "natural" for horses, with regard to equine psychology and their recruitment for human recreation, sport, service, and rider training—carrying a rider can hardly be considered "natural" to a flight animal. The simple act of sitting on a horse's back inevitably requires conditioning the flight animal for an unnatural purpose. This is accomplished through repetitive movement on gymnastic patterns, like a circle.

Traditional longeing offers a controlled learning environment using body language, voice commands, longe line and whip, side reins, and the circle itself as training tools. Longeing helps the horse adapt to the tasks of riding and develop the necessary balance to carry a rider. But, if longeing or any training is attempted

What we are doing with all the specific adjustments in longeing is taking a more active approach to balance...to prepare the horse, which has not necessarily evolved to be ridden, for the exercises of riding.

PAUL BELASIK

without sufficient knowledge, there can be negative repercussions.

The main assets needed from the horse are training, rideability, and temperament. Well-schooled, mature horses accustomed to longeing riders are the best choice (fig. 3.5). They need to be kind, calm, sound, balanced, supple, and comfortable to ride. And as with any riding activity, you should always choose a longe horse appropriate for your weight, height, and level of experience.

Nice movers that can maintain a balanced frame on the circle make wonderful teachers of the *following seat* (I'll explain this on p. 171). Their rhythmical gaits provide a steady "beat" to follow and help you establish cadence in your own movement. Despite a longeur's best efforts at horse control, until you achieve complete control over your body movement, you can cause fluctuating tempos, irregular rhythms and transitions, as well as unbalance the horse through your postural adjustments. A valuable horse accommodates these mistakes and patiently helps you learn. These horses include seasoned "longe-masters," baby-sitter types that "take care" of riders and vaulting horses that are trained to accept a rider's movements, however unconventional.

To help you develop a good seat, your ideal horse should be forgiving, but definitely not insensitive or dull. The only way you'll know when you get things right is from his response to your aids. A trained horse can demonstrate what it feels like to ride in self-carriage—a vital lesson that will support your continuing progress as a rider.

Fig. 3.5 *A good-natured riding horse generously participates in your equestrian activities when worked conscientiously. To preserve his willingness and trust, you strive to become the best rider you can be, whether hobbyist or competitor. Gus is an experienced longe horse, well-schooled on and off the longe line. Here, he is stretching forward and down during a warm-up.*

Experienced longe horses may not be readily available at every riding stable. However, your instructor may know of a good prospect that could be trained for longeing, maybe even your own horse!

Longeing Environment

Arena or Round Pen

The surface of any riding arena, ring, or round pen should be built upon a firm foundation with an average 4- to 6-inch layer of compacted base material for drainage and support. This is topped with a layer of footing—2 to 4 inches high—that cushions the horse's legs and provides traction and spring. Coarse, angulated sand is often used and can be enhanced by mixing in

Fig. 3.6 *A seasoned longeing horse is an invaluable teacher that can consistently help you build a secure riding foundation, as well as provide insight as to how you should "feel."*

NOTE TO INSTRUCTORS

If you do not have a suitable horse for longeing riders, your lesson program would greatly benefit from the acquisition or training of at least one mount that could teach the following seat to a wide range of students. Choose the most trained horse available and evaluate his gaits, temperament, rideability, ground manners, acceptance of bit and side reins, and responsiveness to longeing aids (fig. 3.6). Longe an experienced "test rider" who can perform suppling exercises to first determine and then improve the horse's tolerance for unusual rider activity on his back.

Often, an older, higher level dressage horse that is reliably quiet and consistent in your hands will make a good longe-line teacher for students, even if they are not yet skilled enough to ride him on their own. Safety should always be a primary concern—do not "over-horse" novices with a "big" mover, or one so finely-tuned, he is disturbed by a rider's inadvertent awkwardness.

A trained longe-lesson horse is worth his weight in gold and is a valuable "co-teacher" who can help you do your job. On the longe, when unencumbered by the rider, a schooled longeing horse should readily be able to assume his familiar carriage—haunches engaged, back muscles lifted to carry weight, and stretching over the topline, in other words, "on the bit." The time it takes to train him is an investment in your career and your students' riding futures. (See Appendix, p. 227 for resources.)

***Note:* Horses that habitually counter-flex, fall in, hollow their back, or move at excessive speeds are unsuitable for rider longeing without additional training.**

wood or rubber products. As local materials and weather conditions vary, hiring an experienced contractor is a good idea when constructing or improving an existing arena or ring (fig. 3.7).

The footing should be groomed regularly so that it is smooth, level, and maintained at an appropriate depth—usually between 2 to 4 inches, with 3 inches or less recommended for flatwork. A vaulting arena

Fig. 3.7 *An ideal longeing environment is an enclosed arena with safe footing designed for riding. Here, Gerardo quietly warms up Gus prior to a lesson.*

generally has softer and springier footing to absorb the shock of frequent dismounts.

When footing is too shallow and is hard-packed, it increases concussion on both the horse's legs and rider's body, and inhibits freedom of movement. The opposite is also true: if excessively deep or spongy, such footing can heighten the risk of leg injury while longeing, especially when you ask for more ground-covering paces. Avoid longeing when a surface is slippery.

Do not allow the footing to pile up against the sides and create a groove in the track, particularly in a round pen. The arena should be large enough for a 20-meter longeing circle (approximately 66 feet in diameter) while also allowing sufficient space between the circle and arena's sides as a cushion. Remove hazards such as jump standards, chairs, rocks, or poles. And, if sharing an arena, other riders should be asked to avoid the vicinity of your longeing circle.

Circle Size

When longeing in walk and slow trot you don't require a full 20-meter circle; in slow gaits, a smaller circle can be useful so the longeur is closer to the rider and able to do bodywork and adjust the rider's position as necessary. Longeing at faster gaits like a working trot and canter are safer on a larger circle—the full 20 meters. (For size perspective, vaulting rules require a minimum circle of 15 meters and the German National Equestrian Federation (FN)

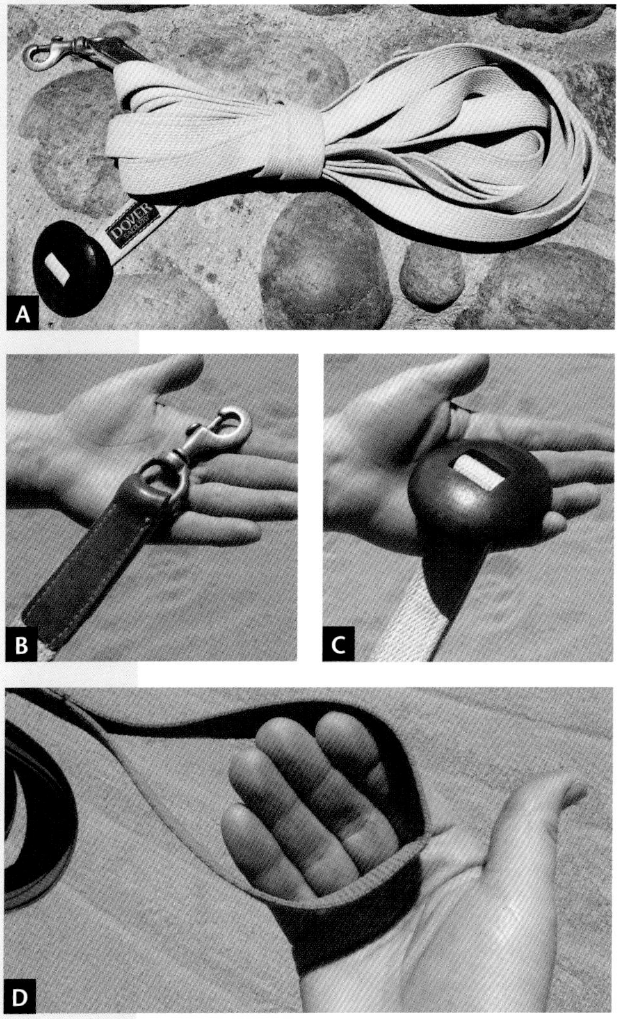

Figs. 3.8 A–D *A cotton web longe line is soft, flexible, has a good grip, and feels comfortable in the hand (A). Note the swivel snap at the end to allow the line to remain untwisted (B), and the rubber end stop (C). Some longe lines come with a hand loop rather than an end stop, as seen here on a nylon example (D).*

advises against longeing a horse on anything smaller than a 12-meter circle.

Optimum Environmental Conditions

An environment conducive to learning includes the suitable horse I've already discussed in comfortable well-fitted tack (p. 43) being longed at slower gaits, and an instructor (and/or a longeur) who creates a supportive atmosphere with a relaxed tone. A quiet setting with minimal distraction is best, because obviously this will inspire the rider to focus and relax. However, activity and noise around horse facilities are inevitable, so a horse that is accustomed to the goings-on will help keep the rider calm. The rider needs to be encouraged to let distractions fade into the background and focus her attention on the sound of her breath.

Longeing Equipment

Longe Line

I prefer a web cotton longe line (or "rein"). Soft and flexible, cotton facilitates a better feel of the horse (figs. 3.8 A–D). Nylon ones can be stiff, and abrasive to your hands. A 25- to 26-foot line enables a 15-meter circle used for longeing in walk and slow trot. A 33- to 35-foot line enables a 20-meter circle for faster gaits. I prefer the latter because it offers more circle size, but the shorter one may be more manageable to some people.

Longe lines often come with features such as: a hand loop at the end (although putting your hand and wrist all the way through is unsafe and can trap your hand); a rubber stop called an "end stop" that serves as a "hand stop" at the end of the line; leather "hand stops" all along the line for increased grip (gloves recommended); or identification markers that show you where to hold it to create specific circle sizes. A nice feature is a swivel-jointed clip to attach to the bit ring. It's easier to attach than a buckle, and helps prevent the line from getting twisted.

I do not recommend a stud chain attached to a longe line. When clipped to the inside bit ring, a chain weighs the line down and it swings around the horse's face. When taken through the inside bit ring, up and over the horse's head, and attached to the outside bit ring, (as discussed on p. 44) the chain will tighten across the horse's poll. The resulting pressure can cause pain and may result in strong objections from the horse, such as head tossing. Pardon the pun, but this can cause a "chain reaction": with his head thrown high, if the horse comes up against the side reins, it may lead to entrapment panic (see The Longeur's Role, p. 62). A chain may well be useful at times on a lead rope to help restrain a young or undisciplined horse, but this type of horse is not yet a suitable candidate for longeing a rider.

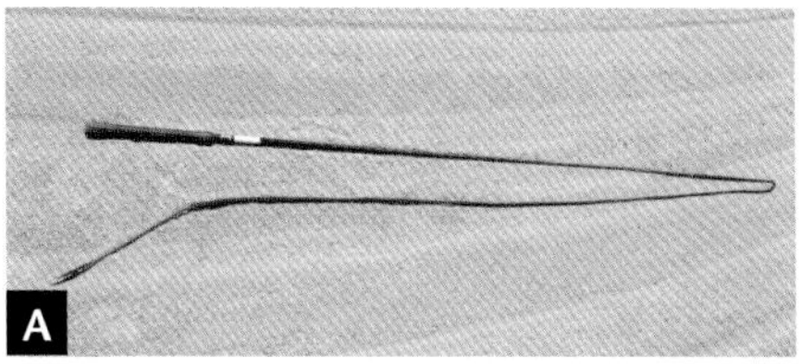

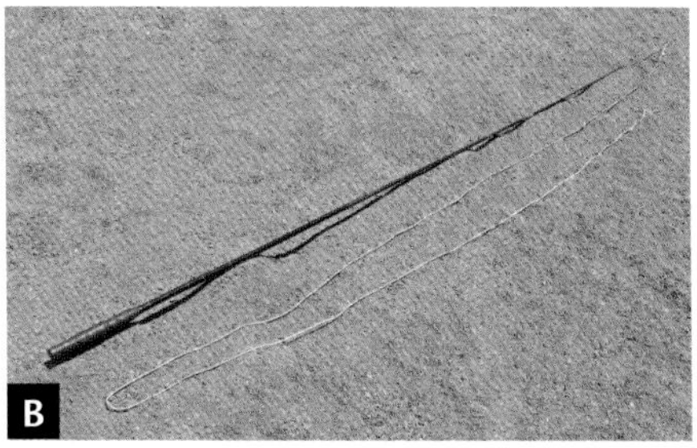

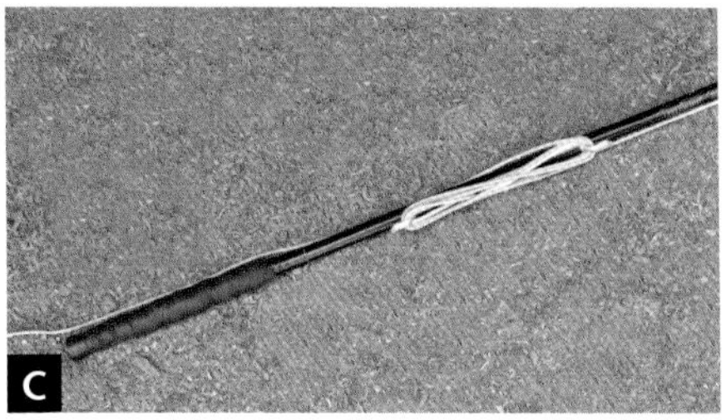

Figs. 3.9 A–C *The most common longe whips are approximately 12 to 15 feet long, including the lash (A). A more expensive and longer one (up to 27 feet) is the telescope variety (B), which has an additional feature to store the longer lash safely (C).*

Longe Whip

Longe whips are constructed of synthetic materials such as a plastic or fiberglass shaft, a rubber grip, and nylon cord (figs. 3.9 A–C). Inexpensive nylon whips are widely available and often consist of a 6-foot shaft with a 6-foot lash that has a "popper" at the end. Some more costly whips are the telescoping type with the shaft and lash extending to a combined length of 25 to 27 feet, which conveniently retract to a shorter length for transporting. The additional length is useful when horse training, as a light touch of the lash can be used to influence a horse's hind leg. A longer length can also help motivate those horses that respond better when the whip is in closer proximity to their haunches. The shorter ones are useful as a visual driving aid when longeing riders.

Snaffle Bridle

The horse's tack for longeing a rider should include a standard snaffle bridle with a properly adjusted noseband (regular—with or without a flash—or dropped) with the longe line attached to the inside bit ring (fig. 3.10). Use a smooth snaffle bit (single- or double-jointed) with a loose ring, D-ring, eggbutt, or full cheek—the bit selection depends on the

Fig. 3.10 *A snaffle bridle with a loose ring bit. Note the longe line is attached at the bottom, the side rein next, and the bridle rein on top.*

horse. Since the outside bit ring will press against the horse's face, a small ring is inadvisable as it can slide into the mouth. A full-cheek snaffle, by design, offers protection against the bit sliding through, and rubber bit guards can be used with other snaffles to help stabilize bit position. Avoid shank bits and curb chains, as the leverage they provide is unnecessary. The reins should be knotted and secured (see sidebar).

(Note: when longeing a horse without a rider, the reins can be intertwined and secured through the bridle's throatlatch.)

Side Reins

The function of side reins is similar to an educated rider's hands holding the bridle reins. They encourage flexion at the poll and acceptance of the bit, while contributing to a desirable carriage. When adjusted correctly (not so tight as to be overly restrictive, and not so loose as to have no influence at all) they offer the horse some freedom to move within the contact, enabling him to make subtle postural adjustments with his head and neck. This promotes relaxation and reduces the likelihood of him feeling trapped within the confines of the side reins.

Side reins typically come in leather, cotton web, or nylon varieties. In contrast to the minimal care and long life of nylon or cotton web products, traditional leather side reins must be cleaned and oiled regularly and can stretch, crack, or break over time. Leather has the advantage of being easier to adjust, as additional holes are easily created with a leather punch. Adding holes to nylon can be accomplished by using a heated nail to melt through the material, but unfortunately, cotton web reins cannot accept additional holes. Those suitable for rider longeing need to have some type of built-in flexibility, such as rubber donuts (less stretch) or elastic inserts (more

Figs. 3.11 A & B *A side rein with a rubber "donut" in the middle offers longer wear and some elasticity, which depends on the stiffness of the "donut" (A). A side rein with an elastic insert at the end offers more elasticity or stretch than one with a "donut," although it may wear out more quickly (B).*

A

B

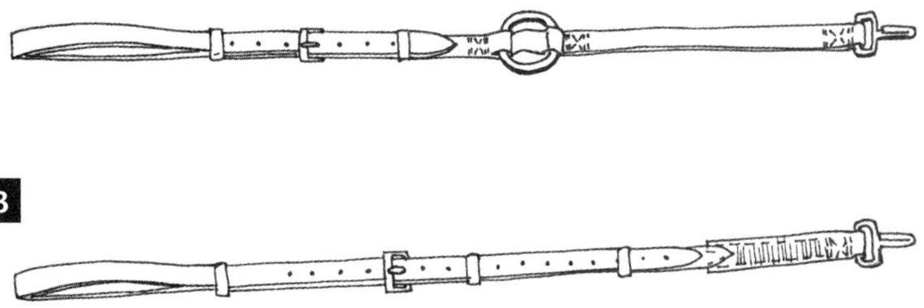

stretch), which help promote relaxation in the horse (figs. 3.11 A & B).

You need a pair that can be adjusted to fit "now" as well as accommodate your horse's advancements in training, which means progressing from a longer length to a shorter one. Most side reins allow for a good amount of adjustability. You can find side reins that adjust either with buckles that require both hands, or a clip that attaches to one of many D-rings built into the rein for fast adjustments with one hand.

When longeing a rider, it is best to select side reins designed to loop around the girth, as opposed to ones intended to clip to a surcingle, which are used mainly in horse training and vaulting. Sliding side reins (Lauffer reins), running draw reins (Vienna side reins) as well as martingales or other gadgets, might have legitimate uses in various horse training situations, but are not recommended for longeing the rider.

It is abusive to use side reins to shorten the horse's neck into a restricted, overly bent posture or to leave them attached on a stabled horse to create a false "head set." I can only compare this to the absurd

HOW TO KNOT THE REINS

Lift the buckle and gather the reins together with one hand in front of the withers, the other grasping the buckle end. Take the buckle end and wrap it around the reins, creating a single knot that should rest on the horse's neck in front of the withers, with an end loop remaining. Based on the tack you are using, apply one of the following techniques to secure the knotted reins (see also Equipment Safety Check, chapter 4, p. 65):

- **Unbuckle reins, thread the narrow tip of one rein through a D-ring near the pommel of an English saddle, and then re-buckle together.**
- **When longeing in a Western saddle, hook the loop over the horn.**
- **Unbuckle reins, feed one through the pommel safety strap (see fig. 3.12), and then re-buckle them together.**
- **When longeing a rider with stirrup irons crossed over the withers, an iron can be slipped through the end loop to secure the reins.**
- **When longeing bareback, do not attach the reins to anything (even if using a bareback pad), simply let the knot rest on the horse's neck, and hook a few fingers through the loop to steady it.**

idea of strapping a person into a yoga pose for some length of time as a method for forcing him into a posture! For safety's sake, never clip side reins to the bit while the horse is tied, loose, confined to a stall, being led in-hand, or while the rider is mounting or dismounting.

The horse should be well accustomed to working in side reins with an experienced longeur before you use him to longe a rider. Have an experienced trainer assist you with their selection and fit, particularly when introducing them for the first time. Improper fit can cause feelings of entrapment, which can result in fear, rebellion, panic, balking, or rearing with disastrous results. To learn what to do if the horse panics in side reins, see chapter 4, p. 62, sections The Longeur's Role and The Rider's Role.

All horses benefit from a regular riderless warm-up first with long, low side reins, which can be then be readjusted for the rider's longe lesson.

It is not necessary to clip side reins to the bit during rider suppling exercises in halt, or during rider warm-up or cool-down in walk. However, in trot and canter their use facilitates a suitable carrying posture in the horse. When not in use, clip them to the saddle's D-rings, (the D-shaped metal rings used for attaching gear and located on either side of the pommel) or to each other over the horse's neck.

Side reins attach *under* the bridle reins on the bit rings, but *above* the longe line (see fig. 3.10). Ideally, they should be adjusted to an equal length, although the *inside* side rein may be shortened to assist with flexion on the circle, if necessary. Their height on the girth, and length from girth to bit depends on the horse's degree of schooling and the nature of the rider's work on the longe. Side reins positioned below the saddle flap encourage the horse to stretch over his back and work in a longer, lower frame, which is a comfortable posture for horses of any level and ideal for warming up on the longe, and longeing a rider in slow gaits. Positioning them higher on the girth and adjusting them shorter is appropriate for longeing in working trot and canter. For horses with more schooling and an uphill frame, the side reins can be shortened and raised further for longeing in collected gaits.

When longeing a rider in slow gaits, the side reins can remain long and low (see fig. 3.19 B). However, when longeing with shorter side reins (see fig. 3.19 C), the horse will need rest breaks to release his active muscles. Thus, side reins should be periodically adjusted or unclipped during more active longing. As a general rule, if the side reins draw the horse's head behind a vertical position (or even worse, pull his chin to his chest), they are *too short*. They should be long enough so that the horse can reach forward with his neck seeking contact, while flexing at the poll, positioning his head with his nose slightly in front of the vertical. He should softly chew the bit, not fight against it, and his head and neck should look as though he is reaching for a bucket of carrots!

If a horse is "cramped" in tight side reins, he will flex incorrectly around mid neck rather than at the poll, and lower his head excessively with his nose behind the vertical. This is a physically damaging posture and, if sustained over time, may result in chronic pain, tension, respiratory problems, improper muscular development, and, inevitably, resistance to the rider's aids.

Saddle and Stirrups

A comfortable saddle, correctly fitted to rider and horse, is fundamentally important. While the photographs in this book illustrate the use of a dressage saddle for longeing, you can use whatever makes you comfortable—English or Western saddles, even bareback pads.

Developing the seat is possible in a variety of saddles, as long as they are correctly balanced. Some riders may discover, as their seat improves, that their current saddle may no longer feel comfortable. A too small saddle limits seat movement and should be exchanged for one that is roomier and enables the rider to follow the horse unrestrictedly.

Stirrups are useful for mounting and confidence-building but when practicing seat work without stirrups, they should be crossed-over or removed altogether. When crossing the stirrups on an English saddle, pull down the buckles first so leathers lie flat under your leg, and rest the stirrup irons on the horse's shoulders. When working *with* stirrups, ensure they are wide enough to fit your foot properly, with treads or stirrup pads for traction. Safety stirrups with rubber bands or flexible hinges are appealing and if they improve your confidence, use them.

Pommel Safety Strap

An essential piece of rider longeing equipment, this is unfortunately sometimes called a "bucking strap," which is actually the name of a piece of rodeo gear that wraps around a horse's lower abdomen to induce bucking! In contrast, the safety strap is a short leather piece that buckles to the D-rings on either side of the pommel of an English saddle and is used as a handhold for riders being longed in the basic seat (fig. 3.12). For those working on their basic seat in a Western saddle, the horn or the prominent pommel on either side of the horn (also called the swell or the fork) could serve as a rider handhold while longeing.

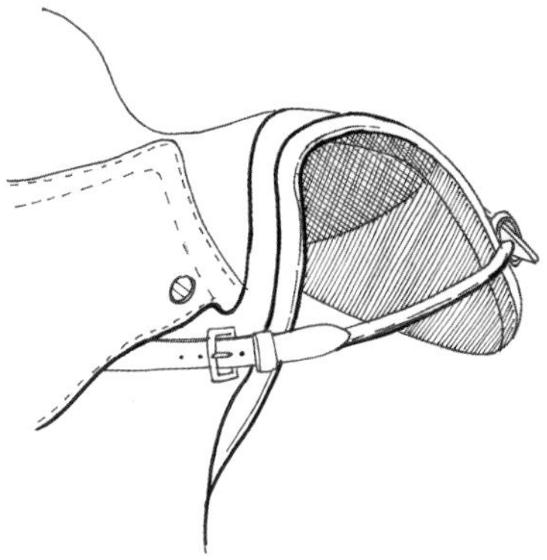

Fig. 3.12 *A pommel safety strap is a short piece of leather that buckles to the D-rings of an English saddle and serves as a handhold for riders when longeing.*

Optional Neck Strap

This can be an old stirrup leather or belt buckled comfortably around the horse's neck (see fig. 2.7). It makes a suitable handhold for working in a forward seat (two-point) but is too far forward for working in basic seat. However, *be careful* when the horse stretches down, the neck strap doesn't slip over his head. A neck strap can be helpful when learning the forward seat

Fig. 3.13 *Polo wraps are one example of protective coverings that support the soft tissues of the horse's legs and help prevent minor injuries.*

position, especially if the horse's mane is sparse with nothing to grab, but it is not necessary for every rider.

Longeing Cavesson

With a longeing cavesson, the line attaches to a ring on the cavesson's noseband rather than the bit. This is useful when first training horses to longe, and some trainers prefer to use a longeing cavesson over the bridle. Today, the longeing technique most often seen involves attaching the line to a snaffle bridle without a longeing cavesson. (This has become widespread in vaulting, as FEI rules require the longe rein be attached directly to the inner bit ring.) In this program, I take a similar approach—rather than attaching the rein to the noseband of a longeing cavesson, I attach it directly to the snaffle bit. When longeing the rider, this arrangement contributes to a safer, more controlled environment as the person longeing has a more direct means of communication with the horse's mouth.

Protective Leg Covering

Working in halt, walk, and slow trot may not necessitate the use of splint boots, sport boots, bell boots, or polo wraps. However, when longeing a fresh horse without a rider, or when longeing a rider in faster gaits, it is good practice to protect the horse's legs with supportive wraps or boots as a precaution against brushing, overreaching, or missteps (fig. 3.13).

Artificial Aids

Only an "educated" leg should consider using *spurs* as a communication device in refined equitation, and I do *not* recommend their use for rider training on the longe line, which is teaching seat development by using *natural* "driving" aids. In any case, spurs get in the way of some suppling exercises and can disturb the horse. You can learn to carry a whip properly and change it between hands while being longed, however, it can get in the way. I do use a *dressage whip* or *crop* as a "prop" in an exercise (see Double Whips, p. 142).

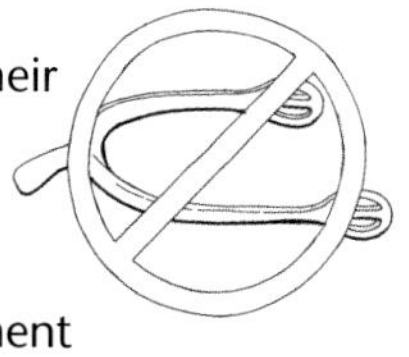

General Longeing Tips

The person longeing should know how

to handle the longe line before attempting to longe a rider. Permitting horses to race around a longe circle at high speeds or in a crooked, imbalanced frame represent the most common mistakes made by inexperienced longeurs. A common error involves side reins: they are frequently introduced too quickly and too tightly—often with disastrous results. Or, they may be attached too loosely for no effect at all. Improper training of any kind has the potential for physical problems or injuries in the horse, and an unfamiliarity with correct longeing may cause some trainers to avoid this technique altogether.

In contrast, proper longeing improves the horse's gaits, willingness, suppleness, confidence, and self-carriage. To be effective, it requires educated hands to manage the equipment, and safely handle the horse through the longeing process. A skilled longeur can encourage a horse to develop a correctly balanced frame in all gaits, with and without a rider.

While some believe horses become "bored" or "soured" by longe work, a sensitive horse that is less stressed or challenged on the longe circle may be *relaxed*, but not bored. Horses are more attuned to what's going on around them than humans, and even if lulled into a tranquil state by longeing, this is far more desirable to most riders than an overly stimulated creature. "Souring" a horse is more likely due to an unrelenting training approach than the nature of the work. Diminishing a horse's good nature can occur whenever training disregards the horse's well-being, or is taken to extremes. "Reading" the horse, knowing when to stop and when to push on is essential for longeing and all training situations.

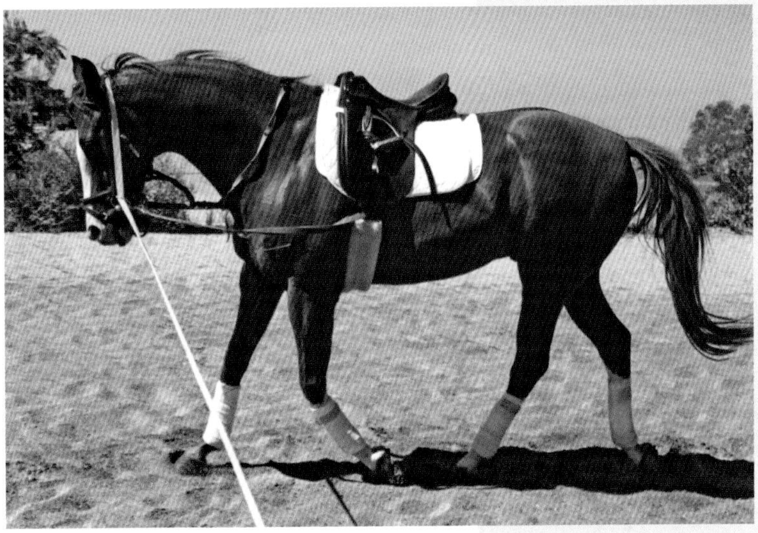

Fig. 3.15 *You can secure the longe line over the top of the horse's head like this when you need more control.*

Using the Longe Line

The longeur uses the longe line to flex, stretch, or position the horse, as well as for half-halts, speed reduction, and supporting his voice commands in downward transitions. The longe line can be drawn directly toward your hip, or taken to the side and used as an opening/leading rein. However, if the longeur must engage in repeated jerking or pulling it suggests the horse's training—or the longeur's—is insufficient for rider longeing.

If a horse needs additional restraint, you may opt to insert the longe rein through the inside bit ring, take it up over the horse's head behind the ears, and attach it to the opposite bit ring (fig. 3.15). This causes the bridle to function as a "gag

Fig. 3.16 *This is a nice picture of the horse correctly positioned between the longe line and longe whip. The contact is steady with no loop in the line.*

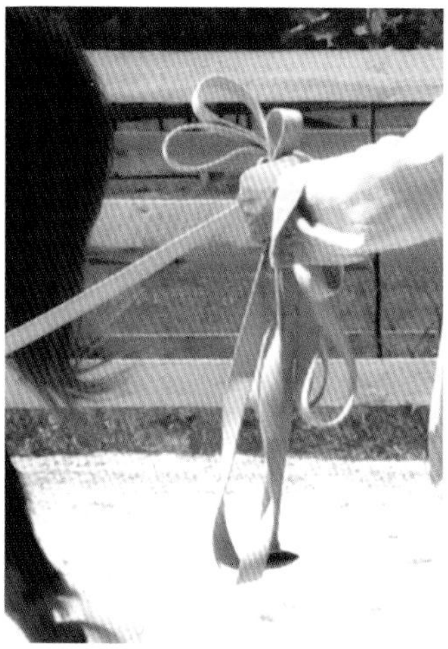

Fig. 3.17 *I'm holding the longe line in my "inside" hand (left) and it is folded correctly.*

Fig. 3.18 *Here, I am bridging the longe line with the folded part in my outside hand (right) and feeding it through my inside hand (left).*

snaffle," placing increased pressure on the horse's poll and corners of the mouth when the rein is taken. This tactic is more severe and best for educated hands.

How to Handle the Longe Line

- Maintain a central position in the circle and work the horse evenly around you, or walk a parallel circular track if you need to stay closer to the horse or rider.
- Keep the horse positioned between the longe line and whip (fig. 3.16).
- The line should not be wrapped around your hand but folded so it can gradually be let out to increase circle size (fig. 3.17).
- Remain aware of the line and its relationship to your body. Never allow it to become wrapped around your hands (it can easily become tangled) or fall about your feet, and always keep it clear of the horse's legs.
- Keep a light steady contact between the longe rein and bit, taking the "loop" (slack) out of the line so it does not drag on the ground (see fig. 3.19 B).
- Hold the entire longe line in your inside hand; or "bridge" the rein, placing the folded portion in your outside hand and feed it through your inside hand to the bit (fig. 3.18).
- Gently wave the line *horizontally* to help slow the horse and invite him to stretch downward; wave it *vertically* to help push the horse out on the circle. Use minimal arm movements; primarily use your wrist.
- Gather the line in folds when approaching the rider (see fig. 3.1). For hands-on bodywork, stuff the line under an arm or disconnect it

momentarily, putting it off to the side if the horse will stand quietly in halt. If the rider needs frequent adjustments and bodywork, an assistant should be enlisted to hold the horse as you instruct.

Using the Longe Whip

Two important things to remember, first, the whip should never be used to punish the horse! Second, cracking it is usually counterproductive--even though it may get some forward movement, it also startles both horse and rider. For safety, keep whip use silent and use it as a specific aid only (figs. 3.19 A & B). A *rider* longeing session should never become a *horse training* session—if the horse does not respond your visual whip aids, or he is frightened by them, he may require additional desensitizing and schooling before you use him to longe riders.

The position and movement of the longe whip transmits a variety of specific signals from the longeur's hand to go or stop, accelerate or decelerate, lengthen stride, or move out on the circle.

Active driving aids are delivered by pointing the whip toward the horse. When using active whip aids, the horse is ideally positioned between the rein and whip, as you continually rotate to face him as he travels around the circle. When longeing a rider, you may or may not need active whip aids to communicate; this will depend on the responsiveness of the horse.

Figs. 3.19 A & B
Here, I am keeping the whip silent at my side since the horse is moving forward at the required speed.

Passive aids are offered when the whip points away, either to the side or behind you. Placing the whip handle under your arm so it faces backward and down retires it as a driving aid (see fig. 3.1). I often position the whip in this manner when working with an experienced longe horse that responds well to voice aids and body language. I also keep it behind me when gathering the longe line to approach the horse, such as when both my hands are needed

Fig. 3.19 C
Determine a horse's sensitivity to the whip prior to a rider's longe lesson by warming him up before the rider mounts. Here, I have raised the whip to about hock level when requesting the trot.

to adjust rider or tack, or to change rein. I like to hold the whip in this neutral position rather than putting it on the ground, but if you must, use caution when picking it up. Advise the rider to hold on and do not look down at the whip—watch the horse and reassure him as you pick it up. Remain attentive to the whip's effect, even if you believe the horse is thoroughly desensitized and will not react, horses have a way of surprising us, so it's better to be safe than to be caught unaware.

To determine his sensitivity to the whip, longe the horse on his own, before the rider mounts. Point the whip just behind his haunches and hold it in a low position when requesting walk. Raise it level with the ground or about hock level when requesting trot (fig. 3.19 C). The whip may be lifted to croup-level or higher for canter, or the lash cast overhead. To energize the gaits, wave the lash back and forth low to the ground, or to push the horse out, point the whip at his shoulder or girth, and scoop the lash gently toward him in an underhand fashion. To halt, you can place the whip behind you or touch its tip to the ground in a neutral position. Some longeurs cast the whip overhead and touch it to the ground in front of the horse to request a halt; I have seen this whip aid used in vaulting. Be sure the horse you are longeing is familiar with your whip aids before longeing a rider.

To sum up, here are quick-reference general guidelines for using the longe whip:

- Hold the whip in a low position when requesting walk.
- Raise the whip to about hock level when requesting trot.
- The whip may be lifted to croup level for canter.
- You can wave the lash back and forth low to the ground to energize the gaits.
- To push the horse out, point the whip at his shoulder, or scoop the lash gently toward the shoulder or girth.
- To halt, place the whip behind you or touch its tip to the ground in a neutral position.
- Place the whip under your arm so it faces backward to retire it as a driving aid or when gathering the longe line to approach horse and rider.
- Avoid placing the whip on the ground, but if you must, use caution when picking it up.

Guidelines for Longeing the Rider

Try to minimize your use of voice aids. Combine concise vocal cues, visual whip aids, and body language to communicate with the horse. Your ability to give aids more physically, as opposed to audibly, will help the horse differentiate between your "conversations" with him versus the rider. Consider that riders on the longe may be counting aloud or talking, and you may be instructing them verbally. If accustomed to nonverbal aids, the horse will stay tuned into your body language, longe rein, and whip. Your specific use of gestures, posture, and eye contact for communicating with the horse are all the more important.

Here are some general points to consider when longeing the rider:

- Longeing the rider requires prior longeing experience, common sense, adherence to safety guidelines, good observation skills, and the application of progressive skill-building exercises. If you are an instructor working alone, you must constantly assess safety by seeing the "big picture," evaluating *your* relationship with horse and rider, and between rider and horse.
- Give the horse an opportunity to loosen up on the longe before the rider mounts. A buck or two helps get the "kinks" out, especially if a horse has been sedentary for some time, and riderless longeing is when behavior like this should be allowed, within reason. Horses benefit mentally and physically with a longeing warm-up, but for their own safety, do not allow them to race around the circle out of control. Ensure the appropriate corrections are quickly applied if the horse counter-flexes (bends to the outside of the circle) or begins cross-cantering.
- Stand upright and relaxed, shoulders squared, head balanced. You will need one eye for the horse, the other for the rider. Ground yourself through your feet and keep your center of gravity low using abdominal breathing to stabilize your posture (fig. 3.20). If you lose balance or stumble, you may lose hold of the line, which could endanger horse and rider. If the horse is strong, engage your abdominals, press your heels into the ground, bend your knees and take a step back if necessary.
- You can convey a steady beat to horse or rider when either appear to be faltering—a rhythmical nod of your head and eye contact with the horse can inspire a steady pace, as can emphatically stepping in place, or moving your body to the beat as you walk a parallel circle (fig. 3.21). The horse will watch and respond to your body language. Counting aloud is especially helpful to establish rhythm in the rider (see chapter 9, p. 171, for counting tips).
- When changing rein, it's better to keep the whip under your arm, pointing backward, than to place it on

Fig. 3.20 *The longeur should stand upright and relaxed, feet square, using breathing to stabilize his or her posture as I am doing here.*

the ground (figs. 3.22 A–E). Use the change of direction to reward the horse; you might momentarily unclip one or both side reins while the rider practices a few deep breaths or suppling exercises in halt, then re-clip and proceed in the new direction. When sending the horse away on the circle, use caution—stay behind his inside shoulder and out of the kick zone.

- Most riders and horses enjoy *relaxation* work, as it offers a low-stress interaction that does not involve strenuous effort. Some even become extremely tranquil or too "blissed out." If this occurs with the rider, energize with vigorous breathing. If it occurs with the horse, give him time to revive gradually in walk, before expecting him to snap to attention and go to work.
- Keeping the horse in a slow jog is magical when encouraging a rider to absorb the sitting trot. It quickly dissolves a rider's resistance to movement, relaxing the seat before bringing the trot up to tempo (see fig. 3.23).
- Alert the rider to upcoming transitions so they can prepare. Prompt the rider to inhale first then exhale as you ask the horse to transition (more about this in chapter 10, p. 196).

Fig. 3.21 *Stepping in place, as Jenny is doing here, nodding your head, or otherwise rhythmically moving your body while you longe a horse can help him keep a steady pace.*

Guidelines for Riders Being Longed

Consequences of Forced Longeing

Does the mere mention of rider longeing conjure up images of relentless sitting trot and mercilessly pulling your seat into the saddle until your arms give out? As a student, I endured longe lessons like that. Which is why, as an instructor, I choose to longe riders with a more encouraging approach.

Compelling a body to perform is counterproductive, and if associated with pain, longeing jeopardizes the cooperativeness of rider and horse. Pain inhibits learning, and when moving too fast or making physical changes too soon, we simply tire and fail to absorb the subtler insights longeing can provide. Forceful longeing can result in muscle fatigue, soreness, bruises, saddle rubs, increased anxiety, or falls. It is not an experience riders are eager to repeat, or enter into in the first place. The anticipation of painful consequences is off-putting, and if longeing is approached with a "no pain, no gain" mentality, relaxation and *feel* are inaccessible.

Intentionally pulling to secure your seat can lock up arms, shoulders, neck, and upper back and sabotage our efforts. This can make it harder to sit a horse and is a prime example of excess strength thwarting our best intensions. If the horse begins careening around so fast that you envision being catapulted off, by all means, *hold on*! But forcing your seat into the horse can

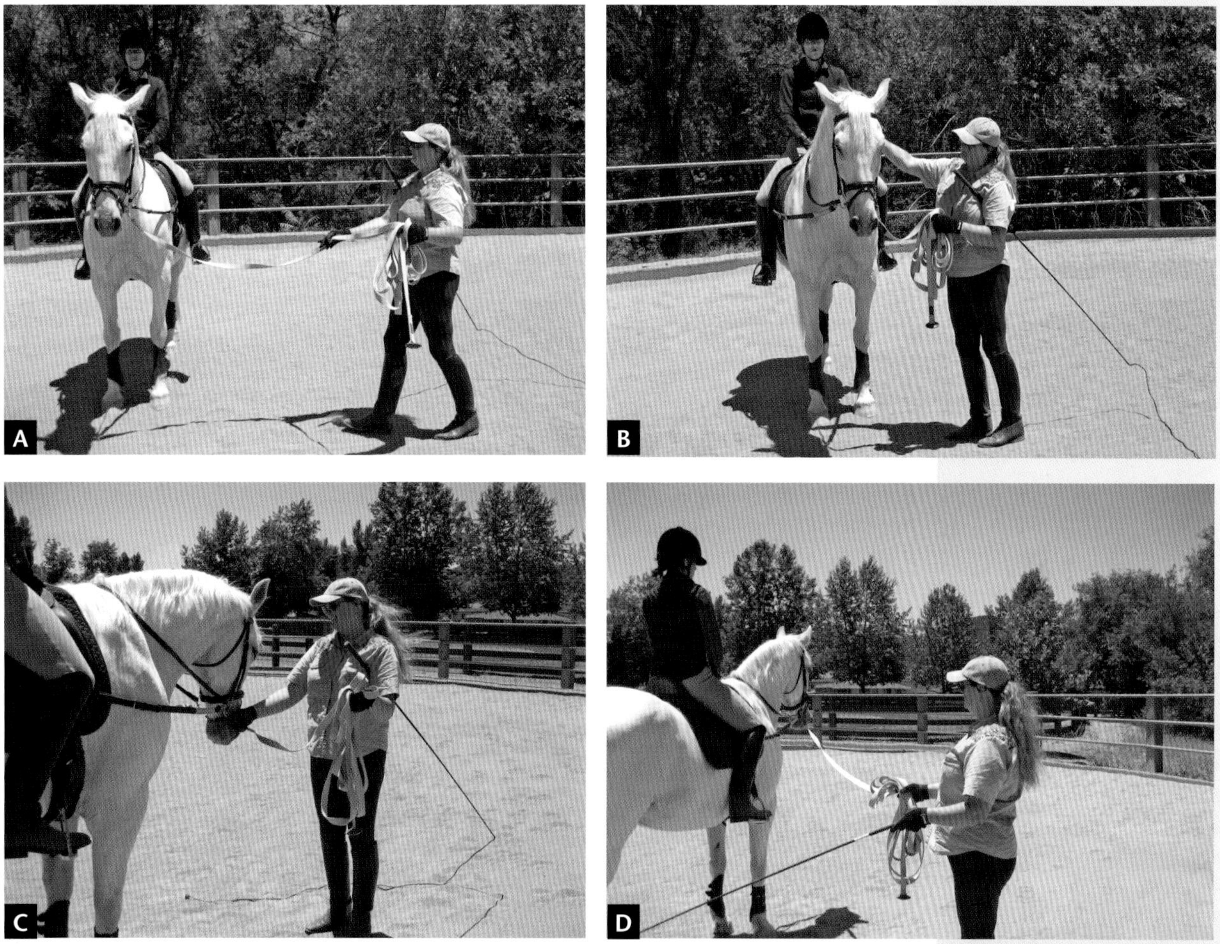

Figs. 3.22 A–E *When changing rein, hold the whip under your arm, pointing backward as you approach horse and rider (A). Use the break as an opportunity to reward the horse as you unclip the longe line and reposition it for the new direction (B & C). Stay behind the horse's inside shoulder as you cue the horse to move off on the circle, and retire the whip behind you once he is moving well forward at the required gait (D & E).*

Fig. 3.23 *A slow jog can help the rider relax at the sitting trot before bringing the trot up to a more forward—and difficult to sit—speed.*

actually cause him to accelerate, as it inadvertently drives him out from underneath.

There is, however, a force that will produce positive results in riding—the natural force of gravity. This powerful ally constantly furnishes a downward attraction, connecting us to the horse below. So why must we force our seat down, unless *opposing* gravity? When we ride forcibly, our muscles clench and our body fights gravity by moving up and away from the horse. *Slowing the pace* enables us to relax and *befriend* gravity, as we let go of resistance and allow our seat to sink into the horse effortlessly (fig. 3.23). Working slowly and mindfully also helps us contend with centrifugal force—the pull toward the outside of the longe circle.

I assure you, longeing does not have to be grueling to be effective. When working *with* gravity, our seat deepens authentically, without force. And when we can maintain seat balance at slow speeds, we are more prepared to move into the working gaits and beyond.

Attire

When being longed, wear riding clothes such as breeches or long pants, boots with a low heel, and an approved safety helmet. Throw away the sticky substance that can adhere your leg to the saddle; come prepared to learn how to do it correctly! Do not wear spurs.

Unmounted Warm-Up

As Eckart Meyners says in his book, *Fit for Riding:* "Riders would make it easier for their horses if they warmed up before they mounted" (see p. 227). A short routine that includes conscious breathing and stretching at the stables is recommended (fig. 3.24). You can practice standing exercises just about anywhere; sitting exercises can be done in a chair, on a mounting block or bale of hay; and you can bring a yoga mat or lay a horse blanket on the ground for exercises lying down. Even a short 5- to-10- minute warm-up can help you "de-stress" and release tension before getting on the horse. To facilitate relaxation and *feel* on horseback, prioritize *suppling* before *strengthening.*

Set an Intention

To achieve goals, it is helpful to set an intention for each longeing session, at the same time remaining flexible and able to address unexpected issues. Your intention can be general, based on basic objectives, such as: *"I intend to integrate conscious breathing throughout my ride today,"* or specific, based on personal challenges: *"My intention is to lengthen my thigh position."* At the end of each session, if you have not yet accomplished your task, appreciate the fact that you are at least taking purposeful steps toward your goals.

Fig. 3.24 *This rider is demonstrating an unmounted version of Chest Expansion (see p. 130), which is a hatha yoga technique.*

Do-It-Yourself Bodywork

Riding without reins leaves you *hands-free* to practice bodywork—applying simple touches to target troublesome areas and guide yourself into a balanced, relaxed position (fig. 3.25). Your own hands can influence areas within reach (anterior torso, seat). For other areas (back, lower legs) your instructor's hands can help. A strategically placed hand increases awareness and prompts an appropriate response to instructions. By enabling you to assess muscle texture and determine how a body part may be performing (are your thighs hard and gripping, or soft and yielding?), hands encourage tight muscles to release and weak muscles to engage. Using hands-on techniques helps relay sensory information to your brain and provides a pathway for messages to travel quickly between mind-body, improving coordination.

Fig. 3.25 *The touch of a hand can provide a direct link from mind to body by moving awareness to a specific spot, which helps you focus thoughts and accomplish desirable physical changes.*

How to Structure a Session

Longe lessons are usually shorter and more intense than other riding lessons, especially when focusing on working trot and canter. For active work on the longe, 30 minutes is usually sufficient, though when you begin with *relaxation* and *suppling* exercises, *bodywork*, and mounted *yoga* in halt and walk, you can easily spend 45 minutes to an hour on the longe line without unduly stressing yourself or the horse. Rather, you will more likely walk away from longeing feeling relaxed and energized, as if you just stepped off a yoga mat! Suppling exercises in halt and walk at the start prepare you for the active work in the faster gaits; concluding each session with them makes a great cool down.

It is important to develop both sides of your body evenly, so be sure to change direction every 5-to-10 minutes, and factor in time for rest breaks. Below is a sample time frame to illustrate how a one-hour longe session can be structured. Your experience on any given day will depend on your fitness level, the horse, the longeur, and circumstances.

Sample Longe Session

5 min. halt	***Relaxation and bodywork***
5 min. walk left	***Warm-up***
5 min. walk right	***Warm-up***
10 min. trot & walk left	***Seat work***
10 min. trot & walk right	***Seat work***
5 min. canter left	***Seat work***
5 min. canter right	***Seat work***
10 min. walk & halt	***Cool-down***
5 min. free walk	****Final relaxation***

***After longeing, hand-walk the horse or take him for a short ride on a loose rein. Your final relaxation can be longer than five minutes, and offers quiet time to reflect on lessons learned.**

Long-Term Longeing

For maximum benefit, you may opt to be longed exclusively for several weeks, months, or longer to establish a firm foundation in rider basics and equitation. Or, if you have a head start on your seat already, in addition to regular riding lessons, you can implement a longeing program to reinforce and refine skills and prevent bad habits.

The rationale is simple—the more you are longed, the better your seat becomes. By removing obstacles and instilling correct riding habits, longeing can save years of frustration that stems from feeling disconnected and unable to control the horse.

Work within Limits

Despite goals, intentions, and a desire for a good seat you must respect the horse's mental and physical limitations—as well as your own. Avoid longeing to the point of fatigue, or pain. In the faster paces it can be hard work, so emphasize quality, not quantity. Take an encouraging approach by rewarding the horse often, and include frequent rest breaks.

If riders proceed without a secure seat and basic skills, it can result in horses being ridden forcibly and insensitively, with too much reliance on excessive grip, a stronger bit, or the use of whips and spurs for "communication." These tactics can cause a horse to object strenuously. If, however, he lacks the disposition to challenge the rider,

or is unsuccessful in his attempts, he may go numb—a lack of sensation envelops him like a protective coat of "body armor."

This is a survival technique adapted by the horse to block pain and discomfort caused by the rider's conflicting aids. Equine body armor shields the horse from unconscious "abuse" that is perpetuated by a rider's lack of seat development. I have seen riders use a whip nearly every stride, and/or spurs, with absolutely no reaction from the horse. These riders say their horse is "dull," resisting, behind the leg, not going forward...but he has likely gone numb intentionally. When a horse is dulled to all natural and artifical aids, there is nothing left to drive him, yet the rider battles on.

Fortunately, when longed without a riding crop, dressage whip, or spurs, and encouraged to release tension, eliminate grip, and focus on *feel*, a "conflict-weary" rider can learn to bring passivity into his riding, while also tempering muscular activity. Under these conditions, an "armored" horse can emerge a different animal, often in the first session! I have witnessed horses, once completely blocked against the rider, "suddenly" respond to fewer aids, and gratefully shed their armor as sensitive riding replaces "fighting."

Riders are understandably shocked at a dull horse's rapid transformation, especially since they perceive they didn't "do" anything to initiate a change. But this is exactly the nature of passivity—results arise through "*non-doing*." Although conflict on horseback is common, it is a relief to know that many modern battles can be resolved through longeing, where the sensitivities of the rider are developed and those of the horse reawakened.

Longeing and Learning

Without the need to control the horse, being longed gives you the opportunity to learn by *listening*, cultivating receptivity in mind and body. You are familiarizing yourself to the gaits and developing a kinesthetic relationship with the horse before *talking* to him with your *active* aids. To listen, you need one "ear" on the horse, one on the longeur, and an "inner ear" on yourself. By "ear," I mean the ability to absorb and process information gathered with self-awareness—so put your antennae out! As you learn to allow the horse's movements to pass through your body without resistance, you become better prepared to learn the language of equitation.

The only "weapon" we employ is body language, the coordinated sequence of individual movements, absolute awareness and concentration, and a strong will. All of that can be learned and, believe me, our horses help teach us.

KLAUS FERDINAND HEMPFLING

CHAPTER 4

Safety Considerations

It is always safer to be well balanced on a firm base of support, i.e., the rider's seat, by being slightly behind the vertical, than perched forward on the crotch/fork, rocking and continually rolling forward on an insecure base of support, using the reins to hang-on with, and placing too much weight incorrectly in the stirrups, with both legs clinging to the sides of the horse well behind the girth. Quite a familiar sight with beginners and novice riders, and the cause of many problems, and accidents.

CHARLES HARRIS

I'll begin my Riding Without Reins longeing program with an overview of three important points to bear in mind as you get started:

1 Safety procedures
2 Mounting and dismounting
3 Introduction to relaxation techniques

Safety Procedures

Emergency Preparedness

Safety orientations are standard when traveling in commercial vehicles like airplanes or boats. It is with far less consistency that safety procedures are provided in commercial horseback riding programs. Students are not always advised how to handle a horse out of control, and do not spend sufficient time developing a balanced seat—the rider's first line of defense. Below I have some suggestions for both the longeur and the rider.

Due to the horse's unpredictability, everybody should acquire a working knowledge of equine behavior and learn in advance what their options are. As the instructor, it can be terrifying to watch a helpless rider consumed by panic not knowing what to do—let alone be that rider! Sometimes in these situations, the instructor cannot "cut through" the rider's fear—he also tends to lose his sense of hearing as well as his sense of space and time. Loud outbursts or screaming can panic the horse even more. I certainly don't want to dwell on thoughts of falling off—but it is crucial to know how to respond to emergencies that may occur in everyday riding—even on the longe—and to remain calm and cool in a crisis.

The Longeur's Role

A critical factor in safe longeing is horse control. While the longeur takes on this responsibility, distractions may startle even the quietest animal, ripping that control (and sometimes the longe line) out of the longeur's hands. Knowing how to prevent a crisis involves standard equestrian safety precautions, one of which is choosing a suitable horse for the job.

Deep breathing can be practiced by the longeur to resonate calm from the center of the circle and ease anxiety in rider and horse. The longeur should remain aware of his posture, movement, and voice and know how these aids can influence the emotional state of the team being longed. Low resonant speaking tones promote relaxation, while louder authoritative tones can be used to initiate immediate action. Any movement by the longeur should be with balance and control and abrupt motions avoided.

The longeur's role also includes important decision-making. For example, if the horse balks or "sucks back," he must determine whether it is safe to push forward, as a key concern of longeing is avoiding "entrapment" panic in the side reins. This happens when a horse feels overly restricted. If he feels he cannot flee forward (since horses don't care to back up) he may rear. When the astute longeur suspects rearing, reassure the horse and unclip the side reins to diffuse the situation. If a horse misbehaves, he can assess whether the rider is endangered and may choose to discontinue longeing if undesirable behavior makes it difficult for the rider to relax—even when the culprit is the rider's own horse.

The longeur must be capable of interpreting equine body language and recognize how long the horse can attentively participate. While most enjoy the meditative, low-stress experience of longeing a rider in slow gaits and seem as if they could go on for hours, they can get charged up in faster paces and last only a short while. Watching the horse's expression, listening for *stress-induced behaviors* like teeth grinding, and tail swishing—the horse typically communicates alarm, restlessness, and agitation before acting on it—provides the longeur a brief window of opportunity to address the situation and prevent it from escalating. Or, notice "tail flagging," head and neck erect, ears perked, eyes wide, which are alarm signals that normally precede a flight response. The longeur must *read* the horse and respect his limits.

The Rider's Role

Since the longeur is standing several meters away, be sure you know how to assist him from the saddle if needed. One technique is to take hold of the knotted reins to help slow or stop the horse if the longeur cannot. And, if the horse exhibits strong behavior or a burst of speed and unexpectedly pulls away, or if requests for a downward transition are ignored, the rider's assistance with the reins may be required. Safe stopping techniques are described in more detail below.

Another safety measure is the "emergency dismount," which involves quickly dropping stirrups and vaulting off. This may be necessary if the horse threatens to rear due to feeling trapped by the side reins—the longeur may call for an emergency dismount for the rider's safety if there isn't enough time to approach and remove the side reins. This tactic is also useful if the rider suddenly loses his seat balance, and if coming off seems inevitable, the safest solution may be to vault off rather than clutch tack, the horse's neck, or precariously hang off his side (which could cause a spook) and falling. (See p. 69 for instructions on the emergency dismount.)

In time, as riders gain independence, their role becomes more complex as they eventually take over all aspects of horse control from the longeur. This is another reason why it is so important to build a strong foundation and take advantage of safe longeing opportunities to develop confidence, trust, and the skills that help keep riding safe.

Safe Slowing and Stopping

There may be times when the rider will need to assist the longeur by slowing or stopping the horse using the bridle reins

Fig. 4.1 *When something unexpected occurs as is happening here with the horse getting too strong, Gerardo thinks quickly, stays calm, and uses the reins to help contain the horse.*

Fig. 4.2 *When the horse is getting too strong, take both reins above the knot and give a series of strong tugs on one rein and then the other.*

(fig. 4.1) Here are a few examples of situations that might require this action:

- When a horse suddenly turns in on the circle or comes off-track, the longeur may ask you to pick up your outside rein to help guide him back out.
- When a horse becomes too strong in his gait, you may need to take up both reins to help slow him down.
- On rare occasions, your reins may be required to stop a frightened horse.

Reaching up for knotted reins may require the forward *light* seat. Use of these reins will likely override the side reins influence, but avoid pulling backward on both reins simultaneously as this could cause the horse to brace against you. Have an instructor give you a safe-stopping lesson in halt before you are longed, and offer the horse much praise for allowing you to practice these strong rein techniques as he's standing still. Here are two methods:

Check Rein

To slow or stop a horse, take both reins above the knot and with the outside rein, exert a direct tug then release (take and give), or a series of strong tugs on this rein in rhythm with the gait to achieve the desired slowing. Or, you might "check" one rein in this manner, then the other (fig. 4.2). Should you need to use this technique while longeing, the longeur should offer guidance and simultaneously decrease circle size by gathering the longe rein to contain the horse.

Pulley Rein

If the longe line breaks or is pulled from the longeur's hands, a mild variation of the pulley rein could effectively prevent the horse from running off. This rein is a strong technique used to regain control by turning him in a tight circle. Remember, the longe horse may be wearing side reins, which may limit your ability to turn: with increasing flexion from the inside pulley rein, the outside side rein attached at the girth will limit bend and thus your ability to tighten your circle.

Fig. 4.3 *This picture shows a rider demonstrating an emergency pulley rein (see text) off the longe. The technique would be the same if the longe line broke, for example. In that case, you would hold the reins above the knot.*

To execute a pulley rein, take both bridle reins above the knot. Shorten the inside rein to flex the horse's head toward the circle center. With your other hand holding the outside rein, press your fist into the horse's crest, or grab a handful of mane to help steady you since the pulley rein could cause a horse to change course abruptly. Simultaneously, push your legs out in front as you lean back and rotate your torso into the circle to stay balanced as the horse's tempo decreases and he eventually stops (fig. 4.3).

Equipment Safety Check

Fitting Your Helmet

A helmet should be level and snug on your head, sitting just above your eyebrows.

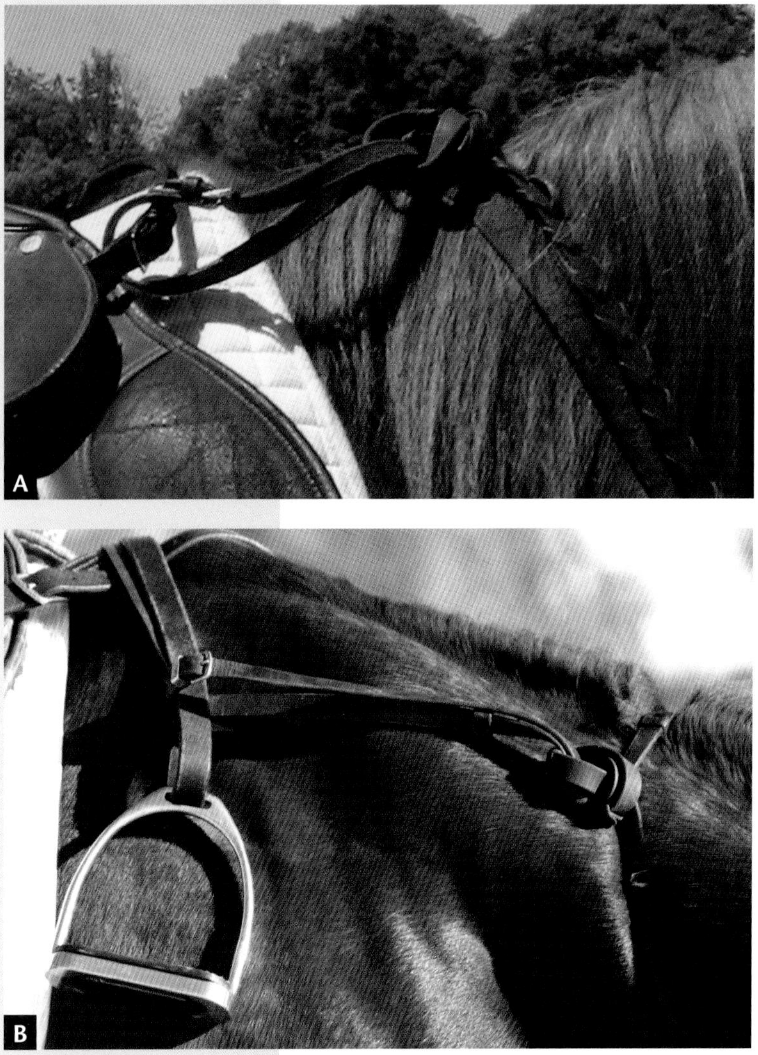

Figs. 4.4 A & B *Knot the reins around the horse's neck, leaving a loop. The knot should lie in front of the withers and the loop can be buckled to the saddle's D-ring, around the pommel safety strap (A), or when riding without stirrups, you can cross them over the horse's withers and slip a stirrup iron through the loop of the rein to keep it in place (B).*

You can test the fit by shifting the helmet forward and back—you'll know it's fitting correctly if your forehead and eyebrows move with it. (Try this in front of a mirror, to be sure.) The harness straps should meet below and slightly in front of your ears; the back of the harness should prevent the helmet from sliding forward. All straps including the one under your chin should be snug, not overly tight. If your helmet has ever sustained a direct impact, you need a new one.

Knotting the Reins

When a horse stretches over his back, he lowers his head and neck, so it is important the reins are secured to other tack and do not slip over the horse's head. Never remove the bridle's reins; always keep them available should you need to use them to help slow or stop the horse (figs. 4.4 A & B).

Tack Check

The fit, position, and security of all riding tack should be checked before mounting including bridle, bit, saddle, stirrups, and girth. Tighten the girth, check saddle and pads are positioned correctly, and leathers on the stirrup bars are secure. Make sure each strap of the bridle is positioned correctly and the bit is hanging properly in the horse's mouth.

Longeing Equipment

Ensure you have a safety strap, and neck strap if longeing in two-point. The longeur may have the longe line attached as you mount, but the side reins should not be connected until you are ready to begin longeing. The longeur should pick up the whip after you mount—it is better to lean it against something rather than lay it on the ground. The longeur should walk with the whip discreetly, holding it under one arm, out of the horse's view.

MOUNTING AND DISMOUNTING
Mounting with Breath

Introduction

The way you mount reveals a great deal about your physical control. I sometimes see riders perform ungraceful landings, even when using a mounting block! No horse deserves an insensitive thump from a rider's clumsy efforts—the operative word is *control*. If you have ever plopped into the saddle and landed heavily upon a horse, do not skip this step.

The ability to mount from the ground is a fundamental skill that all able-bodied riders should acquire. However, because you are about to be longed without reins, you will be guided to use a mounting block while the longeur holds the reins for you. Using a block causes less strain to the horse's back and enables you to mount with greater ease so you can pay closer attention to controlling body and breath.

Mounting will be described from the left side but can also be done on the right as an exercise in symmetry for you and the horse. Carefully prepare horses for right-sided mounting (and dismounting), as many could be startled by unfamiliar activity on the right. Some horses are skittish around mounting blocks. This could become a future training project but for now, if your horse does not stand at the block, apply the instructions while mounting from the ground.

BENEFITS

• Promotes relaxation • Improves balance, coordination, and self-control • Helps prevent the horse from moving off before you are ready •

HOW-TO

Step 1 Position the horse in a square halt, left stirrup aligned with mounting block. (Lightweight blocks can be picked up and positioned at an optimum distance. Otherwise, the horse must be positioned to the block.) The longeur stands on the off (right) side of the horse pressing down on the right stirrup to steady the saddle, holding the longe and/or bridle reins to keep the horse in place.

Step 2 Stand near the horse, facing forward, and place your left foot in the stirrup. Reach for the mane with your left hand; your right hand momentarily on the cantle (fig. 4.5).

Step 3 Inhale, bringing your right hand to the pommel while springing off your

Fig. 4.5 *Step 2: Jenny is getting ready to swing her leg over, one hand reaching for the mane and the other momentarily resting on the cantle.*

TIP

Do not "fish" for the right stirrup while you're in the air, hovering over your horse's back—*sit down first*. Should the horse move during mounting, securing your seat is more important than taking your right stirrup.

right foot, raising your body, and stepping into the left stirrup. Both legs will momentarily touch; keep left knee against saddle and avoid poking the horse with your left toe.

Step 4 Exhale as you fold forward from the hips, support with hands, bring your right leg over the hindquarters with bent knee, lower your right thigh, and gently sit down—all in one smooth motion.

Step 5 Inhale bringing your torso upright, letting right leg hang briefly. Exhale settling fully into the saddle, finally placing your right foot in the stirrup. Continue breathing; adjust stirrups.

Remember to:

- Inhale step up; exhale sit down
- Face forward
- Avoid clenching seat muscles

Vault-Off with Breath

(Emergency Dismount)

Introduction

This dismount should be learned in halt before attempting it from a moving horse. It is the rider's version of a vault-off and the classic emergency dismount. Perform it first from the left side. Once mastered, practice vaulting off the right (as shown) for another exercise in symmetry, and for times when the right side is safer for a dismount.

BENEFITS

• Improves courage and athleticism • Provides a viable option for handling a crisis situation • Promotes safe controlled landings • Helps avoid rider injury •

HOW-TO

Step 1 Take both feet out of the stirrups. Inhale to prepare, while stretching up, straightening both legs and swinging them slightly forward to generate momentum for the next step, which should occur in one smooth, synchronized motion.

Step 2 Exhale and fold down from the hips, bringing your belly to the horse and taking weight onto your hands, on the withers or pommel. Look forward through the horse's ears as you simultaneously swing both legs up behind you over the hindquarters, touching heels together. Practice swinging your legs a few times returning to the basic seat in between (fig. 4.6 A).

Step 3 To dismount, as you're exhaling and when legs are at their highest, slightly rotate hips toward the right, pushing off and away to the right side of the horse, keeping legs together (fig. 4.6 B).

Step 4 As you land near the horse's shoulder, keep feet parallel with knees and ankles bent to absorb the impact (fig. 4.6 C). Look forward the entire time. Inhale as you straighten into an upright position, and if you feel inspired (and if it won't spook your horse), extend your arms up and out like a gymnast (fig. 4.6 D). Exhale and congratulations—you did it!

INTRODUCTION TO RELAXATION TECHNIQUES

Guided Relaxation in Halt

Introduction

As the longeur attends to the horse, reading the following relaxation technique aloud can be assigned to another assistant. It should be read slowly, pausing between each suggestion, to allow time for the rider to process and respond. This relaxation is best practiced without reins or stirrups; eyes closed if comfortable, or with a soft gaze.

BENEFITS

• Helps "ground" and connect you to the horse • Provides a simple progressive relaxation technique • Relieves stress • Enhances awareness • Improves postural alignment • Transitions you from pedestrian to equestrian •

HOW-TO

Take a deep breath and as you inhale, feel a wave of relaxation wash over you (fig. 4.8). As you exhale, slowly allow yourself to sink deeper into the saddle. Keep breathing as you move awareness to your feet. Wiggle your toes, and then relax them. Inhale through your nose as you slowly circle your ankles, and exhale through your mouth with a sigh, letting ankles softly hang down. Continue to breathe deeply and allow your lower legs, shins, and calves to become heavy; just let them go. Soften the backs of your knees and feel your knees sink downward. Inhale and move awareness to your thighs; exhale as you release your upper legs, allowing them to lengthen and stretch, becoming heavy, and soft. Keep breathing and let both legs dangle off the hip joints, letting them drape down around the horse; simply release them to gravity.

Breathe in deeply and move awareness to your abdomen, feel it inflate gently with breath. Stay here for another breath and each time you exhale, release all tension from your abdomen. Now move awareness to your seat. Keep breathing and allow your seat muscles to soften and spread out across the saddle. Notice how your seat feels deeper and more connected with the horse. Inhale and move awareness into your lower back; feel it widen, the muscles spreading out left and right. Exhale and let your sacrum sink as your seat melts into the saddle even more.

Continue breathing and move awareness into your middle back, then your upper back, softening and releasing tension with every exhalation. Feel stress melting away as you become more and more relaxed. Stretch up through your spine letting your back muscles remain heavy. Now inhale and move awareness to your rib cage, then your upper chest. Feel breath moving through your torso. Exhale, and release all tension from the front of your body.

Become aware of your shoulders. Notice that they align directly above your hips. Now, inhale, slowly raise shoulders toward your ears, and hold your breath for a moment while you squeeze and continue to lift shoulders. Exhale with a big sigh, letting your shoulders "thump" back into place. Repeat again—inhale shoulders up, hold your breath while squeezing them, and let your shoulders thump down as you exhale. Continue breathing deeply, feeling more relaxed. Now, draw shoulder blades together, stretching them down toward your waist. Feel your chest open, your torso become more upright.

Fig. 4.8 *Christa is performing her guided relaxation technique.*

Now, inhale and let your arms hang from shoulder joints, heavy and loose. Exhale; give them a gentle shake, and then release. Feel relaxation travel from shoulders into elbows, wrists, palms, and fingers. Give your arms to gravity; let them go completely limp. Inhale, lengthening the back of your neck, and notice your chin is level with the ground. Exhale with a sigh feeling a release of tension across your scalp. Keep breathing and move your head slowly until it's balanced lightly on your neck. Feel relaxation spread across your face as you soften your forehead, temples, the corners of your eyes, eyelids, and the bridge of your nose. Inhale through your nose, and exhale through your mouth with a sigh releasing jaw, tongue, cheeks, and throat.

Take another breath and notice how anchored your seat feels, how connected with the horse. Exhale and sink even more while stretching up through your torso. Take one final deep breath and notice how good you feel!

Start to wiggle your fingers and toes, if your eyes are closed open them, and with a soft gaze look through your horse's ears. Notice how relaxed you feel.

Control Your Emotions

Being longed "holistically," that is with the emphasis on your *whole*—body and mind—acknowledges your physical, mental, and emotional aspects and offers a multi-faceted approach to learning and achieving self-discipline. It provides an opportunity for self-discovery, and rather than a series of mechanical lessons learned by rote, it encourages introspection of what you are doing on the horse and why.

Aside from your obvious need for physical coordination on horseback, one of the greatest challenges riders face is emotional control. Two emotions that commonly surface when riding are anger and fear. Because of riding's inherent risks, when these emotions arise on horseback, they should be immediately diffused before a dangerous situation escalates. The reassurance of a trusted instructor can help, as will slowing the pace and using deep breathing to regain calm. If necessary, you can dismount, resume if able, or try again another day. When you feel calm and secure, you can avoid anger...and confidence grows, giving rise to courage. And when you feel courageous, you allay fears.

For safety's sake, while longeing do not compel your body into a posture or perform an exercise that causes pain or disturbs the horse. Avoid "trying too hard" as skills must be allowed to evolve over time—be patient with yourself and flexible with goal setting. There is no timeframe in which progress is expected or required; practice at your own pace and respect your physical and mental capacity for mounted work. Remember *you* are ultimately responsible for your body even under the supervision of an equestrian professional. Seek qualified instruction and always strive to make safe decisions for you and your horse. If you have prior injuries or physical limitations, obtain the advice of your healthcare practitioner before longeing.

With the longeur directing the horse, you can tap into a holistic learning opportunity not feasible when riding with reins—closing your eyes (fig. 4.9). This promotes an inner-focus and gathering of sensory information that can result in rapid advancements. With eyes closed, you can:

- Center—place attention on your physical center, just below the navel, deep in your abdomen to lower your center of gravity, deepen breath, and improve connection.
- Monitor thoughts—if self-defeating, you can release on an exhalation and replace with affirmative statements, key words, or counting to manifest desired changes.
- Visualize—picture sitting in perfect balance. If you have trouble visualizing, just pretend you can do it. This can prompt the same response and jump-start your imagination.
- Perform mental body scans—start at the tip of your toes, moving awareness to the crown of your head or

Fig. 4.9 *When you are balanced, focused, free of tension, and in control of mind-body-breath on horseback, your riding can become a meditative experience in motion.*

vice versa, while spreading relaxation through your body. If you notice the same tight areas every time, target your suppling efforts on this chronic tension.

- Interpret the horse—learn about the horse's mental state through your sense of touch and lower body contact, by detecting tension, energy surges, tempo changes, and more.
- Listen—decipher the meaning of sounds such as the pattern of the horse's hooves striking the ground, his vocalizations, tail swishing, teeth grinding, or loud exhalations.
- Become absorbed—in the moment, in the movement. This can lead to a flow-experience of skill in motion that redefines riding as a moving meditation.

PART III

ESTABLISHING THE BASIC SEAT

(Suppling Exercises for the Whole Body)

Athletes today are not satisfied with simply being given commands; they want to know why and how things work. An understanding of why you must change something increases your motivation to make that change, which facilitates the learning process.

KYRA KYRKLUND

Introduction to Part III

The Riding Without Reins program continues in chapters 5, 6, and 7 with the first of the Four Phases (see p. 25)—a variety of suppling, centering, and breathing exercises designed to structure your riding position and establish a *basic seat.* Except for two exercises, all this suppling bodywork is learned at the halt on the longe. (In Part IV, p. 146, when a rider's seat is established, they are performed in all the gaits.)

I've divided these exercises into three sections: in chapter 5, you begin by organizing your *midsection* or "center"; in chapter 6, you move to the *lower body*; and conclude with *upper body* exercises in chapter 7. By exploring these distinct parts of the body, and the relationship between them, you can learn to arrange yourself into a coherent whole to more mindfully participate with the horse's movement.

In this phase (Phase One: The Uneducated Seat—Rider as Passenger) the object of the lessons is to help you work through the first of the Four Phases and establish your foundation for good riding. These are the first steps toward developing rider self-control.

Important note: These suppling and awareness exercises are *not* just for beginners, they are for ALL riders, no matter how much experience they might have. As you'll see in later chapters, I've suggested that many of them be used daily by all riders as a mounted warm-up, and when performed at walk, trot, and canter they are the basis of the more advanced work on the longe as you proceed through Phase Two: The "Following" Seat, and Phase Three: The Active Seat. You'll incorporate the Basic Circle's Eight Objectives: Awareness, Relaxation, Breathing, Alignment, Suppleness, Rhythm, Coordination, and Feel, to "work within" each exercise (see The Basic Circle on p. 19, and What Are the Eight Objectives? on p. 156).

A seemingly simple, routine activity such as mounting can become a rewarding multi-layered challenge—even for long-time riders—when the Eight Objectives are taken into consideration while doing it. And blending conscious breathing with movement adds a new dimension to everything you do on horseback, while promoting your balance, safety, and enjoyment of riding and facilitating proper seat development on the longe.

As I will continue to do at the beginning of each of the four phases of seat development, in order to give you a general idea of how a rider longeing program can be structured and what to expect, I will show you a sample of a typical daily longeing session with Phase One exercises (see sidebar).

Phase One: The Untrained Seat—Rider as Passenger

Sample Longe Session

1 Prepare for being longed with a five, ten, or 15-minute unmounted warm-up routine that can include stretching exercises, yoga asanas (poses), and pranayamas (breath work). For discussions of these, refer to p. 6. Cultivating a repertoire of desirable riding skills on the ground beforehand will support your efforts in the saddle and enable you to identify strengths and weaknesses and, in particular, where you normally hold tension. Your growing self-awareness will help devise a personalized pre-longeing warm-up that can be varied as your seat skills develop.

2 After your instructor or longeur completes an equipment safety check, practice Mounting with Breath (p. 67) to develop a balanced technique using a mounting block to get on safely and correctly, landing tactfully in a controlled manner on the horse's back.

3 Practice Vault-Off with Breath in halt (p. 69) to become versed in planned, controlled, safe dismounting and to know what to do if your instructor calls for an emergency dismount during longe work, or when you are riding off the longe.

4 With your feet in the stirrups initially, practice Safe Slowing and Stopping in halt (p. 63) so you know how to take the knotted reins and use them to reduce the horse's speed when necessary.

5 Drop your stirrups while your instructor helps you with Guided Relaxation in Halt (p. 72). This teaches you to perform a "mental body scan" by moving awareness sequentially through each body part to gather information and initiate relaxation. Practice this technique to de-stress, prepare for body movement, and to learn how to relax *at will* on horseback.

6 Practice Centering Breath (p. 87) in halt to lower your center of gravity and stabilize your seat. It is best to Release Legs to Gravity (p. 84) during mounted relaxation, breath work, and the upcoming alignment work.

7 Once you feel centered and relaxed, your instructor can help you align your pelvis correctly using the Centered Pelvis exercise (p. 91). After an evaluation from all sides (front, back, left, right) you will be guided to make the correct postural adjustments in halt. Your goal is to first become familiar with your habitual way of sitting, and then learn the corrections you'll need to establish a balanced sitting posture on a stationary horse. This knowledge better prepares you for making the appropriate seat adjustments while in motion in the gaits.

8 Now that your pelvis is upright and centered, practice Four Corners (p. 95) in halt to become aware of how you distribute weight on your seat bones and how your weight shifts can correspond to the horse's legs. This is an important step in achieving lateral balance on the longe circle.

9 Practice Slow Pendulum (p. 96) to assess range of motion in your hip joints. Be gentle with yourself—even long-time riders may have limited flexibility in their hip joints and are quite surprised to learn how "stuck" they are when they begin seat training. Releasing the hip joints is key to absorbing the gaits for all riders! Practicing this sport-specific exercise (or the Scissor Stretch variation, p. 103) at the beginning of each ride, on and off the longe line, facilitates the development of an independent seat and leg by mindfully suppling these crucial joints.

CHAPTER 5

The Midsection: Breathing and Suppling Exercises

Be brave! It requires a lot of courage to relax the hip and pelvis musculature. Just dare to relax your hips and pelvis and entrust the pelvis to the movement of the horse because this is the only way to be in complete harmony with the horse.

SUSANNE VON DIETZE

Purpose of Suppling and Breath Work

The exercises in this chapter, performed initially on the longe line at the halt and walk, target your body midsection—from waist to mid-thigh—the area that riders call "the seat" or the "center." No matter which of the Four Phases of seat development you are working on (as described on p. 25 in chapter 2), or what level rider you are, I encourage you to explore each of these exercises on the longe. What you may discover about your body and breath could astonish you!

These exercises are invaluable for eliminating grip and learning balance. They aim to secure your seat by keeping your center of gravity low in your body, close to the horse. Many include *instructor bodywork*—simple touches your instructor can do to sculpt your position and help you relax—and *rider bodywork* you can do yourself. The touch of hands is a powerful means to bring awareness to specific body parts, and can be as simple as placing one hand on your abdomen below the navel, the other on your lower back. This allows you to "encircle" your physical center—a powerful headquarters for controlling breath and energy, and where your center of gravity resides when you are ideally balanced.

The chapter begins with an indispensable passive stretch to release leg tension and open your hip joints. Then, by sustaining this posture during breath work, gravity continues to lengthen the tendinous soft tissues of your legs to better prepare you for the bodywork ahead. Rider bodywork in this chapter is subtle and includes exercises to align your pelvis, distribute weight, and increase range of motion in the hip joints. Practiced on a regular basis, these centering exercises that focus on your midsection can facilitate your balanced position and independent seat and legs.

Breath Work

The breath work pertains not only to the exercises in this chapter, but to all subsequent suppling exercises and seat work—in fact, everything you do on horseback. Breathing deeply into your center helps dissolve tension and promotes a calm mind and balanced posture. In contrast, shallow irregular "chest breathing" or holding the breath perpetuates tension and rider top-heaviness that causes imbalance and disconnection with the horse.

Work with a soft gaze or eyes closed, and unless otherwise directed, rest hands on thighs, or hold the safety strap. Practice without stirrups whenever possible and, although it may seem like you're "doing nothing" in passive exercises, gravity exerts a tremendous pull on your legs. If they become fatigued, take back your stirrups. Overexertion due to prolonged passive stretching can cause soreness—even though gravity does the work, you feel the effect. Practice mindfully; do not underestimate the power of gravity.

While holding a position for several

breaths or a few minutes during breath work and bodywork, you can access inner layers of mind-body learning. Perform a mental body scan and ask yourself (or have your instructor ask you) pertinent questions that prompt you to examine how you are feeling and what you are thinking and doing. With the information gathered, you can evaluate your rider basics and improve them. Refer back to chapter 2 to review the Eight Objectives in the Basic Circle: Awareness, Relaxation, Breathing, Alignment, Suppleness, Rhythm, Coordination, and Feel, and use fig. 2.10, The Basic Circle, as a priority checklist to "work within," during each exercise. Also, see What are the Eight Objectives? p. 156, for practical application.

Only with a correct position can correct aids be given. The elegant, calm and quiet position is rooted in function, not only in a sense of aesthetics. The beautiful position is really beautiful because it is effective…I know that one can never have a truly perfect seat and position, but we must always strive to be as close to the ideal as possible.

WALTER ZETTL

Release Legs to Gravity

Allows gravity to passively lengthen your legs and reduce grip

BENEFITS

• Reduces muscular tension • Improves leg passivity • Encourages freedom in the hip joints • Contributes to a deeper seat and correct leg position • Prevents conflicting leg aids and loss of stirrups •

Figs. 5.1 A & B *Step 1: Let both legs dangle from your hip joints. If your upper legs feel tight, place your hands on the inside of your thighs to coax them to widen and release their grip. Or, lift your thighs a fraction of an inch and let them gently plop down; shake them out. You can also briefly massage your thigh muscles to encourage looseness.*

HOW-TO

Step 1 Breathe normally and sit comfortably. Let both legs hang unrestrictedly from the hip joints (figs. 5.1 A & B). Let their weight passively stretch and lengthen thighs. Completely let go. "*Do nothing.*"

Step 2 Let toes hang; do not be concerned with "heels down."

Step 3 Take a deep breath. As you exhale, imagine your seat spreading out and widening across the saddle, from left to right.

Step 4 Keep breathing, letting your seat sink into the horse, releasing tension with each exhalation. Remain here for a few deep breaths.

Remember to:

- Align shoulders over hips
- Avoid "setting" legs into position

TIP

This passive stretch is ideal for warm-ups, cool-downs, halt and walk breaks—whenever releasing tension and grip is necessary. Just drop your stirrups and let your legs dangle, lengthen, and relax.

INSTRUCTOR BODYWORK

There are a variety of exercises in this book where you can lay one or both hands on a rider's leg, as I am doing here, and simply jiggle it in place, gently prompting the release of tension. Always work both legs, encouraging the rider to develop symmetrically.

Fig. 5.2 *I am helping Christa release tension in her legs.*

Breath Awareness

Generates awareness of your breathing habits as a precursor to breath control

BENEFITS

• Cultivates focus and the ability to be present • Provides information on breathing style, depth, pattern, mechanics, and posture, while mounted •

Fig. 5.3 *Step 1: Direct attention to your breath. Notice how it sounds, feels, and moves through your body.*

TIP

You can practice this exercise anywhere—while sitting, standing, lying down, and walking. Awareness on horseback develops more readily when we tune into body and breath *off* the horse, as well.

HOW-TO

Step 1 Direct attention to your breath. Without changing it, notice how it sounds, feels, and moves through your body (fig. 5.3). Is it deep, shallow, uneven, or regular? Do you hold your breath?

Step 2 Observe your upper body during inhalation. Do you lift your shoulders and arms? Does your abdomen move in or out? Do you open your chest; arch your back? Simply notice movements or postural changes without judgment.

Step 3 Observe your upper body during exhalation. Do shoulders and arms drop? Does your abdomen tighten or relax? Is there movement in your upper chest? Do you round your back and shoulders?

Step 4 Observe your lower body during inhalation. Do seat muscles tighten or relax? Do you feel lighter or heavier in the saddle? Do you close or open your upper legs?

Step 5 Observe your lower body during exhalation. Notice if your seat shifts—back/front, left/right, up/down. Can you tell whether you're sitting more heavily on one side or the other?

Step 6 Spend a few moments observing your breath then gently shake out arms and legs.

Remember to:

- Become an observer
- Use this exercise as a precursor to breath control
- Keep legs released to gravity

Centering (Abdominal) Breath

Deepens your connection and instills relaxation in mind-body-horse

BENEFITS

• Maintains low center of gravity • Anchors seat • Cultivates rhythmical cadence in breath, movement, and horse • Improves use of postural muscles and connection with gaits • Promotes stability, relaxation, and calm • Strengthens abdominals • Releases lower back tension • Enhances all rider basics •

HOW-TO

Step 1 When relaxed, we breathe abdominally. Conscious abdominal breathing can be learned like any other riding skill, and eventually becomes automated and natural (fig. 5.4). Place your dominant (active) hand on your lower abdomen below the navel. Place your non-dominant (passive) hand on your lower back—palm against spine, if comfortable. Imagine your hands have a magnetic pull that attracts breath deep into your center.

Fig. 5.4 *Step 1: Centering Breath teaches you to control and deepen your breath at will.*

Step 2 *Inhale* through your nose. Feel your abdomen inflate like a balloon. *Exhale* through your mouth using your active hand to help push out air, while flattening your belly and drawing abdominal muscles *inward* and *upward*, performing an *abdominal lift*. Your passive hand reminds back muscles not to clench during the breathing process. (This instruction is referred to frequently in this book as "exhaling with an abdominal lift.")

Step 3 Inhale and release abdominals. Feel breath rush in as your abdomen expands. Exhale, pushing with your active hand while pulling abdominals toward spine. Keep back muscles soft.

Step 4 Continue for several breaths, engaging abdominals with exhalation, releasing them with inhalation. If you become lightheaded, breathe normally. Remove hands; shake out.

Remember to:

- Assist abdominals with active hand
- Soften back muscles with passive hand
- Draw shoulder blades together and down (imagine wearing a heavy garment that weighs them down)

TIP

If this feels opposite of how you normally breathe, you are not alone. When asked to take a deep breath, many inhale into the chest while sucking in abdomen and lifting shoulders. This "chest breathing" raises our center of gravity and causes top-heaviness—very ineffective when riding.

Centering Breath teaches us to control and deepen our breath at will. It strengthens postural muscles and invites a deeper inhalation, with hands-on bodywork for improved awareness and the ability to *direct* breath. Breath control is a vital tool that greatly improves performance and makes physical riding tasks seem easier.

Advanced Centering Breath

Creates a fluid, cadenced pattern of breath and movement

BENEFITS

• Maintains low center of gravity • Anchors seat • Cultivates rhythmical cadence in breath, movement, and horse • Improves use of postural muscles and connection with gaits • Promotes stability, relaxation, and calm • Strengthens abdominals • Releases lower back tension • Enhances all rider basics •

HOW-TO

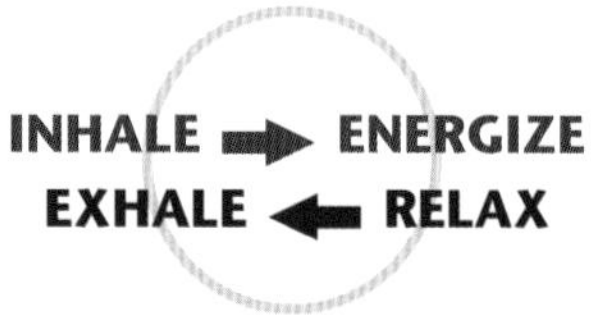

Step 1 Once familiar with Centering Breath (see p. 87), you can develop regularity by matching the length of inhalation with exhalation. With hands on your lower abdomen and lower back as in the last exercise, count silently, inhaling 1-2-3-4 and exhaling 1-2-3-4, segueing without pause. Repeat for several breaths to establish consistency. You can create a fluid cadence first in halt, then in motion (see chapter 9, p. 171).

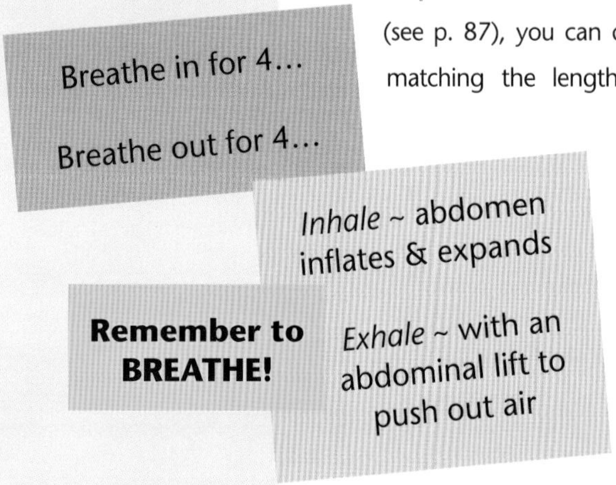

Breathe in for 4...
Breathe out for 4...
Inhale ~ abdomen inflates & expands
Remember to BREATHE!
Exhale ~ with an abdominal lift to push out air

Fig. 5.6 *Practice Centering Breath throughout your day. Take breathing breaks and put little notes in strategic places at home, in the car, on your computer, etc., to remind you of this exercise.*

Step 2 When you can reliably perform *abdominal lifting with exhalation* and keep your lower back relaxed with *hands on*, practice Centering Breath *without hands* to test mind-body coordination.

Step 3 To fully master the exercise, remove hands *and* count silently to regulate the length of inhalation/exhalation with the alternating activity/release of your abdominals.

Remember to:

- Keep lower back relaxed
- Match duration of inhalation with exhalation

Complete Breath

Inflates lungs more completely to improve your position

BENEFITS

• Increases oxygen intake • Provides greater release of tension • Elevates sternum and rib cage • Supports upright balance of torso • Encourages back muscles to release • Teaches the rider to "sit tall" without rigidity •

Figs. 5.7 A–C
Step 1: Inhale into your center; move one hand to your side inhaling more into your ribs; then move it to your sternum and fill your upper chest with breath.

HOW-TO

Step 1 Prepare to experience a more complete inflation of your lungs. This exercise involves a *three-part inhalation* that moves breath distinctly through *abdomen, rib cage,* and *upper chest,* followed by a *complete exhalation.* To start, place both hands on lower *abdomen,* breathing normally. In a moment, you'll inhale into your center, then one of your hands will move to your *rib cage,* which expands sideways, and then it moves to your *upper chest* and encourages the sternum to lift. That hand returns to center, then both hands push out the exhalation. With an *abdominal lift upon exhalation* (see Centering Breath, p. 87), continue lifting through the front of your body to keep torso upright.

Step 2 Inhale into your center; move one hand to your side inhaling more into your ribs; then move it to your sternum and fill your upper chest with breath (figs. 5.7 A–C).

Complete Breath cont.

Fig. 5.8 *Notice how good you feel!*

Step 3 Exhale, using both hands on your center to assist, as you lift abdominals and continue lifting through the front of your torso to support rib cage and sternum—do not let them collapse with exhalation. Simultaneously, relax your back muscles from neck to seat. Allow your back muscles to sink, as your skeleton remains balanced and upright (fig. 5.8).

Step 4 Repeat the *three-part inhalation* directing breath into your torso with one hand. As you exhale, draw shoulder blades together and down while lifting through the front of your torso.

Step 5 Inhale completely once more. Exhale, soften your seat, and lift upward through the crown of your head, chin level with the ground. Feel back muscles drape off your skeleton (fig. 5.9). Resume normal breathing; shake out hands.

Remember to:

- Maintain seat balance
- Keep torso upright with exhalation
- Avoid arching lower back with inhalation

Fig. 5.9 *To help back muscles relax and hang off your frame, imagine the slow drip of honey drawing them downward, creating a sense of heaviness—literally pooling more weight in your seat.*

INSTRUCTOR BODYWORK

Place a hand on the rider's upper back. Feel for the shoulder blades and apply gentle pressure drawing them downward to help with skeletal alignment and muscular release of the back.

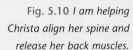

Fig. 5.10 *I am helping Christa align her spine and release her back muscles.*

Centered Pelvis

Evaluates pelvic alignment with bodywork to correct your seat balance

BENEFITS

• Increases anatomical awareness • Cultivates stable secure seat • Enables ongoing postural refinement • Teaches mechanics of weight distribution for balance and weight aids • Eliminates "swayback" or rounded back while maintaining natural spinal curves •

HOW-TO

As a rider, you learn to adapt your sitting posture to the horse and distribute weight correctly to balance your seat. Making specific *pelvic adjustments* enables you to establish a central position between the back/front "edges" of our seat bones (*longitudinal balance*) and the left/right halves of your seat (*lateral balance*). With flexibility and control, you can maintain a centered pelvis that adjusts to the horse's movement. To center the pelvis, an instructor is needed to evaluate your position, and then help you make the appropriate adjustments. In the pages that follow, I present ways to correct longitudinal balance first, and then when you are stable in this, the lateral balance.

Fig. 5.11 *Off the horse, most of us sit asymmetrically, relying on furniture for postural support. Common rider faults result when you attempt to recreate your familiar "chair seat" on horseback. Seat balance can be acquired bareback and is not the responsibility of the saddle, although correctly fitted tack can assist us to develop a centered pelvis and upright posture for a balanced basic seat.*

Longitudinal Seat Balance (Back/Front)

Evaluation: Have an instructor visually assess longitudinal balance to determine if your pelvis is tipped forward due to an arched or hollow back, or tipped backward due to a slumped, rounded back. Misalignment requires adjusting to bring your pelvis into a neutral position. (Note: If your seat is already well balanced from back to front, move ahead to Lateral Seat Balance—see p. 94.)

To Flatten an Arched/Hollow Back and Correct Forward Pelvic Tilt

If your instructor says you're tipping forward, lean back onto the vertical and ensure you feel both seat bones. Then place your hands around your center and practice Centering Breath. During exhalation, simultaneously press your back hand down over your sacrum (the wide bone in your lower spine), guiding it into an upright position,

Fig. 5.12 *During exhalation, press your back hand down over your sacrum, guiding it into an upright position, tucking your tailbone underneath.*

Fig. 5.13 *Here, I'm asking the rider to push her lower back to fill up my hand.*

INSTRUCTOR BODYWORK

If the rider's pelvis is tipping forward, place a hand on the shoulder and gently guide the torso back onto the vertical. (If you cannot reach, have an assistant hold the horse so you can use a mounting block.) Then place a soft flat hand, palm touching, on the small of the rider's back. If excessively hollow, there will be a significant gap between hand and back. Ask the rider to push the lower back into your hand to "fill up" your hand. The rider accomplishes this with a Centering Breath, and simultaneously tucking her tailbone during exhalation to flatten the lower back. Before removing your hand, prompt rider to *remember how your touch feels.*

tucking your tailbone underneath (fig. 5.12). This lengthens and straightens your lower back. Avoid clenching seat muscles or gripping with thighs. Continue until your instructor visually confirms your upright pelvis.

To Straighten a Rounded Back and Correct Backward Pelvic Tilt

If your instructor says you're behind the vertical, lean forward into an upright position, ensuring your seat is in the deepest part of the saddle. Then with hands around your center, practice Centering Breath (fig. 5.14). Upon inhalation, let your abdomen protrude while slightly arching your lower back. Press inward with your back hand, if necessary. Avoid clenching seat muscles or gripping with thighs. Continue until your instructor visually confirms your upright pelvis.

Fig. 5.14 *Using Centering Breath, Christa is ensuring her seat is in the deepest part of the saddle.*

TIP

Once the pelvis is centered *move awareness* through your body to notice if anything else changed. Did your legs tighten or push forward? Has torso alignment altered? Take mental notes. (I will address leg and upper body position in upcoming steps.) Remember what a hand feels like on your lower back, as this can help you adjust independently in motion on the horse.

INSTRUCTOR BODYWORK

Place a hand on the portion of the rider's back that protrudes most behind the vertical; this may be the middle or upper back. Gently guide the rider's torso onto the vertical. With a significant realignment, the rider may discover the seat bones are now too far forward in the saddle. Ask the rider to scoot back toward the middle of the saddle. Then, recheck alignment. If the pelvis still tilts backward, place a hand on the lower back and ask the rider to inhale and push her belly out while simultaneously arching the lower back, pulling it away from your hand. Or, if the rider's back is now hollow, use the flattening technique on p. 91.

Fig. 5.15 *I am guiding the rider's torso onto the vertical to correct a backward tilt.*

Lateral Seat Balance (Left/Right)

Evaluation: Have an instructor assess your lateral seat balance from behind the horse to determine if you are balanced evenly or sitting heavier on one side (fig. 5.16). If you need adjusting, practice the bodywork described in the next paragraph. If you are balanced evenly on both seat bones, proceed to the next exercise (see p. 95).

Fig. 5.16 *When checking a rider's lateral seat balance from behind, develop an eye for "composition," or the arrangement of a rider's body on horseback. By visualizing a grid you can better assess symmetry, see where corrections are needed, and more specifically guide the rider into a balanced position.*

TIP

When your seat is level, it may look right to your instructor, but *feel wrong* to you if you don't normally sit in balance. Rely on the instructor's evaluation until this posture becomes familiar to you. Try sitting on your hands in a chair for more awareness, as information about your unmounted sitting posture can help you understand your riding seat.

To Correct a Laterally Uneven Seat

Take your hands behind and slip them under your seat bones (fig. 5.17). If you cannot feel them, pull your buttocks muscle back until you do. Sit upright, breathing abdominally, seat bones on the tips of your fingers. Without leaning over the sides of the horse, alternately lift and lower hips, left and right, feeling weight shift between seat bones. For assistance, press with fingertips to push seat bones up alternately. Sitting on your hands proves how subtle weight shifting can be and encourages the use of specific pelvic movements that do not disturb your upper body position. Remove and shake out your hands while distributing weight evenly from left to right. Have your instructor confirm when your seat is balanced laterally.

Fig. 5.17 *Slip your hands under your seat bones to evaluate your lateral seat balance.*

Four Corners

Distributes your weight on four distinct points of your seat

BENEFITS

• Increases awareness of pelvic movement and weight shifts • Promotes dexterity, subtlety, security, and control of the seat • Helps anchor seat balance on the circle •

HOW-TO

Step 1 Combining pelvic adjustments to shift weight forward, back, left, and right teaches you to subtly place weight over any particular corner of your seat, or leg of the horse. Start with a Centered Pelvis (see p. 91). Inhale and tilt your pelvis slightly forward by arching your lower back; do not lean upper body forward. Exhale and become aware of the weight shift to the front edges of your seat bones. Keep breathing and remain here as you start lifting and lowering hips alternately. Feel weight shift left to right on your front edges. Return to center.

Step 2 Inhale, stretch up. *Exhale with an abdominal lift* (see Centering Breath, p. 87), tucking your tailbone under to slightly flatten your lower back. Notice the weight shift to the back edges of your seat bones; do not round your upper back. Keep breathing and remain here as you start lifting and lowering hips alternately. Feel the weight shift left to right on your back edges. Return to center.

Step 3 Now, combine these adjustments to navigate the four corners in a clockwise direction starting with the left front. Inhale and slowly shift weight forward to the left front, then right front. Exhale as you shift weight to the back right, then back left. Continue clockwise around the corners once more; return to center.

Step 4 Repeat this exercise in a counterclockwise direction starting with the right front. Inhale as you shift forward—right fore, left fore. Exhale as you shift back—left hind, right hind. Repeat; return to center.

TIP

These pelvic movements should be isolated and imperceptible to all but an experienced eye. If you must exaggerate to experience a weight shift, your torso can be inclined forward, back, left, or right for learning purposes only. Make every effort to reduce upper body displacement until only your pelvis is involved in weight shifting. An appreciation for the importance of this ability will grow relative to your equitation skills.

Remember to:

- Keep torso upright
- Avoid rounding shoulders
- Isolate the pelvis

Slow Pendulum

Opens hip joints and improves flexibility

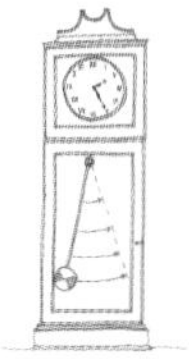

BENEFITS

• Warms up rider while mounted • Opens eyes as well as hips • Increases awareness of mobility in hip joints • Improves flexibility • Contributes to independent seat and leg • Encourages directing breath to a target • Dissolves tension • Promotes isolated leg control without disturbing upright balance of pelvis and torso •

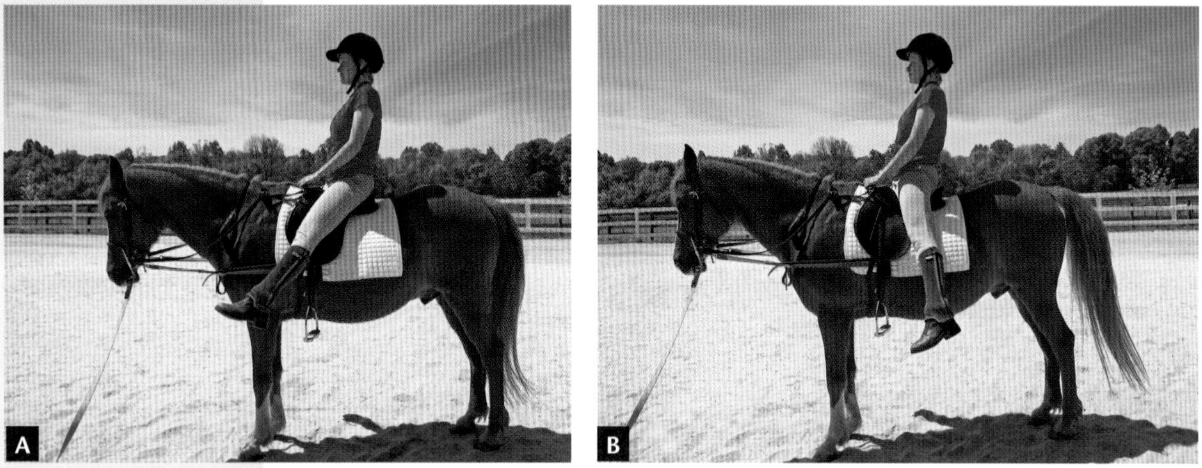

Figs. 5.19 A & B
Step 1: Straighten one leg in front of you. Release the opposite leg to gravity (A). Step 2: Inhale and draw the active leg slowly behind you without leaning forward, losing your seat, or bending your knee (B).

HOW-TO

Step 1 If centering your pelvis (see p. 91) caused your legs to move forward, or if they habitually stick out in front of you while riding (i.e. chair seat), your hip joints may be "stuck." Inflexibility in the hip joints is an extremely common riding obstacle and addressing it is absolutely necessary for a balanced, independent seat. To prepare for the more active stretch of drawing your leg back from the hip joint, first straighten one leg (active) and hold it in front of you with pointed toes, stretching it from the hip joints (fig. 5.19 A). Do not lean back or rest your leg on the saddle. Release the opposite leg (inactive) to gravity.

Step 2 Inhale and draw the active leg slowly behind you without leaning forward, losing your seat, or bending your knee (fig. 5.19 B). Exhale and maintain this extended position for a few breaths. Keep the leg straight, toes pointed. If your leg does not move far, do not force or strain.

Step 3 As you inhale, direct breath into any tight areas in your seat. As you exhale, ensure your opposite leg is still uninvolved. When ready, release the active leg; return to center.

Step 4 Repeat several times with the same leg, keeping it extended longer if desired. Then repeat the exercise on the opposite side. Notice if one hip joint feels tighter than the other. If so, practice more on your stiff side. Practice carefully; do not overdo this exercise.

Remember to:

- Isolate active leg
- Remain upright
- Avoid bending knee
- Move slowly and mindfully

TIP

Riders are often surprised at how challenging it is to isolate one leg—you may find your inactive leg really wants to be involved! Avoid using the opposite leg for balance or allowing it to tighten. Gently shake it out to release tension.

Take care when practicing—move your leg back *slowly* to avoid cramping as you direct breath into tight areas. If you reach your "edge" and find there is little to no range of motion, that's okay—start today and with routine practice, your hip joints and leg/seat independence will improve. This exercise (like Scissor Stretch, see p. 103), does not allow your seat to follow the horse's movement so is best performed in halt and walk.

Figs. 5.20 A & B *I'm identifying the location of the hip joint, then to keep Christa's leg straight, I place one hand on her knee and the other on her ankle before slowly guiding her leg back from the hip.*

INSTRUCTOR BODYWORK

Riders frequently bend at the knee in attempting to move their leg back. This brings the lower leg back but prevents the rider from realizing the full benefit of this exercise, which is to loosen the hip joint. Identify the location of the joint, then to keep leg straight, place one hand on the knee, the other on the ankle and slowly, gently guide the leg back from the hip. Many riders are very tight, so be cautious and communicate with the rider when assisting—never force the leg.

Putting Finishing Touches on the Basic Seat

You are now centered, balanced, breathing deeply and evenly. Your torso is upright, legs relaxed, hip joints suppled, and you're ready to put the finishing touches on your basic seat and prepare for the suppling exercises (fig. 5.21). The more you develop your basic seat, the more effective your riding can become no matter what discipline you decide to pursue. Your basic seat will carry you from being just a passenger, to a follower, leader, and eventually trainer, if you so desire. It is a valuable asset to polish and refine throughout your riding experience.

Adhering the Seat

Locating your *seat bones* and learning to shift weight between them helps anchor you and prepares you for balancing on the longe circle. But *adhering* to the horse, rather than simply concentrating all your weight on these bony pelvic points, soften your seat muscles to let weight spread across a wider surface area. Widen your lower back, hips, buttocks, and thighs as your weight sinks below your seat bones, deepening the seat. The thighbone (femur) is the largest in your body and is designed for supporting weight. When you let weight from your torso sink into the backs of your thighs (a suitable weight-bearing surface) your seat takes on an adhesive quality. A deep, wide seat not only helps you feel connected and secure, but is more comfortable to the horse and invites his back muscles to lift and carry you.

Strengthening the Seat

The *abdominal lift during exhalation* (see Centering Breath, p. 87) builds strength in core muscles for postural stability. Abdominals are the hardest working muscles in seat development, followed by the thighs, which strengthen over time by riding without stirrups and working in the forward seat. The abdominals play a major role in riding and students of any age, discipline, and skill level can increase abdominal use through an ongoing practice of Centering Breath.

Riders can also benefit by cross-training for abdominal strength—there are a variety of complementary fitness practices that help develop seat skills off the horse, such as yoga, Pilates, martial arts, fitness ball, gymnastics, or any exercise that cultivates upright posture and core muscles. It is important, though, to isolate abdominal activity from the lower back muscles, as when the back is engaged, it can actually push the horse away. The tighter and more tense the rider's back, the more the horse is driven away by the tension. If intentional, a strong lower back can be used as a driving aid. Or, if inadvertent, it can cause the horse to speed up without the rider understanding why. A horse that seems hard to slow or stop may be triggered by unconscious lower back activity. This can result in a loss of horse control,

Fig. 5.21 *This rider is breathing deeply and evenly, and is centered and balanced. Her torso is upright, legs relaxed, and hip joints suppled.*

which may increase excessive leg and arm strength (grip), which is what imbalanced riders rely on for security. This chain reaction can be broken by longeing in slow gaits and practicing suppling exercises to release unnecessary activity, while the appropriate muscular strength for riding is cultivated.

CHAPTER 6

The Lower Body: Suppling Exercises

In attempting to obtain suppleness it should be remembered that good humor is conducive to relaxation, which in turn leads promptly and directly to confidence.

UNITED STATES CAVALRY SCHOOL, FORT RILEY (from *American Military Horsemanship*)

Building a Sturdy Base

Riding Without Reins now builds on the work on your *midsection* presented in chapter 5, and offers a series of exercises that address the *lower body* to promote *independent control* of your limbs. Like all bodywork, the process of suppling lower body muscles and joints is multilayered, and an ongoing task appropriate for riders in any phase of seat development, at any level.

Continue using The Basic Circle (p. 19) with the Eight Objectives: Awareness, Relaxation, Breathing, Alignment, Suppleness, Rhythm, Coordination, and Feel, to "work within" each exercise (see p. 20). This enables you to obtain maximum benefit by consciously assessing your strengths and weaknesses each step of the way.

The exercises in this chapter will prompt you to remain *centered* as you learn to organize and isolate the segments of your legs. They include techniques to:

- Supple hip, knee, and ankle joints
- Widen your straddle
- Eliminate unnecessary grip
- Establish a flat thigh contact
- Deepen your heels

And because your lower body must serve as a sturdy a base for your torso, you'll be introduced to postures "above" the horse that lighten your seat; raise your center of gravity; and challenge your stability. To finish, there are stretches that start toning and limbering your back, and a fun exercise to bring a little humor to your work!

Learn all these exercises in halt; as with the others, you can perform these in the gaits later on (see chapter 9, p. 171). Remember to work slowly and mindfully; never force or strain. Most exercises are ideally practiced without stirrups using a soft gaze or eyes closed. Unless otherwise indicated, begin in *basic seat* and *breathe abdominally* as described in Centering Breath (see p. 87). Rest hands on thighs, let them hang, or hold the safety strap as necessary.

"Return to Center"

As you proceed with the suppling exercises in this chapter, *return to center* means coming back to your basic seat. Because the basic seat is a whole-body achievement, it combines balanced posture with a state of relaxed mental focus and the absence of emotional stress.

The basic seat is both a comfortable starting and ending place for all suppling exercises. To *return to center* anchor your seat, stretch up through your spine, balance shoulders over hips, let arms hang soft and heavy, wrists and fingers relaxed, thighs dangling from hip joints, the back of your knees soft, lower legs hanging, with feet beneath your hips. Without stirrups, toes and ankles relax; with stirrups, heels drop, ankles flex. Keep your mind quiet, calm, and focused on the rhythmic sound of your breath.

Scissor Stretch

Increases flexibility in hip joints and integrates leg movement with breath

BENEFITS

• Improves range of motion in hip joints • Cultivates independent legs and seat • Warms up legs • Increases awareness of both halves of pelvis •

HOW-TO

Step 1 Inhale and stretch one leg forward, the other backward (fig. 6.2). Point toes and straighten legs, creating long lines of energy from hips to toes.

Step 2 Exhale and slowly switch position of legs.

Step 3 Repeat several times, "scissoring" legs and alternating positions *slowly*, coordinating movement with breath. Return to center.

Fig. 6.2 *Step 1: Inhale and stretch one leg forward and the other backward.*

Remember to:

- Maintain upright torso
- Keep legs straight
- Move slowly with awareness

TIP

This exercise is ideal for a *rider warm-up* on and off the longe. Because your pelvis is not able to follow the gait while scissoring, an unfamiliar horse may hesitate or take slower steps. The longeur should encourage him to walk on.

Frog

Deepens seat and strengthens abdominals by opening the straddle

BENEFITS

• **Warms up rider in saddle** • **Strengthens abdominals** • **Flattens lower back** • **Stabilizes and deepens seat** • **Widens straddle** • **Reduces excessive grip** • **Helps rider learn to "sit back" and find rear edges of seat bones** •

Fig. 6.4 *Step 2: Exhale with an abdominal lift (see Centering Breath, p. 87) and simultaneously lift your knees outward and upward while leaning back slightly to sit on the back edges of your seat bones.*

HOW-TO

Step 1 Hold pommel or safety strap. Inhale, stretch up, and release legs to gravity.

Step 2 *Exhale with an abdominal lift* (see Centering Breath, p. 87) and simultaneously *lift your knees* outward and upward while leaning back slightly to sit on the back edges of your seat bones (fig. 6.4).

Step 3 Inhale, relax abdominals and lower knees with control, coming back to the vertical.

Step 4 Repeat for several cycles.

Step 5 On your last exhalation hold Frog as an isometric posture. With knees at maximum width/height, engage your abdominal muscles throughout inhalation/exhalation for several breaths. Then release, slowly lower legs, and return to center.

TIP

Rather than pushing knees up by bracing calves and ankles, think of *lifting with abdominals* and let lower legs dangle, feet relaxed. Separating knees to *widen the straddle* takes priority over lifting. Frog may reveal that your seat is too far back. To correct, reposition seat bones more forward, in the saddle's deepest part. If your legs are now too forward, practice Slow Pendulum (p. 96) or Scissor Stretch (p. 103) to release hip joints so that legs can be suppled to hang down below your center. When performing Frog in trot or canter, practice only the isometric version (Step 5) or the subtler Modified Frog (p. 106), while maintaining seat rhythm.

INSTRUCTOR BODYWORK

Take the rider's lower leg—one hand on her knee, the other underneath her foot. Gently lift, guiding it into the Frog or its modified version (see p. 106). Help reduce bracing by gently swaying the rider's lower leg and rotating the ankle to release the tendency to "set" the foot in a "heels down" position.

Fig. 6.5 *I'm taking Jenny's lower leg—one hand on her knee, the other underneath her foot—and gently lifting it into the Frog position.*

Remember to:

- Exhale *lift*...inhale down
- Emphasize width over height
- Dangle lower legs and feet
- Avoid hollowing lower back

Modified Frog

Eliminates knee pinch to prevent grip and stabilize seat balance

BENEFITS

• Deepens seat • Eliminates grip • Widens straddle • Improves leg control • Shifts rider weight back • Transfers weight from front of thighs and inner knees to back of thighs and seat bones •

HOW-TO

Step 1 Similar to isometric Frog, but the knees lift minimally—a fraction of an inch to a couple of inches. Sustain for several breaths, maintaining seat rhythm. Then release, return to center (fig. 6.6).

Step 2 When practicing *with* stirrups, spread toes in your boots to help hold stirrups as you lift heels gently, widen your straddle, and shift weight to the back of your seat.

Remember to:

- Lift knees minimally
- Practice gently
- Emphasize width over height

Fig. 6.6 *Step 1: This exercise doesn't lift the knees as high as Frog (see p. 104).*

Dancer

Lengthens and stretches thighs while opening the hip angles

BENEFITS

• Lengthens thighs • Opens hip joints • Widens straddle • Deepens seat •

HOW-TO

Step 1 This is a modified version of a classic yoga asana and a traditional longeing exercise. To begin, inhale and stretch up. Exhale, reach down, and take hold of your foot, ankle, or shin as your knee bends and points downward (fig. 6.7).

Fig. 6.7 *Step 1: Inhale and stretch up, then exhale, take hold of your foot, ankle, or shin as your knee bends and points downward.*

Step 2 Inhale, draw your heel up toward the cantle. Exhale, extend thigh to be as vertical as possible. Release your opposite leg to gravity.

Step 3 Maintain for several breaths, relaxing into the pose. Slowly lower leg, and return to center. Repeat to the opposite side.

Remember to:

- Stretch knee downward
- Keep opposite leg passive
- Avoid gripping

Legs Away

Loosens inner thighs to increase range of motion in hip joints and widen straddle

BENEFITS

• **Supples hip joints** • **Widens straddle** • **Tones leg muscles** • **Improves balance in motion** •

TIP

Legs Away can also be practiced with bent knees in forward seat with stirrups. If combining Legs Away with Standing in Stirrups (p. 113) from a lighter seat, be cautious, as with shorter stirrups your center of gravity will be higher above the horse.

HOW-TO

Step 1 Drop stirrups. Hold pommel or safety strap. Inhale and slowly straighten both legs down and point toes.

Step 2 Exhale, and lift legs out to the side, away from the horse's barrel (fig. 6.8). Soften the backs of your knees if necessary. Ensure elbows haven't turned out!

Step 3 Maintain posture for several breaths. Then release, lower legs slowly, return to center.

Fig. 6.8 *Step 2: Exhale, and lift legs out to the side, away from the horse's barrel.*

Remember to:

- Relax arms, elbows in
- Maintain upright balance
- Stretch in small increments—do not force

Ankle Suppling

Improves shock absorption and encourages proper foot position

BENEFITS

• Increases ankle flexibility • Helps prevent toeing-out • Improves shock-absorbing quality of ankles • Contributes to a deep, stable seat •

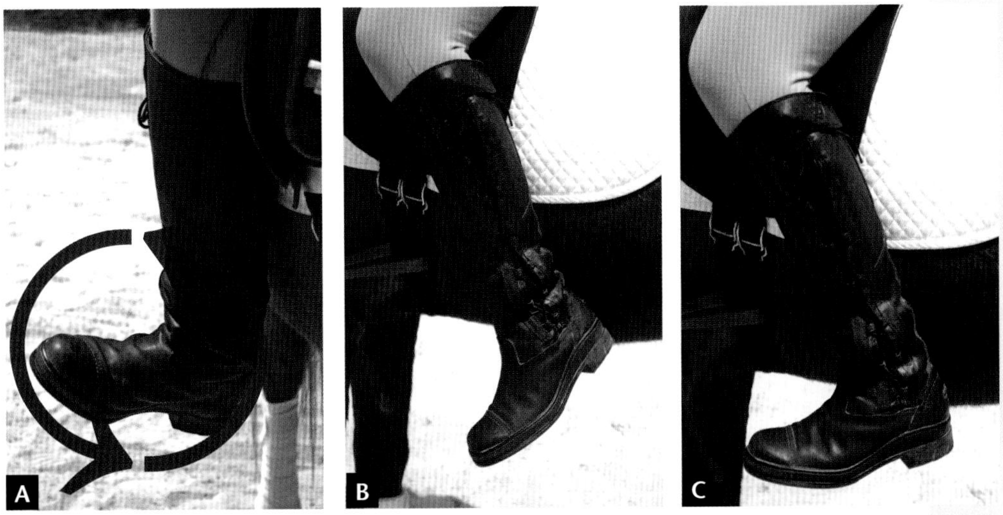

Figs. 6.9 A–C *Step 1: Inhale and stretch up, then exhale, flex both ankles, and keep breathing while slowly circling them (A). Step 2: Inhale and point toes downward to extend ankle joints (B), then exhale and flex ankles by lifting toes (C).*

HOW-TO

Step 1 Inhale, stretch up. Then exhale and flex both ankles, with toes turned upward and inward. Keep breathing and slowly circle both ankles toward the horse (fig. 6.9 A). Make several rounds; then stop and circle them away from the horse. If you tend to toe out, repeat inward circles. Release your feet; return to center.

Step 2 Now, inhale and point toes downward to extend (open) ankle joints. Exhale and flex (close) ankles by lifting toes. Ensure knees do not open and close. Repeat for several breaths. Return to center (figs. 6.9 B & C).

Remember to:

- Practice without stirrups
- Isolate the movement

TIP

Keep lower legs relaxed; do not push feet out in front of you. Emphasizing inward rotation counteracts toeing-out.

Ankle Suppling cont.

INSTRUCTOR BODYWORK

To help the rider isolate this movement and make ankle circles—not lower leg circles—place one hand on ankle, the other under the toe of the rider's boot. Gently rotate foot slowly in both directions. Then point and flex the foot while holding it stable to prevent the lower leg from shifting. Have rider repeat without your assistance.

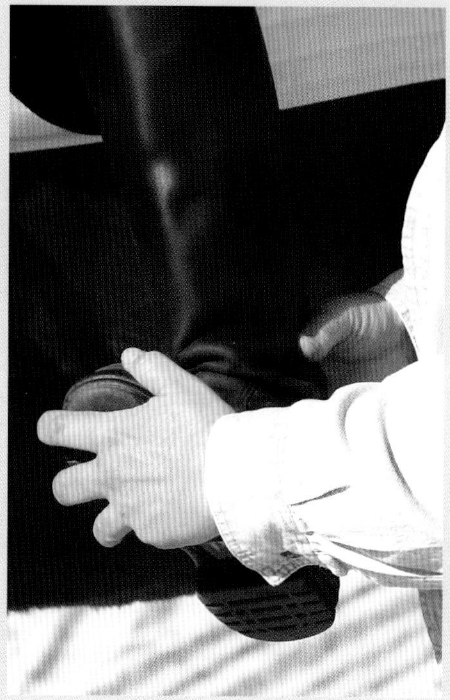

Fig. 6.10 *I'm helping Christa isolate this movement and make "ankle circles," not "lower leg circles."*

Thigh Rotation

Establishes flat thigh contact and limbers hips with a deep stretch

BENEFITS

• Increases hip joint flexibility • Flattens thighs • Tones calves • Contributes to seat independence and correct leg position • Establishes a deeper seat • Helps prevent toeing-out •

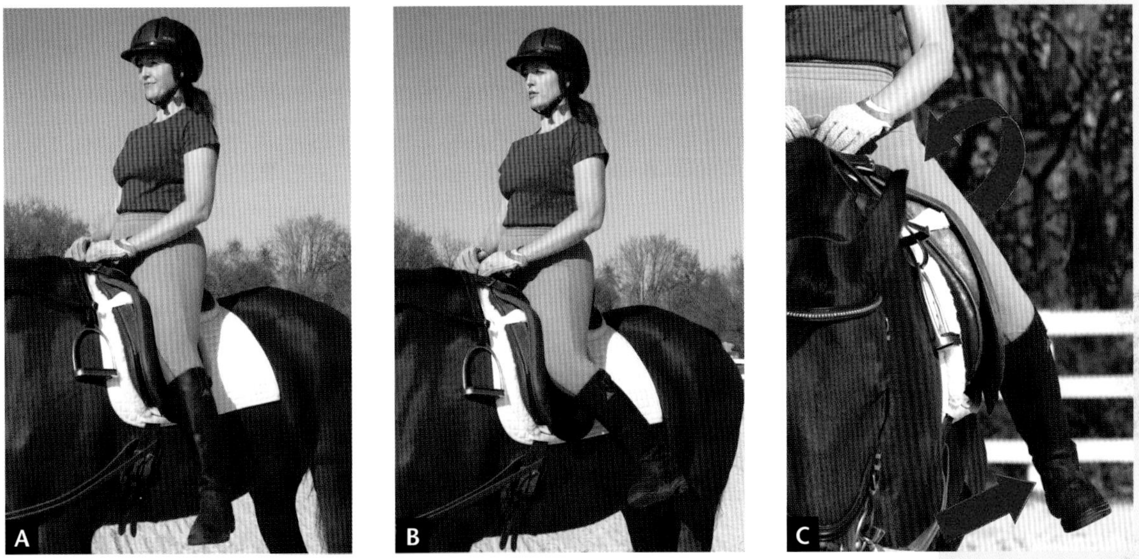

Figs. 6.11 A–C *Step 2: Simultaneously turn both knees into the saddle as you draw your heels away, distancing your lower legs from the horse and causing your thighbones to rotate inward.*

HOW-TO

Step 1 Drop stirrups and release legs to gravity. Inhale; stretch up. Exhale and assume an imaginary stirrup position with knees bent, heels down and aligned under hips, lower legs near barrel. Keep breathing and move slowly to avoid cramping—this stretch can be powerful.

Step 2 Simultaneously turn both knees into the saddle as you draw your heels away, distancing your lower legs from the horse. This will cause your thighbones (femur) to rotate inward, toward the horse (figs. 6.11 A–C). Move awareness to your arms—did you involuntarily rotate them? Ensure arms and elbows do not change position.

TIP

Turning knees in while pulling heels away can cause an unconscious jutting of the elbows—you may find yourself doing the "funky chicken!" Remember to keep your arms and elbows relaxed.

Thigh Rotation cont.

Step 3 Maintain the posture for a few breaths, directing inhalations into tight areas in your seat while exhaling out tension. Release legs; return to center. Repeat as desired.

Remember to:

- Flex ankles and knees
- Breathe into tight areas
- Watch your elbows!

INSTRUCTOR BODYWORK

Use your hands to help the rider rotate and flatten her thighs against the saddle. Reach under the back of her thigh, drawing the large muscle out from underneath; repeat on the other side.

Fig. 6.12 *I'm helping Jenny rotate and flatten her thighs against the saddle.*

Standing in Stirrups

Promotes balance by aligning legs below the center of gravity and deepening the heel

BENEFITS

• **Encourages awareness, balance, and proper foot position in stirrup** • **Eliminates knee grip** • **Helps prevent "riding on toes"** • **Stretches hamstrings** • **Improves leg position** • **Prepares rider for rising trot** •

Figs. 6.13 A & B *Step 2: Inhale and push your body higher by lifting heels, standing on toes, and extending your ankles (A). Step 3: Exhale, flex your ankles and allow your heels to sink down. As your seat lowers, remain standing (B).*

HOW-TO

Step 1 With one hand on pommel, the other on cantle, inhale and stand up in stirrups, elongating through your spine. Exhale; secure your balance.

Step 2 Inhale and push your body higher by lifting heels, standing on toes, and extending (opening) your ankles. Note the instability this causes (fig. 6.13 A).

Standing in Stirrups cont.

Fig. 6.14 *Stand in your stirrups with your heels down for security.*

TIP

Momentarily offsetting balance by lifting heels illustrates the instability caused by "riding on toes," a common fault that results in excessive grip. Practice lifting/lowering heels in halt and walk, but stand in stirrups *with heels down* for security in trot or canter (fig. 6.14). If you fall backward while standing, your legs are likely too forward. To correct, widen straddle, and draw legs back and underneath you.

Step 3 Exhale, flex (close) your ankles and allow heels to sink down. Notice how this offers more stability. As your seat lowers remain standing; do not sit down yet (fig. 6.13 B).

Step 4 Repeat lifting/lowering in stirrups for several breaths—up and down on toes. On an exhalation, ensure heels are down, and slowly return to center.

Remember to:

- Ensure knees do not pinch
- Align legs under center
- Remain standing

Two-Point Position (Forward Seat)

Strengthens legs and supples knees and ankles for a balanced light seat

BENEFITS

• Lightens the seat • Teaches balance • Increases challenge of other lessons • Improves leg position, flexibility, and strength • Encourages heels-down position • Prepares rider for faster paces, jumping, and hills •

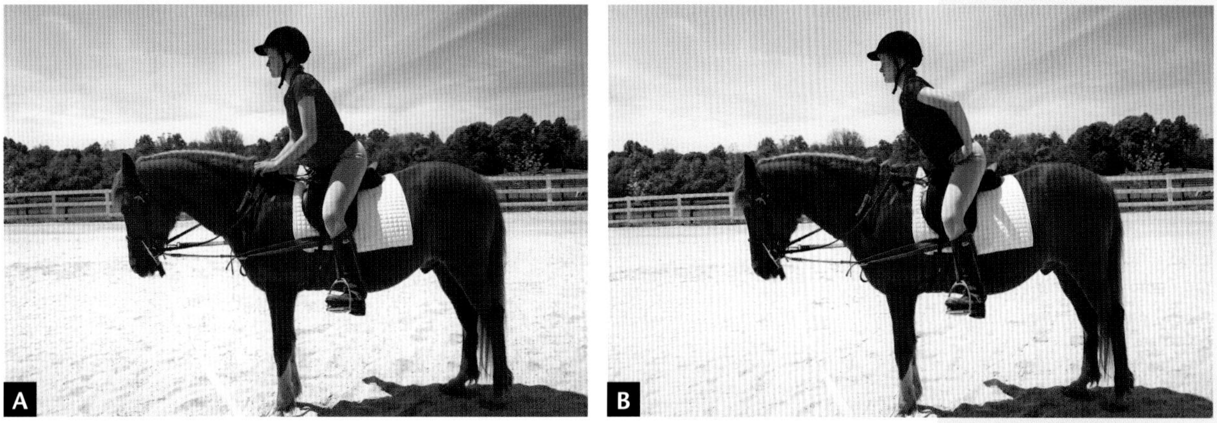

Figs. 6.15 A & B *Step 1: To begin the first step, exhale and reach for the neck strap or a handful of mane, lifting your seat as you incline forward from the hip joints with a flat back (A). Step 4: Once you are centered and balanced, place your hands on your hips (B).*

HOW-TO

Step 1 Inhale, stretch up. Exhale and reach for the neck strap or a handful of mane, lifting your seat as you incline forward with a flat back from the hip joints. Push your buttocks back over the saddle's deepest part (fig. 6.15 A). Flex knees and ankles; keep legs below hips. Avoid arching lumbar spine, or rounding shoulders.

Step 2 Breathe abdominally and relax into the position. Check knees—do not pinch the saddle or carry weight on your knees. Allow weight to sink into the backs of your thighs and down into stirrups. Notice ankles flex, heels lower, toes lift. Wiggle toes and spread them out in your boots. Ensure stirrups remain on the balls of your feet.

Step 3 Inhale and elongate through your spine from tailbone to the crown of your head. *Exhale with an abdominal lift* (see Centering Breath, p. 87) for stability as you relax your back muscles.

Two-Point Position cont.

Step 4 Once you are centered and balanced, place hands on hips. Remain here for several breaths, then exhale, slowly lower your seat and return to center (fig. 6.15 B).

Remember to:

- Shorten stirrups one or two holes
- Incline forward from hip joints
- Avoid pinching with knees

TIP

For more of a challenge, Two-Point Position can be teamed with arm exercises. It can also be practiced without stirrups. First assume imaginary stirrups—knees and ankles flexed, heels down. Pinching knees or the front of your thighs into the saddle in an effort to lift the seat can disrupt balance and cause instability. Instead, use the back of your inner thighs for weight-bearing and lightening the seat; do not lift very high.

INSTRUCTOR BODYWORK

If the rider's pelvis tilts forward, place a hand on the lower back to help flatten the lumbar spine (fig. 6.16 A). Have the rider *exhale with abdominal lift* (see Centering Breath, p. 87) while tucking tailbone and pushing lower back into your hand. To check for pinching and weight bearing at the knee, slip your fingers between inner knee and saddle. If tight, gently pry it loose (fig. 6.16 B). If rider's wrist is bent, guide into a straight, neutral position; check moveability of the elbow by flexing. Repeat bodywork on opposite side (fig. 6.16 C). When rider places hands on hips, recheck lower back and knees.

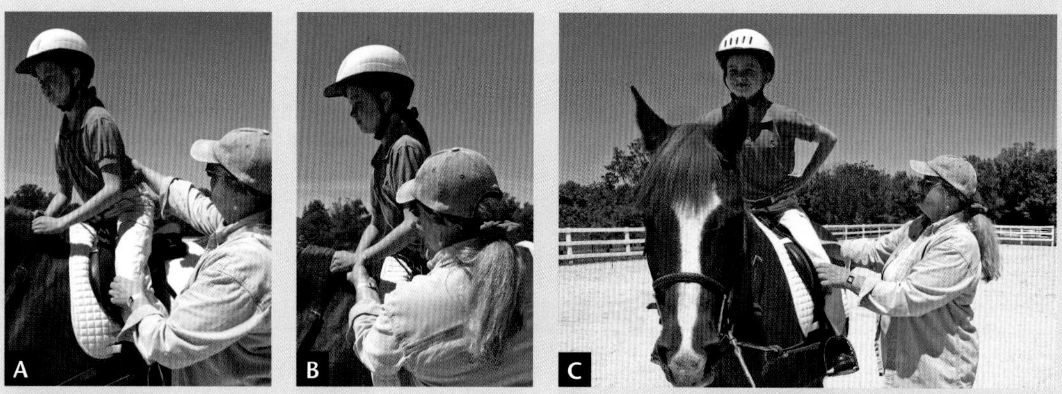

Figs. 6.16 A–C *I'm fixing Marissa's pelvis, which has lifted forward, straightening her wrist, and checking for pinching at the knee.*

Chin to the Mane

Adds versatility and flexibility while toning leg and back muscles

BENEFITS

• Balances and strengthens rider • Encourages ability to move from one position to another •

HOW-TO

Step 1 Begin in Two-Point Position (see p. 115), holding mane or a neck strap. Inhale, elongate through spine.

Step 2 *Exhale with an abdominal lift* (see Centering Breath, p. 87) and fold forward from the hip joints down to the horse's neck. As you lower your chin to the mane, keep your back flat and shoulder blades together. Your seat remains over the deepest part of saddle, heels below hips, and elbows pointed downward (fig. 6.17).

Fig. 6.17 *Step 2: As you lower your chin to the mane, keep your back flat and shoulder blades together.*

Step 3 Stay here for several breaths. Scan your body for tension and release any muscles that don't need to be working—relax into the position (see Guided Relaxation in Halt, p. 72).

Step 4 Inhale, return to Two-Point Position; then exhale and return to center.

Remember to:

- Look through the horse's ears
- Draw shoulder blades together
- Align legs under hips

TIP

We commonly round the shoulders and upper back when leaning forward, so remember to keep your upper back flat by drawing your shoulder blades together.

Gentle Back Bend

Releases the rider's back while developing trust in the horse

BENEFITS

• Stretches spine in opposite direction from forward bending exercises (see p. 117) • Encourages open angles at hip joints • Releases back muscles • Expands chest • Builds rider's trust in self and horse • Offers a comfortable relaxation position (depending on cantle height) •

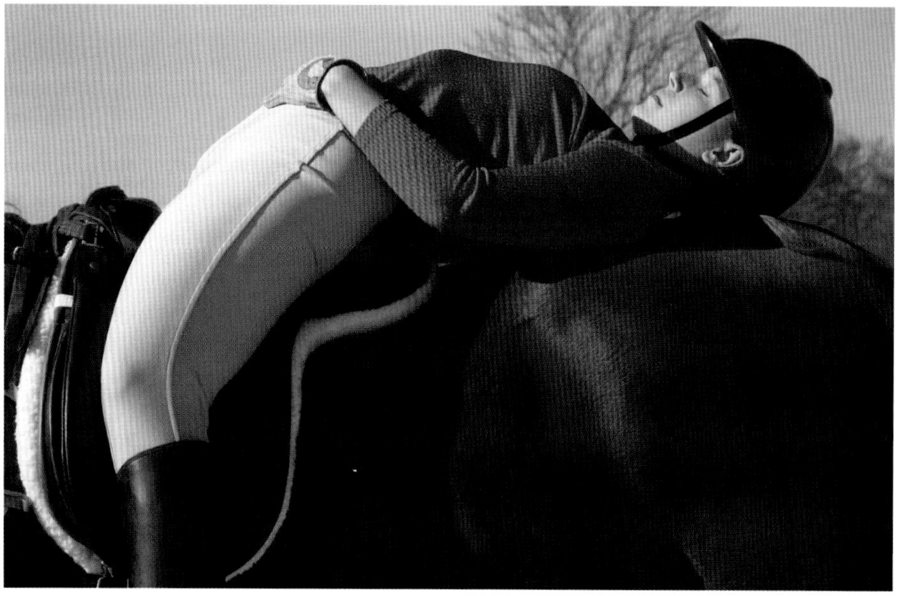

Fig. 6.20 *Steps 1 & 2: Inhale, and lean back slowly until your head rests on the horse's croup. Remain in this position as long as you and the horse are comfortable.*

TIP

If your saddle has a high cantle, try this exercise bareback instead.

HOW-TO

Step 1 Drop stirrups, inhale, and lean back slowly until your head rests on the horse's croup (fig. 6.20). If you require assistance, have an instructor spot you.

Step 2 Exhale with an audible sigh for a greater release of tension as you relax into the horse. Continue breathing deeply and remain here as long as you and the horse are comfortable.

Step 3 Inhale into your center to come upright, pushing hands against cantle to help raise torso. Then exhale and return to center.

Remember to:

- Practice without stirrups
- Work with a spotter

Around the World (The Mill)

Cultivates balance and coordination with a sense of playfulness

BENEFITS

• **Develops balance, coordination, courage, and control** •

Figs. 6.21 A–D *The Around the World exercise, step-by-step.*

HOW-TO

Step 1 In *basic seat*, face forward or "North." Place your right hand on pommel, left hand on cantle. Inhale and stretch up, straightening your *right* leg. Exhale, lifting right leg up and over the horse's neck to sit sideways, legs together, facing "West" (figs. 6.21 A & B).

Step 2 Inhale and straighten your *left* leg. Then exhale and lift it up over the hindquarters to straddle the horse to the rear, facing "South" (fig. 6.21 C).

Step 3 Inhale and straighten your *right* leg, then exhale and lift it up and over the hindquarters to sit sideways, legs together, facing "East" (fig. 6.21 D).

Step 4 To face "North," inhale and straighten your *left* leg, then exhale and lift it up and over the horse's neck to return to center. The sequence can be reversed and repeated.

Remember to:

- Keep torso upright, head balanced
- Move legs over horse without touching
- Momentarily release handholds to let leg pass

CHAPTER

7

The Upper Body: Suppling Exercises

A stable upper body is the prerequisite for following the horse's movement. Stable does not mean rigid, but rather steady, well-adapted to the situation... The secret of effortless, harmonious riding is to be found in a balanced upper body!

SUSANNE VON DIETZE

Promoting Rider Self-Carriage

This chapter on suppling exercises for the *upper body* continues your progression in Riding Without Reins by building on chapter 5, "The Midsection: Breathing and Suppling Exercises," and chapter 6, "The Lower Body: Suppling Exercises." For riders at any phase of seat development (see the Four Phases, p. 25, chapter 2), practicing upper body exercises at the halt helps increase *independence* in hands, arms, and shoulders while suppling the spine. By combining traditional longeing exercises, mounted yoga, and hands-on bodywork, this series of exercises promotes a rider's self-carriage by cultivating an upright skeletal alignment with muscular relaxation and joint mobility.

The bodywork in this chapter is intended to release chronic tension from common areas such as your neck, shoulders, and upper back. You will be guided to flex your spine (including your neck) forward, backward, to the sides, and rotationally, as in the twisting exercises. You'll also learn to coordinate rhythmical arm movements with breath and seat, and to center your hands in preparation for holding the reins.

When practicing upper body exercises, *do not move erratically*—always control your arms. If you're a novice rider, be sure your trainer has accustomed the horse to arm movements before attempting them yourself. Again, learn exercises first in halt; later when you have mastered a following seat you can practice them in the recommended gaits (see lists on pp. 178, 184, and 190). When holding a posture for a few breaths, or practicing an exercise for several moments, remember to use the Basic Circle's Eight Objectives (The Basic Circle, p. 19, and sidebar, What Are the Eight Objectives? on p. 156) to "work within," and hone your rider basics.

Riding is movement and harmony. Incorrect riding is strain and torment. Should we ask our horses to carry us if we ourselves are not limber, fit and dexterous? No, we should not.

KLAUS FERDINAND HEMPFLING

Head & Neck Stretches

Relieves stress and improves flexibility with mild stretching

BENEFITS

• Releases tension from delicate areas where it is often stored • Promotes flexibility of cervical spine • Integrates breathing with slow conscious movement •

7.1 A & B *Step 1 ("Yes"): Exhale, lowering your chin to your chest, then inhale and lift your head up, tilting it back to look upward if you are comfortable.*

TIP

Practice in the gaits to release head and neck tension whenever you feel braced or stiff in that area. Head movement should gently follow the gaits, not bob excessively. For more suppling, combine "yes" and "no" movements for a controlled circular rotation of the head.

HOW-TO

Step 1 "Yes": Inhale, stretch up through your spine. Exhale, lowering chin to chest. Inhale, lift head up, and tilt it back to look up, if comfortable (figs. 7.1 A & B). Repeat for several breaths, inhaling upward, exhaling downward. Return to center.

Step 2 "No": Inhale and turn your head to look over one shoulder, your chin level with the ground. Exhale here and release your shoulders. Now inhale again while turning your head to look over opposite shoulder. Exhale here with a sigh, for a greater release of tension. Continue for several breaths, inhaling to move, exhaling to release. Return to center.

Remember to:

- Move slowly with awareness
- Release shoulders and draw them downward
- Keep torso balanced and upright

Bent Willow

Enhances relaxation with a deeper release for neck and shoulders

BENEFITS

• Relieves stress from neck and shoulders • Improves range of motion in the neck • Cultivates relaxation and poise •

HOW-TO

Step 1 Inhale one arm overhead, reaching up. Exhale, bringing the palm of that hand to rest on your head, fingertips above ear. Gently guide ear toward your shoulder and stretch the opposite side of your neck. Let gravity take the weight of your head and arm; do not push it down. Continue breathing, drawing shoulder blades together and down.

Step 2 To increase neck stretch, reach for the ground with your opposite hand. Hold for a breath or two. When ready, on an inhalation bring head upright then exhale and slowly lower arm. Return to center, and repeat to the opposite side.

Fig. 7.3 *Step 1: Gently guide your ear to your shoulder and stretch the opposite side of your neck. Let gravity take the weight of your head and arm.*

Remember to:

- Elongate through spine
- Align shoulders over hips
- Let gravity assist you

Shoulder Rolls

Encourages independent hands by increasing absorption of the gaits in shoulders

BENEFITS

• **Promotes independence in shoulders, arms, and hands** • **Encourages joint mobility and correct posture** • **Breaks up chronic tension and improves relaxation** •

Figs. 7.4 A–C *Step 1: Inhale both shoulders up toward your ears and exhale as you roll them back and down (A). Step 2: Inhale one shoulder up, then exhale and roll it back and down. Repeat immediately with the opposite shoulder (B & C).*

HOW-TO

Step 1 Inhale both shoulders up toward ears; exhale as you roll them back and down. Repeat for several breaths. Return to center (fig. 7.4 A).

Step 2 Now inhale one shoulder up. Exhale and roll it back and down. Repeat immediately with the opposite shoulder (figs. 7.4 B & C). Continue alternating shoulder rolls with breath for several cycles. Return to center.

Remember to:

- Isolate shoulder movements
- Relax forearms
- Integrate breathing

TIP

Rolling the shoulders sounds like a simple task, however, your hands and forearms like to get involved. For independent hands, you must isolate shoulder movements so that you do not inadvertently hold the reins with your shoulders and upper back muscles. Start this exercise by holding onto the safety strap or pommel to prevent hands from lifting up, or rest them on your thighs. Work up to practicing Shoulder Rolls with imaginary reins (p. 155), and then while Carrying Cups (p. 143).

Practice shoulder rolls frequently, on and off the horse. Try them when driving a car or bike, with your hands on the steering wheel or handles, or while carrying a drink in one or both hands—use these props to isolate shoulder movement from your hands.

Arm Raise with Breath

Improves mind-body coordination and connects rhythmical movement with breathing

BENEFITS

• Integrates abdominal breathing with slow controlled movement • Increases relaxation • Improves rhythmic awareness, coordination, independence, and balance • Supples shoulders and upper back •

Figs. 7.5 A & B *Step 1: Inhale while slowly raising your arms out the sides with your palms up, reaching above your head (A). Step 2: Exhale while slowly lowering your arms back to your sides with your palms down (B).*

TIP

Match the length of inhalation with exhalation while coordinating arm movements. When in motion on the horse, integrate arm movement with breath *and* seat rhythm.

HOW-TO

Step 1 Let your arms hang from shoulder joints alongside your body. Inhale as you straighten your arms and slowly raise them out to the sides, palms up, reaching above your head, with arms and fingers energized, palms facing (fig. 7.5 A).

Step 2 Exhale palms down while slowly lowering arms until they return softly back to your sides (fig. 7.5 B).

Step 3 Repeat for several breaths. Return to center; shake out arms.

Remember to:

- Release legs to gravity
- Maintain seat balance/rhythm
- Energize through fingertips
- Move slowly with control

Crescent

Feels great as it aligns your torso and supples your spine to each side

BENEFITS

• Elongates spine and releases tension from back muscles • Integrates abdominal breathing with slow controlled stretching • Enhances relaxation • Improves upright alignment and balance in motion •

HOW-TO

Step 1 Inhale and begin with an Arm Raise (p. 128). Then exhale, clasp hands together overhead, release shoulders.

Fig. 7.7 *Step 2: Inhale, stretch up with your palms turned toward the sky, then exhale and relax your seat while slowly flexing to one side.*

Step 2 Inhale as you turn palms upward, and push them toward the sky. Exhale; relax your seat, while slowly flexing to one side, stretching from tailbone out through the top of your head. Lift your head up out of your shoulders and avoid looking up, or bringing your chin to your chest. Hold for a few breaths.

Step 3 Inhale back to a vertical position, pushing palms toward sky. Exhale, anchor seat, and slowly flex to the opposite side. Ensure both seat bones remain grounded as you stretch through your head. Hold for a few breaths (fig. 7.7).

Step 4 Inhale once again to a vertical position, pushing palms upward. Exhale, slowly lower arms, and shake them out. Return to center.

TIP

Match the length of inhalation with exhalation. Because your torso will hang over the side of the horse, practice in halt and walk.

Remember to:

- Avoid thigh grip
- Anchor seat bones
- Keep head aligned with spine

Chest Expansion

Dissolves shoulder stiffness and corrects a rounded upper back and collapsed chest

BENEFITS

• Draws shoulder blades together • Opens chest • Improves postural alignment • Releases shoulder tension • Strengthens back and arms •

HOW-TO

Step 1 Inhale, stretch up, and clasp your hands together behind your back. Exhale and draw your shoulders down, lifting your arms up and away from your body. Check pelvic alignment to ensure your seat remains centered and avoid rolling onto the front edges of your seat bones (fig. 7.8).

Step 2 Look forward with a soft gaze. Remain in this position for several breaths, lifting your arms and feeling openness through the front of your body. Return to center; shake out your arms.

Fig. 7.8 *Step 1: Inhale, stretch up, and clasp your hands behind your back. Then exhale and draw your shoulders down as you lift your arms up and away from your body.*

Remember to:

- Anchor seat bones
- Avoid arching lower back
- Lift sternum

> **TIP**
>
> If you have trouble clasping your hands, try holding a dressage whip, crop, or lead rope with both hands behind your back, then lift arms. Chest Expansion is a great exercise to include with rider groundwork.

Camel

Opens your chest and draws shoulders back for a gratifying release of tension

BENEFITS

• Flexes mid-upper spine • Stretches and opens chest • Eliminates back and shoulder tightness • Draws shoulder blades together • Improves posture •

HOW-TO

Step 1 Place hands on cantle. Inhale as you lift through the front of your body, raising your chest, and arching your middle and upper back.

Step 2 Exhale, feel your chest continue to expand, letting your head tip back if comfortable, and drawing shoulder blades together (fig. 7.10).

Step 3 Continue breathing, opening the front of your body, and giving shoulders a good squeeze. Remain in this position for a few breaths, relaxing into the pose.

Step 4 Slowly lengthen the back of your neck, bringing chin level with the ground, as you sit upright, using hands for support. Return to center.

Fig. 7.10 *Step 2: Exhale, feel your chest continue to expand and let your head tip back if you are comfortable as you draw your shoulder blades together.*

TIP

Follow with Big Horse Hug (p. 132) to stretch your spine in the opposite direction.

Remember to:

- Center your pelvis
- Stay grounded
- Support torso with arms

Big Horse Hug

Builds trust as you relax your back and honor the horse

BENEFITS

• Stretches arms and shoulders • Releases back muscles • Encourages rider to reward horse • Provides a counter-pose for Chest Expansion (p. 130) and Camel (p. 131) •

Fig. 7.11 *Step 1: Exhale and bend forward, sliding your arms down and around the horse's neck as you lie across his withers and give him a big hug!*

TIP

While lying across the horse, try to feel your breath moving through your lower back, which lifts gently with inhalation and falls with exhalation.

HOW-TO

Step 1 Inhale, stretch up. Exhale and bend forward while sliding arms down and around the horse's neck as you lie across his withers and give him a big hug! Continue breathing and release your back muscles as you surrender your weight to the horse. Thank him for teaching you. Hold for several breaths (fig. 7.11).

Step 2 Using your hands, push up slowly and roll back onto the vertical. Return to center.

Remember to:

- Keep legs under hips
- Reward the horse
- Relax!

Easy Twist

Rotates your spine and prepares you for correctly balancing on the circle

BENEFITS

• Encourages spinal rotation in both directions • Teaches lateral balance • Improves flexibility, alignment, and symmetry • Releases tension •

HOW-TO

Step 1 Inhale, with an Arm Raise (p. 128). Exhale and while floating your arms downward, rotate your center to one side, placing one hand on the pommel, the other on the cantle. Rotate spine uniformly. Release legs to gravity and remain here for a few breaths.

Step 2 With each inhalation stretch through your spine to the top of your head. With each exhalation, twist a little more. Ensure shoulders are level; relax into the pose. Then release arms, unwind, return to center, and repeat to the opposite side.

Step 3 Notice if there is any difference in flexibility between left and right sides. If so, repeat twist once again on your stiff side.

Fig. 7.12 *Step 1: Exhale, allow your arms to float downward and rotate your center to one side as you place one hand on the pommel and the other on the cantle.*

Remember to:

- Release legs and avoid knee/thigh grip
- Keep shoulders level
- Center and anchor seat
- Avoid arching lower back
- Rotate from your center

TIP

When practicing in the gaits and rotating toward the outside of the circle, keep weight on the inside seat bone for lateral balance while maintaining seat rhythm and vertical alignment. Ensure that you don't collapse at the waist or drop a shoulder, as this could inadvertently cause the horse to fall off the circle. If right-handed, you may naturally twist to the right more than the left. Strive to create symmetrical lateral flexion. Keep head and neck in alignment with the rest of your spine; chin level with ground. Avoid looking down, as this offsets balance. Do not grip with thighs to twist farther.

INSTRUCTOR BODYWORK

In halt, jiggle rider's legs gently to ensure they are not gripping.

Symmetry

Promotes the proper vertical and horizontal alignment in your riding position

BENEFITS

• Ensures horizontal shoulders and hips, and vertical spinal alignment • Energizes and strengthens arms and upper back • Teaches how to direct awareness, breath, and energy through the body •

TIP

When practicing in motion, be sure to also maintain the proper lateral alignment on the circle, with inside hand and shoulder reaching toward the center of the circle. Practice in forward seat (two-point) for additional challenge and strengthening.

HOW-TO

Step 1 Inhale, slowly lifting arms to shoulder height; palms down.

Step 2 Exhale, directing breath through outstretched arms. Keep them shoulder height, drawing shoulder blades together and downward (fig. 7.13). Have instructor check your position and help you adjust as necessary to improve symmetry.

Step 3 Inhale, lengthen the back of your neck, and stretch up through the top of your head.

Step 4 Exhale and direct breath out through your fingertips, like bolts of electricity.

Step 5 Continue for several breaths, slowly lower arms, shake them out. Return to center.

Fig. 7.13 *Step 2: Exhale, directing your breath through your outstretched arms as you hold them at shoulder height and draw your shoulder blades together and downward.*

Remember to:

- Release legs to gravity
- Anchor seat and center pelvis
- Keep shoulders/hips level

Symmetry Twist

Challenges your seat and postural alignment by increasing lateral flexion

BENEFITS

• Promotes seat stability on the circle • Encourages vertical, horizontal, and lateral balance • Supples and rotates the spine • Fosters seat independence •

HOW-TO

Step 1 Begin in Symmetry (p. 134). With outstretched arms, inhale and stretch up through spine.

Step 2 Exhale, and rotate from center, twisting to one side, keeping arms parallel with the ground, shoulders level. Check for grip; release legs to gravity. Continue for a few breaths, directing energy out through fingertips with exhalation (fig. 7.14).

Fig. 7.14 *Steps 2 & 4: Rotate, twisting to one side with your arms parallel to the ground and your shoulders level. Release your legs to gravity and "energize" your arms and fingers.*

Step 3 Inhale, stretch up, return to Symmetry.

Step 4 Exhale, slowly rotate center to opposite side, energizing arms and fingers. Keep head and neck in alignment with spine; chin level with ground. Continue for a few breaths.

Step 5 Inhale, return to center, slowly lower arms, and shake them out.

Remember to:

- Stretch up through spine
- Avoid gripping
- Keep arms and shoulders level
- Maintain seat balance/rhythm
- Start the twist from your center

TIP

Do not rotate head or upper body more than lower body and avoid collapsing at the waist. Keep shoulders over hips. When rotating to the outside of the longe circle, maintain weight shift on inside seat bone for lateral balance.

Side Stretch

Supples and elongates your torso to help you sit taller and more relaxed

BENEFITS

• Stretches both sides of body equally • Supples spine and shoulders • Promotes secure seat • Encourages seat independence and upright balance •

HOW-TO

Step 1 Place one hand on your thigh as you inhale the other up slowly, keeping elbow and wrist straight. Anchor both seat bones evenly and extend up through fingertips. *Exhale with an abdominal lift* (see Centering Breath, p. 87) that continues up the front of your body as you reach up and over toward the opposite side. Only stretch as far as you can without losing seat balance (fig. 7.15).

Fig. 7.15 *Step 1: Exhale with an abdominal lift that moves up the front of your body as you reach up and over toward the opposite side.*

Step 2 From your center, stretch downward through your tailbone as you simultaneously stretch upward through the top of your head, keeping your neck in line with the rest of your spine. Remain in this position for a few breaths, then inhale arm up as you return to a vertical position, and then exhale your arm down.

Step 3 Repeat to the opposite side, return to center, shake out arms.

Remember to:

- Avoid gripping and arching your lower back
- Anchor opposite seat bone
- Lift through crown of head
- Relax seat muscles
- Keep head and neck in line with spine

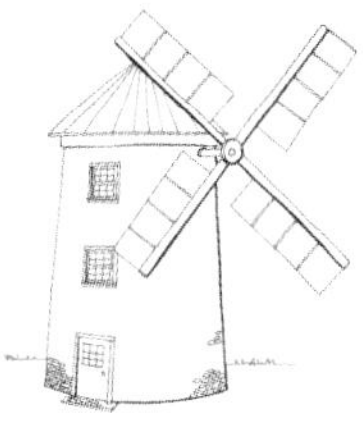

Arm Circles & Windmill

Increases self-control and independence of arms and shoulders

BENEFITS

• **Coordinates movement with breath • Relaxes and supples arms and shoulders • Opens chest • Draws shoulder blades together • Improves posture • Challenges seat balance and rhythm •**

Figs. 7.17 A & B *Step 2 (Arm Circles): Inhale both arms up in front of you, and then exhale as you circle them back and down (A). Step 3 (Windmill): Inhale one arm up in front of you, and as it begins to descend behind you, begin to circle the other arm in the same manner (B).*

HOW-TO

Step 1 Arm Circles: Inhale one arm up in front of you, move it overhead, and then exhale as you circle it back and down. Keep facing forward and avoid twisting upper torso. Continue for a few breaths. Then repeat circle in the opposite direction with the same arm, inhaling up behind you, then exhaling it forward and down. Return to center; repeat with the opposite arm.

Step 2 Arm Circles: Inhale both arms up in front of you, then exhale as you circle them back and down. Continue for a few breaths then stop and circle arms in the opposite direction, inhaling back and up, exhaling forward and down (fig. 7.17 A).

Arm Circles & Windmill cont.

Step 3 Windmill: Make a windmill by inhaling one arm up in front of you, and as it begins to descend behind you, start to circle the other arm in the same manner (fig. 7.17 B). Continue for several breaths, then stop and repeat windmill circles in the opposite direction, inhaling one arm up behind you, and as it descends in front, begin circling the other arm. Continue for several breaths. Return to center.

Remember to:

- Move slowly with control
- Inhale arm up/exhale it down
- Stabilize shoulders
- Avoid rotating torso

Fig. 7.18 *Open your chest and bring your shoulder blades together.*

TIP

When you are practicing this in motion on the horse, make fluid circles and match rhythm of arm movements with breath and seat. Emphasize circling backward to open chest and bring shoulder blades together.

Elbows Opened/Closed

Reinforces elbow placement and your ability to reach forward in balance

BENEFITS

• Increases awareness of elbows • Promotes isolated control of arms • Encourages independence between hands and seat • Reinforces seat stability when reaching forward •

HOW-TO

Step 1 Position hands with imaginary reins (p. 155), elbows bent approximately 90 degrees and aligned near your waist, over hips. Inhale and stretch up, then exhale with an abdominal lift, stabilize seat, and stretch both arms forward, opening elbow joints. Relax arm muscles and shoulders. Inhale both elbows back to their starting place. Repeat a few times.

Step 2 For more coordination, reach forward with one arm at a time, opening and closing elbows, alternating arms, integrating breath.

Remember to:

- Keep wrists straight
- Close fingers in a soft fist
- Relax arm muscles
- Maintain upright torso

TIP

When your arms are held away from your center, they can draw shoulders and upper body out in front of your center of gravity. To avoid losing balance, it is important to stabilize your seat when reaching forward to pat the horse, or when yielding with the rein.

INSTRUCTOR BODYWORK

Stabilize arm by cupping elbow with one hand and placing the other around the rider's fist to keep fingers closed as you gently guide elbows to open and close.

Figs. 7.19 A & B *I am stabilizing and guiding Christa's elbow as it opens and closes.*

Hands Opened/Closed

Limbers your hands and fingers while promoting isolated control

BENEFITS

• Stretches fingers and hands • Promotes coordination and independence •

TIP

Scan and release shoulder and arm tension to ensure your hands do not lift up.

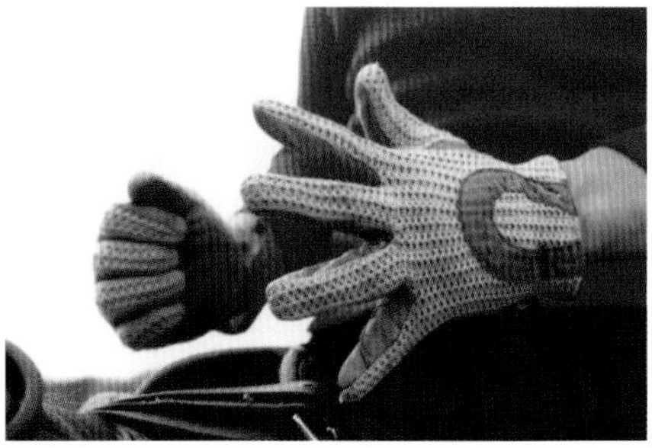

Figs. 7.20 A & B *Step 1: Inhale and open your right hand, spreading your fingers wide. Then, exhale it closed as you simultaneously open your left hand.*

HOW-TO

Step 1 Position hands with imaginary reins, making two soft fists. Inhale and open your right hand, spreading fingers wide. Exhale it closed as you simultaneously open your left hand (figs. 7.20 A & B) Alternate opening and closing hands synchronized with breath. Try switching the pattern and inhaling as your left hand opens, exhaling as it closes and right hand opens. Repeat for several breaths then shake out hands.

Step 2 Variations: Easy—open and close both hands simultaneously. Challenging—integrate opening/closing elbows with hands. For example, open both elbows with one hand closed, one open. Then close both elbows and switch hands. Mix it up!

Remember to:

- Isolate hand movement
- Keep wrists straight
- Relax shoulders and arms
- Maintain deep center of gravity and upright posture

Pass the Glove

Expands your chest and strengthens upper back for better posture

BENEFITS

• Stretches and improves flexibility in arms and shoulders • Releases back tension • Opens chest • Improves balance, posture, and coordination •

HOW-TO

Step 1 Take a riding glove in your left hand and lift it up and over your left shoulder. Reach your right hand behind your back and take the glove (fig. 7.21).

Step 2 Now move the glove in front of you and lift it over your right shoulder. Reach your left hand behind your back to take the glove.

Step 3 Continue passing the glove back and forth several times. Return to center; shake out hands.

TIP

It's natural to lower your head and neck while passing the glove, but do your best to keep head and neck upright. Practicing this in trot and canter is not advisable because if you drop the glove on the horse's hindquarters it could spook him.

Fig. 7.21 *Step 1: With your left hand, lift a riding glove up and over your left shoulder as you reach your right hand behind your back to receive the glove.*

Remember to:

- Keep movement fluid
- Draw shoulder blades together
- Maintain vertical alignment

> **TIP**
>
> This is fun for a hot day using cool water. You may end up getting a bit wet, but it will feel good if the sun is blazing!

Carrying Cups cont.

your arm and shoulder joints loose, as the longeur asks the horse to walk on. Ensure that you are breathing abdominally and continue for a few rounds of walk. As with Double Whips (p. 142), when you have established your seat in Phase One, and are further on in the Riding Without Reins program and have absorbed the longeing information presented at the beginning of Phase Two: The "Following" Seat, you can try this exercise in slow trot and work your way up to practicing it in canter.

Step 3 For more of a challenge, practice shoulder rolls while carrying cups (fig. 7.23 B). Avoid lifting or moving cups. Remember, shoulders must work independently of hands.

Step 4 When moving, hold cups firmly but keep arms soft. The more relaxed your arms, the looser your joints, the better you will absorb the horse's movement, and the more likely you will have water left in the cups at the end of the exercise.

Step 5 Continue as long as you like, then return cups to assistant; shake out hands.

Remember to:

- Stretch up through spine
- Keep arms and upper back relaxed
- Soften elbow, wrist, and shoulder joints
- Ensure seat remains balanced and rhythmical

PART IV

SEAT WORK IN MOTION: DEVELOP FEEL, RHYTHM, AND INFLUENCE

The seat of the rider has a dual purpose. In one way it is a command center from which directions are issued to the horse. At the same time it is also a kind of information center—a place to collect data from the horse.

PAUL BELASIK

CHAPTER

8

The "Following" Seat

In all the basic gaits, lay special emphasis on the rider "feeling" the movement, expressing what he feels in words, and having a supple seat, one that is free from stiffness, and comfortable. This will provide him with the foundations for the correct application of the aids.

PETRA AND WOLFGANG HÖLZEL

The longeing exercises presented in chapters 5 through 7 gave you an excellent introduction to bodywork to supple and center you in order to help you establish your *basic seat.* Now it is time to move on with seat development with some "seat work"—being longed with the horse in motion.

While working through the phases of seat development, you will spend the most time in Phase Two: The "Following" Seat—Horse "Leads," Rider Follows cultivating your ability to *participate* in the gaits and establish *rhythm* in your seat—seeking neither to disturb nor influence the horse. This requires you to first peel back and remove layers of obstacles such as bracing and gripping, and then build a repertoire of desirable mind-body skills that enable you to absorb the movement. New skills require thousands of repetitions before becoming habitual, so focus on "following" until you achieve an authentic connection in each gait.

You may follow more quickly in walk; it might take longer to participate in trot, but spending sufficient time in sitting and rising trot, with and without stirrups, can help you segue more smoothly into canter work.

As you progress, do not abandon the longeing exercises from Part III that seem "elementary" simply because you know how to do them already. Keep practicing them and remember to "work within" using the Basic Circle of Eight Objectives (see The Basic Circle, p. 19 and What Are the Eight Objectives? on p. 156). This can help you develop a foundation in the following seat, gait-by-gait. And as you progress onward, return to Phase Two anytime you need to tackle obstacles and improve your absorption of the horse.

Phase Two is covered in two chapters: this one, which introduces you to riding the gaits, and chapter 9, which focuses more on the rhythm of your seat. As before, I'm introducing this phase with a sample lesson program so you can get an overview of the work to be covered before you move on to Phase Three: The Active Seat—Rider "Leads," Horse Follows.

Phase Two: The "Following" Seat—Horse "Leads," Rider Follows
Sample Longe Session

1 After an unmounted warm-up, routine equipment check, and review of safety procedures, use Mounting with Breath (p. 67). Then from the saddle, reassess your tension level. If desired, have your instructor or longeur lead you through a Guided Relaxation in Halt (p. 72).

2 Make centering exercises a part of your halt warm-up and practice Release Legs to Gravity (p. 84) as you deepen and regulate your breath with Advanced Centering Breath (p. 88). Reevaluate pelvic alignment and weight distribution, and with the help of your instructor, review Centered Pelvis and Four Corners as needed (pp. 91 and 95).

Practice Slow Pendulum in halt to supple hip joints and increase your isolated control of each leg (p. 96).

3 Continue in your halt warm-up with a variety of lower body (chapter 6, p. 101) and upper body (chapter 7, p. 123) suppling exercises. Make your selection based on the specific results you desire, and the obstacles you still need to address.

4 In preparation for walk, take a deep breath, and as you exhale the longeur will move the horse forward. Immediately notice how his walk affects your seat. If your seat does not seem to be moving (i.e. it feels "stuck," braced, or tight), review "Following" the Walk (p. 172) and the Rhythmical Rider Movement Chart for walk (fig. 9.2), for a clearer understanding of how your seat should move and feel. You may have to emphatically initiate seat movement until your pelvis becomes free and your seat "steps" are synchronized with the horse. Spend as much time as you need practicing seatwork in walk until you can consciously participate in the gait. If frustration sets in, take a break, and practice Centering Breath and suppling exercises in halt until you are ready to try again. Be patient with yourself.

5 Once you have rhythmically connected your seat in walk, return focus to your breath. Practice Centering Breath in Walk (p. 176), and even though you learned this technique in halt, you must now integrate the horse's movement and your own, as well as your breathing pattern, depth, and rhythm. Practice this frequently.

6 Once you are consistently coordinating rhythmical walk steps with breath (which may take several sessions to master), "work within" by using the Eight Objectives of the Basic Circle. Take time to assess and cultivate them: Awareness, Relaxation, Breathing, Alignment, Suppleness, Rhythm, Coordination, and Feel in the walk. The Objectives are your priority, and working on these skills will improve the quality of your riding (see pp. 19 and 156).

7 Practice following the horse and synchronizing breath with transitions, as the longeur asks for halt/walk and walk/halt. Work with and without stirrups, and when you feel comfortable, let go with one or both hands to practice various arm positions in walk (p. 153).

8 To challenge and reinforce your seat select from the variety of suppling exercises outlined in Part III recommended for walk (p. 150). You may repeat some exercises practiced previously in halt and add new ones. Once you are familiar with walk suppling exercises, choose several to develop your own mounted warm-up in walk and to help prepare for seat work in faster gaits.

9 When you are ready to work on your following seat in trot, repeat Steps 4 through 8 in trot and refer to "Following" the Trot (p. 179), Rhythmical Rider Movement Chart for trot (fig. 9.6), Centering Breath in Trot, (p. 183), and the trot suppling exercises (p. 184).

10 When you are ready to work on your following seat in canter, repeat Steps 4 through 8 in canter, referring to "Following" the Canter (p. 186), Rhythmical Rider Movement Chart for canter (fig. 9.10), Centering Breath in Canter, (p. 188), and canter suppling exercises (p. 190).

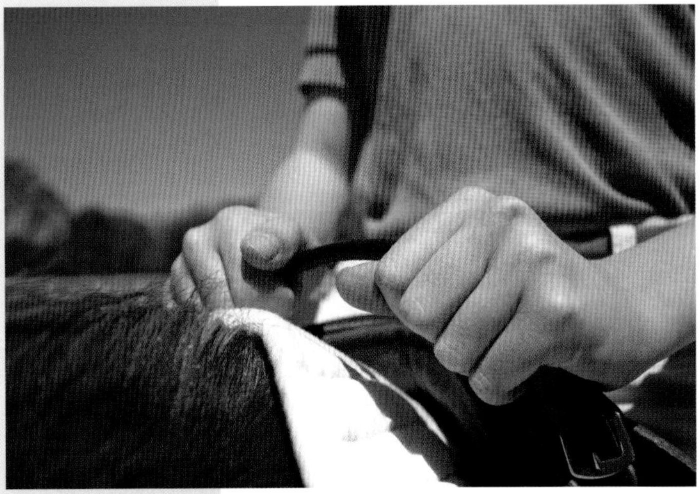

Fig. 8.2 *Holding on with your hands helps steady you so that you can focus on seat development rather than concern for your safety. Hold the safety strap or pommel in basic seat, and the neck strap or a handful of mane in forward seat.*

horse by pulling—gravity draws it down naturally. However, if you consistently feel that you will lose your seat if you don't pull it into the saddle, have the longeur *slow down* the gaits so you can hold more lightly and learn to work *with* gravity, rather than against it.

For lateral stability, place the outside hand on the pommel, inside hand on the cantle. This ensures the correct rotation of your torso toward the inside of the circle, with the outside shoulder slightly forward, and inside shoulder back. Reversing your hands counter-flexes you, disturbs alignment, and can throw the horse off track altering the dimensions of your longe circle.

Letting Go

When you're ready to start letting go, drop your inside hand and hold only with the outside (fig. 8.3). There are various positions to choose for your free hand; you can even allow it to hang down, arm dangling from the shoulder. If it swings or flails around, your arm is too stiff. Shake it out; release again. Because hands and arms are so accustomed to "doing something" it may take deliberate focus to convince them to let go.

Fig. 8.3 *When you're ready, let go with one hand first!*

For a free arm to participate in the horse's movement, its "texture" must be soft, with relaxed muscles and moveable joints. Check your joints frequently: wiggle fingers, rotate wrist/forearm, flex the elbow, and roll the shoulder. Do this for both arms, even though only one may be free. While arms and hands are often assigned different tasks on horseback, both must be monitored for tension. When you "position" your arms and hands, avoid unnecessary clenching of your muscles, as it blocks the joints from absorbing movement. Some arm exercises on the moving horse require "energizing," such as extending an arm away from center. Holding an outstretched arm takes more strength. As long as you ensure joint mobility throughout the rest of your body, you can learn to extend arm(s) without losing your seat.

Once comfortable with one free hand, prepare to let both of them go. Immediately scan for tension and recheck alignment. Freeing both hands can trigger the resumption of familiar but incorrect postural habits—possibly triggering a chain reaction and a concern for safety. For example, letting go might increase feelings of insecurity, potentially causing you to revert to excessive gripping, bracing off stirrups, leaning forward, or counter-flexing. If not corrected, mistakes like these can perpetuate imbalance and a reluctance to let go.

Remember, newly learned skills need reinforcement and repetition before becoming automated habits. If you let go spontaneously, especially if you are a long-time rider in the process of "retraining" your body, instinctive (albeit ineffective) behaviors will override a fresh skill whenever balance wavers...so be wary of letting go too soon. *Wait* until you feel secure, and then let go mindfully to preserve alignment, balance, and confidence.

Positions for Hands When Free

Once you have freed one or both hands from holding on, there are many different ways to carry them. Free-hand positions can be practiced in the basic seat and two-point position, in all gaits. Secure your seat balance before moving your hands away from your center, and when outstretched, energize arms by reaching through fingertips. Reward the horse frequently by stroking or patting.

Released: let arm(s) hang from shoulder joints. (Fig. 8.4 A)

Hips: place hand(s) on hips. (Fig. 8.4 B)

Wings: stretch one or both "wings" out at shoulder level, palms down. (Fig. 8.4 C)

Forward: hold arm(s) straight in front of you, palms down or facing. (Fig. 8.4 D)

Sky: reach for the sky with one or both arms outstretched overhead, palms facing. (Fig. 8.4 E)

Crossed/Front: cross or fold arm(s) in front of you. (Fig. 8.4 F)

Crossed/Behind: cross or fold arm(s) behind your back. (Fig. 8.4 G)

Imaginary Reins: see p. 155

Hands-On Centering

- For one-handed centering, continue holding with your outside hand and place inside hand (whether it is dominant or non-dominant) on your lower abdomen. Your front hand helps

Figs. 8.4 A–G *Free-hand positions can be practiced in basic or forward seat, and in all gaits. They help you center yourself, find your balance, and gain an ability to separate upper and lower body actions.*

TIP

If your front hand creeps up, it reflects a displacement of your center of gravity, which rises up relative to your hand. Have the longeur alert you, as you may not notice your hand has moved. Keep your hand firmly on the lower abdomen and remain aware of its position.

encourage abdominal lifting by pushing inward during exhalation (see Centering Breath p. 87).

- For two-handed centering and an exercise to avoid counter-flexing, place outside hand on lower abdomen, inside hand on lower back. Hands-on centering in both directions improves ambidexterity by allowing hands to alternate active/passive roles.

Hand Positions with Upper-Body Suppling

Hand positions and upper body suppling exercises done with the horse moving require you to split attention between what your seat is doing, and what your hands are doing—engaged in isolated movement or holding a position. When practicing upper body exercises, your seat takes top priority and must remain the primary focus. Assign tasks to your hands, control them, but don't give them your full attention.

Imaginary Reins

To assume the imaginary rein position, first release both arms. Then, bend elbows to approximately 90 degrees and position them near your waist. Let the weight of your elbows drop toward your hips. Make soft fists and hold each one a couple of inches above the buttons on either side of the pommel. With fingers closed, not clenched, your thumbs on top and slightly bent (not pressed flat), wrists straight, upper arms hanging from shoulders, forearms should point toward the bit (fig. 8.5).

Positioning hands close to your center helps keep balance intact. If they unconsciously drift out of place, your hands can upset balance by drawing your upper body forward and/or raising your center of gravity. Exercises that use props such as Double Whips and Carrying Cups (see chapter 7) simulate holding reins and can help you learn to maintain a steady position. To prevent imaginary reins from lifting or bouncing, do not tighten or force your hands into place. Instead, soften arms and check the moveability of wrists, elbows, and shoulders. Practice imaginary reins frequently to encourage hands and arms to absorb motion while maintaining this fundamental position in all gaits.

Learning to "Follow" the Horse

Allowing the Horse to Lead

Your *following seat* yields, adapts to movement, and allows the horse to lead. It requires your release of physical and mental resistance in order to facilitate the freedom necessary for *feel* to develop. And while it is important to maintain the proper alignment, which contributes to rider balance and safety, you must understand that every *mounted* "posture" is in *constant motion*, never static. In "following" the horse, you must not sacrifice relaxation, muscular suppleness, joint mobility, and "feel" *for the sake of form.*

Fig. 8.5 *An imaginary rein position places one or both hands where they will go when holding the reins.*

Learning to follow is a *major* riding goal, and best approached initially in slow gaits on the longe where a feel of position-in-motion can emerge. Use The Basic Circle's Eight Objectives in the order presented (see pp. 19 and 156) as your template. As you become more familiar with it, you'll realize that *following* is more than just "passive sitting." It is a process by which the horse teaches you to *participate* in the movement and become a rhythmical rider—much like a dance student learns choreographed

WHAT ARE THE EIGHT OBJECTIVES?

The Eight Objectives are the basic skills required for riding: the foundation and prerequisites for effective equitation at any level. If the Objectives are not met, the quality of a rider's equitation will be poor, which can make riding seem like a difficult struggle. For all riders, novice to advanced, acquiring the level of basic skills appropriate for their riding activities requires self-monitoring and conscious effort before these skills become habitual.

How are the Eight Objectives met?

The Objectives serve as a "checklist" of priorities (see The Basic Circle, p.19) to be considered during the practice of all exercises, all mounted work, and any cross-training riders do to help develop or refine riding performance. The checklist provides a circular framework (as learning to ride is not linear) for guiding riders to "work within the exercise," or "work within the pose," whether that pose is the basic seat, the forward seat, or any other posture in any suppling exercise, mounted or unmounted.

Why is this important?

This "work within the work" facilitates the acquisition of desirable skills while promoting a rider's safety, enjoyment, and the horse's willingness. Continued attention to basics throughout a rider's career will refine performance. A rider with "good basics" is prepared for advanced work in various equestrian sports, and horse training. Riders with poor basics may feel stuck at the lower levels of competition, and even have difficulty with their horse while their trainer does just fine with it.

How can the Objectives be specifically and practically applied?

On the longe line, whether you're practicing a specific suppling exercise or general seat work in any of the gaits, results can be prompted with thought-and-action-provoking questions, such as:

- **Awareness**: Am I aware of what I'm doing? What am I looking at? What am I thinking about? How does my body feel? How long can I hold a position without getting tired?
- **Relaxation**: Am I relaxed? Where am I tight? Where am I loose? What muscles can I release without losing balance? Are my thoughts self-defeating? What am I afraid of?
- **Breathing**: Am I breathing or holding my breath? How fast, slow, shallow, deep, regular, or irregular is my breath? How can I control and synchronize my breathing with movement?
- **Alignment**: Am I aligned properly? Is my head balanced? Is my torso upright or leaning? Are my legs under me? Is one shoulder higher than the other? Am I correct on the circle?
- **Suppleness**: Am I supple? How can I improve the range of motion in my hip joints? What will help stretch my heels down? How can I soften my lower back and loosen thigh grip?
- **Rhythm**: Am I moving rhythmically? Am I counting my seat movements? Can I feel the gaits pulse through my body? Can I keep a steady beat? Will the horse respond to my tempo changes?
- **Coordination**: Am I coordinating mind-body? Can I contact the horse with my lower legs without tightening thighs and knees? Why do my hands fly up in the air when I'm tense?

- **Feel**: Am I feeling the horse? How does my seat move in each gait? Am I bracing? Why does the horse slow down when I exhale? Can I tell when the horse rounds or hollows his back?

Once I answer these questions, then what?

The answers can be turned into "affirmations"—positive statements to repeat frequently—to initiate positive change and hone basics while performing any exercise, or seat work.

Here are several examples:

- **Awareness**: I notice everything. I look forward with a soft gaze. With each exhalation, I clear my mind of negative thoughts. My body is relaxed, receptive, and open to learn.
- **Relaxation**: It is safe to let go and release my arms and legs to gravity. I allow the horse to move me freely and rhythmically. I am a calm, relaxed rider. My body is soft and absorbent.
- **Breathing**: I breathe deeply and rhythmically. Drawing breath into my center helps anchor my seat. With every inhalation I experience increased energy and stamina.
- **Alignment:** I am centered. My body is in perfect alignment. When circling, I rotate from my center. My arms hang softly by my sides. My pelvis is upright and secure. I am a balanced rider.
- **Suppleness**: I am a soft, supple rider. With flexible joints I easily absorb the horse's gaits. The horse creates a movement pulse in each gait that resonates through my entire body.
- **Rhythm**: I am the rhythm-keeper. I keep a steady beat for my horse to follow. My body and breath blend together in a fluid, cadenced rhythm. The softer I am, the slower my horse.
- **Coordination**: I have an isolated control of each body part. My body is active and passive, supple and strong, gentle and firm. I have an independent seat and leg.
- **Feel:** I am a sensitive rider. I listen and respond to my horse. I am open to receive. I connect with the horse in all gaits. With each ride, I achieve deeper levels of relaxation and feel.

steps by following an experienced lead partner (see chapter 12). With long-term participation, riding—like dancing—becomes less analytical and more intuitive, enabling you to progress into higher levels of activity with ease.

No matter how long you've been riding—a few minutes, or a few years—your ability to follow is impaired if excessive grip, struggle, frustration, or anxiety are recurrent themes. With long-time riders, following may require deliberate restraint to sit passively and let the horse teach without trying to influence him.

The Rider's "Following" Program

Take a sequential approach when learning to follow the horse in the gaits: move from slower to faster and gradually increase the degree of difficulty. Use this general guide to establish, challenge, and confirm your basic skills in all three gaits:

Walk

1. Walk with and without stirrups in the basic seat.
2. Walk with stirrups in the two-point position, then without.

Trot

1. Slow trot sitting with and without stirrups in basic seat.
2. Slow trot with stirrups in two-point position, then without.
3. Working trot rising with stirrups in basic seat, then without.
4. Working trot sitting with and without stirrups in basic seat.
5. Working trot in two-point position with stirrups, then without.

Canter

1. Slow to working canter in two-point or half-seat variation with stirrups, then without.
2. Slow to working canter sitting with stirrups in basic seat, then without.

"Following" the Horse on the Circle

As every rider is unique, there are countless adjustments that may be needed, from moment-to-moment, when learning to follow the circle. It helps to first acquire a theoretical grasp of the alignment between body, horse, and circle and understand how weight distribution affects the horse. Then, you can solidify your tactile skills with the help of an experienced longeing team that includes an instructor to guide you into place while in motion on the circle.

As described in chapter 2 on p. 17, a specific rider's weight shift over the inside back corner/hind leg contributes to seat balance when circling. As the circle is a basic lateral movement, following its track also requires a corresponding lateral adjustment to your torso and shoulder alignment, which involves rotating the spine. To ensure rotation is uniform and not merely a turn of the head and neck, you begin at your center and turn the entire front axis of your body (down the front of your torso, like a line of buttons on a shirt) toward the direction of travel. This brings your inside shoulder slightly back and pointing toward the longeur in the center, with your outside shoulder slightly forward. Your shoulders remain parallel to the horse's shoulders and perpendicular to his spine, which now curves to align with the circle.

Initiating the rotation from your center (lower abdomen/navel) helps keep alignment cohesive. Initiating it instead with your head and neck can result in excessive rotation from the waist up, disconnection between upper and lower body, uneven shoulders, or collapsing at the waist. Upper body misalignment can throw the horse off track, just as incorrect weight distribution in the seat does.

Fig. 8.6 *Practice a modified Easy Twist (see p. 133) toward the inside of the circle to improve alignment and balance on the circle, and help correct a horse that "falls in."*

Horse Falling In and Out

If your longe horse *falls in* on the circle, practice a moderate version of Easy Twist (p. 133) to the inside. With your inside hand on cantle, outside on pommel, sit back and start to twist, glancing over your inside shoulder toward the hindquarters (fig. 8.6). Your horse should begin gliding back onto the track, as long as your pelvis doesn't tilt forward and your legs don't grip. These undesirable behaviors burden his inside shoulder and cause him to fall in. A gentle twist can help you align properly with the circle. Then, when arms release and you face forward again, do not unwind your spine—look through the horse's ears while maintaining a rotation appropriate for the circle size, as confirmed by your longeur and horse.

Postural misalignment on the circle may be one-sided, although in some cases, if you cause the horse to fall in to the left, for example, you might have the opposite effect on the right and cause him to fall out. Increasing rotation may feel awkward to one side, but to the other, our spinal rotation may feel perfectly natural and need no correction. This is because most of us favor one direction, usually determined by our dominant hand. There can be exceptions due to other repetitive activities we engage in outside of riding. And while our habits may go unnoticed off the horse, riding in balance requires a *symmetrical* use of our body and the ability to rotate around our spine equally well, left and right.

Fig. 8.7 *Blending conscious breathing with transitions promotes balance during each change, whether upward, downward, within gaits or between them. Here, Jenny prepares to move from canter to trot.*

"Following" Transitions

Blending *conscious breathing* with transitions—upward, downward, within gaits and between—promotes balance during each change of gait (fig. 8.7). As the instructor or longeur prepares the horse, you prepare by taking a deep breath. Upon exhalation, with your abdominals lifting and your back muscles soft, the transition ideally occurs. For example, from trot to walk: the longeur might say, *"Prepare for walk. Inhale; stretch up! Now, exhale....aaaaannnnnd walk,"* coaching by voice both your exhalation and the horse's downward transition to walk.

Timing your exhalation to correspond with a gait change and keeping your seat supple contributes to stability in *all* transitions and allows for absorption of movement. As your seat becomes more active you'll eventually request transitions yourself while being longed.

During *upward* transitions, avoid leaning forward as this puts you in front of the horse's center of gravity as well as your own, throwing balance off before a transition occurs. To steady and absorb the increase of forward thrust in upward transitions sit on your back edges (see Weight Distribution, p. 17), tuck your tailbone, and flatten your lower back. Continue breathing abdominally as you follow the faster pace.

During *downward* transitions, refrain from leaning or tilting your pelvis backward, pushing your legs out in front of you, or tightening your lower back. Slowing or stopping the horse can backfire when buttocks and lower back muscles tighten, as this pressure can drive the horse out from

Fig. 8.8 *A following leg does not yet intentionally influence the horse. With the longeur in charge of horse control, you learn to follow by cultivating passivity in your legs. They lengthen as they did in halt when released to gravity, and remain released from hips to toes to absorb the movement pulses in walk, trot, and canter.*

underneath and may inadvertently result in acceleration. To avoid interfering with a downward transition, remain upright as you engage your abdominals and soften your seat.

If you struggle to follow transitions, move awareness through your hip, knee, ankle, and shoulder joints. If you detect immobility or discover areas that are blocked, gently work your joints and loosen your muscles *during transitions* for more flexibility. Locking joints and clenching muscles result in bracing against transitions—uncomfortable for rider and horse.

TIP

In downward transitions without stirrups, check to see if your legs reach forward, looking for stirrups to brace against. Ingrained habits are hard to break!

Develop a "Following" Leg

For a following seat, we must develop a following leg—one that absorbs the horse's movement but is not yet *actively influencing* (see p. 191). "Setting the leg" or focusing on "leg angles" too soon (e.g. "heels down") can be unproductive. If you prioritize form over feeling, and position over relaxation, you can perpetuate muscular grip and joint rigidity (fig. 8.8).

Breaking the cycle of unnecessary grip is a challenge many riders face. By pushing your seat away from the horse with gripping, you actually *prevent* following. And if programmed into body memory, your legs resume their customary gripping behavior whenever you feel unstable or vulnerable. To overcome this, it is preferable to maintain a handhold while being longed (but *never* with reins), which offers a sense of security. This will enable you to coax your legs to release and dangle freely so they can learn to follow the movement.

If your legs block movement, then attempts at positioning (or delivering aids to the horse) are premature because this can cause a frequent loss of seat and stirrups. So remember: *following precedes influencing*, so cultivating *passive* qualities of the leg first enables *active* qualities to evolve accurately. Once you have developed a following leg, you can strive for leg contact and the appropriate leg angles as you become more influential.

Hip Joints

The hip joints are the first point of focus in developing a following leg. Ideally you should supple these joints before concerning yourself with lower leg contact, heels down, or flat inner thighs. While these are important facets of a correct position, they develop sequentially after excessive grip is eliminated and joints are suppled. Hip joint flexibility is facilitated by rider groundwork, specific mounted exercises, and increasing leg passivity on the longe.

Thighs

By releasing legs to gravity, the thighs naturally lengthen while yielding to the gaits. A passive thigh is important as it channels forward energy from the thrusting of the hindquarters, *through* the rider's leg, and toward the bridle. (Closing the thighs has a restraining effect, which can be used intentionally as an *advanced* aid when reducing the forward energy is necessary.) But when learning to follow the horse, check thighs frequently to prevent unnecessary clenching.

Excessively tight thighs is an obstacle related to lost seat balance, high center of gravity, shortened leg position with loss of stirrups, chair seat, lack of forward motion, irregular gaits, and inadvertent downward transitions. It is amazing how problems like these can be resolved more readily once the rider's thighs become passive. Momentary grip may be an appropriate reaction for many riding situations, but if it becomes an ingrained habit, slow work on the longe is the best way to reduce it.

Once hip joints have been loosened, coax thighs underneath; let them be long and loose. Draw them outward gently, giving the horse more room to breathe by widening your straddle. Note that passive thighs may jiggle or jounce—this is fine and a normal part of the release process. Avoid clamping your thighs around the horse to keep them still. Once thighs become pliable, they can be trained to lie flat against the saddle using hands-on bodywork and suppling exercises. Thigh Rotation (p. 111) develops a flatter thigh position, and practicing Frog or Modified Frog (pp. 104 and 106) as an isometric posture helps prevent squeezing and invites more release. If legs swing excessively, they are probably too tight, joints locked, so shake them out and release again.

Backs of Thighs

I make special mention of this part of the leg because it is often overlooked, and many riders seem more aware of the contact they have with the front of their thigh, which is typically involved in gripping. When I see a rider's thighs burrowed into cushy thigh blocks, exerting too much pressure and blocking joints, I gently loosen them with hands-on bodywork to free the front surface. For many long-time riders, peeling this part of their thigh off the saddle can cause the perception that leg contact is suddenly *gone*, despite the fact that the back surface of both thighs remains in full contact with the saddle.

In a basic full seat position, the *back* of the thigh is weight bearing. In fact, shifting weight to this area provides an understanding of what "deepening" the seat really means. While gripping with the front surface may be necessary at times (e.g. in flight over a jump), developing a following seat will move awareness to the back of your thighs. This provides a stable, more comfortable seat surface particularly in sitting trot. And when you are comfortable, you can more readily *feel*. Sitting on the backs of your thighs connects and deepens your seat, improves balance and stability, promotes freedom in knees, and prepares you for posting the trot without stirrups. It also makes bareback riding more comfortable!

Knees

A desirable deep knee position evolves as hip joints loosen and thighs lengthen. The "inner knee bone" (lower end of femur) should contact the saddle, but not bear weight. If knees pinch and become weight bearing, they cannot function as the natural hinges they are. Practicing suppling exercises and hands-on bodywork can alleviate knee grip. Many times, I have hardly been able to pry a rider's knees from the saddle due to excessive pinching—even in halt! Releasing knee pressure enables the rider to learn proper balance, and allows the horse to breathe and move more freely.

If your knees pinch, hold with your hands while longeing and turn your kneecaps out slightly to free them. Because this adjustment might rotate your femur outward, take your hands underneath the thigh and pull the bulky muscle back to help flatten it. Sitting on the back of your thigh rather than weighing down the front allows you to transfer your sense of security away from knees and into your seat. This, in turn, creates more freedom in the knee joints.

It can't be emphasized enough that educating a rider's leg takes time and occurs in stages, section by section. Obstacles must be eliminated before correct posture can take shape.

Lower Legs

To develop a following seat, you allow your lower legs to hang from soft knees. In this phase, you will not be aiding the horse, and lower leg contact is not your first priority. Leg contact increases in importance *after* you loosen joints and eliminate grip. By suppling and developing leg passivity first while allowing seat balance to take

Fig. 8.9 *While riders rarely hear "Don't put your heels down!" that is exactly what will help release a tight, overly active leg. In developing a following leg, the ankle joints become more absorbent if feet are allowed to hang, which improves passivity throughout the entire lower body.*

top priority, you'll hone an even greater ability to position lower legs around the horse dexterously, without reigniting gripping tendencies.

When introducing calves to the horse, a reasonably light touch is sufficient, and the horse helps you determine how much pressure is considered reasonable—too much will cause him to accelerate. The ability to maintain a passive contact and feel the horse with your calf muscles is the next task for your lower legs. In walk, you will feel the barrel swing alternately into your calves. In trot, your receptive calves maintain a connection by pulsing with the movements. To wrap lower legs around the horse in any gait, you must be able to control the degree of pressure it takes to keep them there, so you do not inadvertently drive or disturb the horse.

Ankles and Feet

Because so many riders respond to an instructor's "heels down" mantra by forcing this position, I make special mention of ankles and feet. To learn how to follow the horse, your entire leg yields to gravity while ankles and feet hang down loosely—yes, toes down! This encourages ankles and feet to absorb the gaits, and offsets the tendency to shove feet forward and brace off the stirrups—real or imaginary (fig. 8.9).

A correct riding position includes flexed ankles with heels lower than toes. However, when assuming this, or any posture on horseback, you must not sacrifice joint mobility for the sake of form. Particularly in a two point (light) seat and rising trot where more weight siphons into legs and stirrups, your ankles bear more weight and must function as flexible "springs" or shock absorbers. If ankles are rigid (either with heels down or when incorrectly riding off toes) the integrity of your position, ability to follow the horse, and your balance are threatened.

When developing a following leg, work *without stirrups* frequently and use ankle circles for suppling (p. 109). When riding *with stirrups*, balance the balls of your feet in the irons, toes relaxed and spread out in your boots. This helps feet stay put, not by forcing heels down, but by allowing them to stretch while absorbing movement and the weight of dangling legs.

What to Do with Stirrups

Stirrups are helpful inventions, but they are not required for a secure seat. Stirrups often invite gripping or bracing from an overly active leg that has not yet learned to follow. Riding without stirrups is a solution for reducing grip, developing a dexterous leg, and deepening the seat. Stirrups can be crossed over the horse's withers or allowed to dangle if alternating between riding with and without. If stirrups give you confidence when being longed, use them as necessary.

For best results, ride without stirrups as much as possible. Use the slow gaits for learning to let legs and feet dangle freely. Working without stirrups in walk is easy for most people; it remains quite doable in slow trot; and increases in difficulty in working trot and canter. Stirrup-less practice in the working gaits is challenging and something to build up to—you do not need to begin with it, even if you are a long-time rider.

> **TIP**
>
> Working slowly without stirrups facilitates mounted relaxation, and is one the most effective rider schooling techniques for achieving independence and a secure balanced seat.

Fig. 8.10 *To assume an imaginary stirrup position, keep thighs long while introducing your calves to the barrel of the horse. Then lift your toes to flex your ankles, which tones your lower legs and helps you maintain an appropriate knee bend.*

Trotting on the Longe

Sitting Trot "Without"

When sitting the trot without stirrups, start slowly and work up to a more active trot as you gain confidence. Release legs to gravity (p. 84); sit on the back edges of your seat bones (p. 17), and spread weight wide across your seat. Allow the backs of your upper thigh muscles to soften and bear weight to deepen your seat (p. 162). Use abdominal lifting with exhalation (see Centering Breath, p. 87) for stability; keep back muscles soft so your spine can absorb motion. Let lower legs and feet hang until hips joints, knees, and ankles are supple and excess grip eliminated. Then, to master a following seat without stirrups, establish lower leg contact and assume an imaginary stirrup position (fig. 8.10). In the more active gaits, an "adhesive" inner

Fig. 8.11 *When rising with stirrups in basic seat, remain in the saddle's center and for now, to maintain consistency and not interfere, simply stand in the stirrups. Lead the movement with your center by directing it forward and upward as you stand.*

thigh may be required, but an increase in muscular activity should not interfere with joint mobility, and be released the moment it is no longer necessary (see Adhering the Seat, p. 98).

Rising Trot "Without"

Before rising without stirrups, pick up your "imaginary stirrups." This will provide the muscle tone needed to stabilize your leg and lift the seat. The lightening of the seat is controlled with the backs of your thighs and relies on the horse's momentum to provide the lift. With greater suspension, the working trot is preferable; in jog trot, the horse may barely leave the ground.

Stirrup-less rising does not require hurtling your seat into space—you may only rise an inch or less, which is sufficient. Avoid pulling your knees up and pinching them tighter to rise higher—it is unnecessary, causes postural instability, and disturbs the horse. Rising without stirrups is accomplished by pushing off the backs of your thighs, directing your center upward and forward. It is a great way to eliminate "posting too high," often caused by pushing off toes or knees in an attempt to hoist the seat. Posting bareback is also feasible using the backs of thighs, rather than gripping with knees or the front of thighs.

Rising Trot "With"

When rising *with* stirrups in basic seat, remain in the saddle's center and refrain from propelling your pelvis from the back of the saddle over the pommel (fig. 8.11). At times, this thrusting motion may be considered a driving aid, but to maintain consistency and not interfere, simply *stand* in the stirrups. And to accommodate the horse's momentum and remain in balance, lead the movement with your center by directing it forward and upward as you stand.

During the "up" phase, weight transfers from seat to legs. While some of it is borne by the backs of your thighs, the rest of it siphons through the knees and into the stirrups. As long as your knees are not weight bearing, *standing* causes them to dip down, as weight sinks through. To facilitate this weight shift and prevent pinching, imagine that you are about to "kneel down," and point your kneecaps toward the ground when rising.

Weight continues to drop into the stirrups, causing ankles to flex, and heels to dip down even more when you rise from the saddle. If ankles are braced, your weight shift never makes it that far, and as a result, your center of gravity is pushed higher when you rise, contributing to instability, which causes grip, and the cycle continues until your leg joints remain supple in motion.

> **TIP**
>
> When rising the trot from a two-point position, your weight shifts similarly through your legs, but due to shorter stirrups, leg angles are more closed, and your torso inclines slightly forward from the hip joints to remain in balance.

Taking Back Stirrups

After riding without stirrups for a while, it may feel awkward taking them back. Many believe they ride better without them, which may be true, as an absence of stirrups could mean an absence of bracing. If you habitually brace off stirrups in downward transitions, this tendency often continues even without stirrups, until it is recognized and corrected. Meanwhile, do not fret if riding *with* stirrups feels awkward. As long as you're comfortable without, then continue.

When taking back stirrups, do not lift your knees and fish for them, or bring toes above the irons. Keep your leg in an imaginary stirrup position, toes lifted and turned slightly inward—your stirrups should be right there. If they don't slip back onto your feet, move the toe of your boot(s) from left to right to locate them. Avoid struggling, as this may disturb your seat. It's usually better to continue without stirrups until you can take them back without incident.

You can more readily learn or relearn how to ride with stirrups once a dexterous control of your legs develops. By all means, take them back as necessary to increase confidence or alleviate fatigue when being longed. And when moving feet in and out of stirrups, do this *without looking down*!

Being Longed in Two-Point Position

The two-point position—and all variations of a *light* seat—supplements the basic seat and enables you to become a well-rounded rider. By having more than one postural option, you learn to adapt the quality, depth, balance, and alignment of your seat to the horse's repertoire of movements. This makes you more adept, in or out of the arena, on the flat and over obstacles. A good seat is adjustable and remains centered and balanced in a variety of riding activities.

Dressage enthusiasts can benefit by working in two-point to become more versatile outside the arena, and to offer horses diversity in their work. Hunter/jumper enthusiasts and eventers may prefer being longed in two-point because it's familiar, perhaps the seat of choice. But because knee and thigh grip often goes "unreleased" in forward seat riding, you should spend sufficient time mastering the *basic seat* first, as this will subsequently improve the quality of your two-point.

Fig. 8.12 *Longeing in the forward seat (two-point position) promotes balance, adds variety, increases challenge, stabilizes legs, improves flexibility, and strengthens postural muscles.*

When moving from basic seat to two-point, shorten stirrups one or two holes. Riding with a shorter leg may feel uncomfortable after a while due to increased flexion of leg joints. If your legs become fatigued, drop stirrups to stretch and release legs to gravity. Again, avoid weight bearing with the knees, as this creates a pivotal point for balance that can result in a wobbly lower leg, loss of stirrups, and torso instability. While pressing knees into the saddle can be useful in some situations (e.g. in flight over a jump, riding up steep hills, etc.), when longeing in two-point ensure knees are flexible and absorbing movement, not carrying your weight.

Establish the appropriate rotation on the circle with inside shoulder back, outside shoulder forward (fig. 8.12). To secure seat balance, distribute weight on the back of your inside thigh and stirrup. Two-point can be practiced without stirrups using the back of your thighs to support the seat. Lifting high off the horse is unnecessary—a little is enough.

Introducing Canter on the Longe

Once you are accomplished in the working trot without stirrups, you are ready for canter. Due to the faster pace, a horse being longed in canter will be afforded a larger circle, which moves the longeur farther away from you. At this stage, you must be prepared to rely on your balance and ability to follow, while remaining open to the horse's feedback. You should also be versed in emergency stopping techniques and dismounts. Whenever possible, I introduce the canter without stirrups by using a vaulting surcingle (fig. 8.13 A). While holding the large handles, my students more quickly develop a sense of security that leads to confidence and a *feel* of the canter (fig. 8.13 B).

Many riders feel safer cantering with stirrups. At first, canter in a light seat with stirrups to avoid bumping the horse's back. However, the rigidity can result in an undesirable type of bobbing up and down—almost like posting—that prevents you from feeling the rocking-horse swing of the gait. If you experience this, deliber-

Figs. 8.13 A & B *Holding onto a vaulting surcingle in canter can increase your sense of security, enabling you to release your legs to gravity more readily while learning to follow the gait (A). When you feel secure in canter, work as much as possible without stirrups, alternating between a completely released leg and imaginary stirrups—you can hold on as Christa is doing here (B). What a seat you will have!*

ately tuck your tailbone each stride, even in a light seat with your pelvis above the saddle. Once you can perform this motion in the air, slowly lower your seat to the saddle, and synchronize with the horse. If your horse has a slow, smooth canter stride, you may prefer introducing this gait while seated. Your longeur and horse will help you decide.

CHAPTER 9

"Following" the Gaits with Rhythm

Riding is all about rhythm. The body must be trained to "listen" to the rhythm of the horse. In the beginning, this is best done on the longe with the eyes shut.

SYLVIA LOCH

Rhythmical Rider Movements

Many riders must overcome some degree of unconscious resistance to the horse's movement. Although you may be instructed to move *with* the horse, you are not always sure *how*. While groundwork and mounted suppling exercises alleviate tension and improve your range of motion, it is important to establish a theoretical understanding of how the horse moves, and how your seat moves when following his gaits. With this preparation, you are more equipped to *initiate* seat movement. And with the horse's help, you can intentionally train your seat to participate.

To encourage a tangible grasp of seat movement, I have devised Rhythmical Rider Movement Charts for all three gaits. These briefly describe how your pelvis and shoulders respond to the gaits when unobstructed. The charts also mention the horse's movements and how the longeur can help you connect. With a focus on seat movement, you'll learn about rider biomechanics and develop a kinesthetic awareness on horseback. Once you understand your own physical movements, you can more readily determine the horse's movements by *feel.*

Fig. 9.1 *A well-schooled horse serves as a master of rhythm, maintaining a steady beat for us to follow.*

The horse's gaits are marked by distinct rhythmical hoofbeat patterns. Your bipedal gaits are marked by left and right stepping. When mounted, your two seat bones keep time by "stepping," as they alternate in walk and trot, and simultaneously "scoop" in canter. These seat movements naturally occur when you are free to follow. However, if braced, you must focus on eliminating restrictions and then controlling movements so that following the horse becomes spontaneous.

One of the most effective techniques for learning to control your seat is to count your seat bone "steps," silently or aloud. You will notice that each chart offers a four-beat rhythm for all three gaits. And while the horse's walk is four-beat, trot is two-beat, and canter is three-beat, the charts depict a four-beat gait in all three because *the rhythm is based on rider movements*. Organizing your "steps" into patterns of four, equally spaced beats simplifies rider rhythm and enables you to more easily regulate movements. A four-beat pattern feels natural to most riders, and counting aloud can generate astonishing results by providing "mind-body-horse" with an audible rhythmic focus.

Counting steps creates regularity of seat movements and allows you to more synchronously participate in the complex four-legged gaits of the horse. The next step is learning to blend rhythmic abdominal breathing with movement. To assist, I have also included Rhythmical Rider Breathing Charts that outline how Centering Breath is integrated with each gait.

"Following" the Walk

In walk, the horse affects the *two halves* of your seat separately and you feel your left and right seat bones alternately moving and bearing weight. If your seat is "stuck," you may not readily experience this. However, you can initiate seat movement to get into sync with the horse.

As the horse walks, move awareness to your pelvis, softening buttocks and lower back muscles. Then deliberately tuck one seat bone underneath, immediately followed by the other. Press each one alternately from the back of the saddle toward the front. These are your left and right "steps" in walk. Give each one a beat. Count to four steps, and then repeat. This will help establish a rhythmical cadence and may literally feel as if you are "walking" on your seat bones, or gliding and making parallel tracks (imagine cross-country skiing or skating on seat bones). (See fig. 9.2.)

Avoid pressing your seat bones in toward the horse's spine, which would throw your hips from side to side, and cause you to collapse at the waist. To encourage forward movement, imagine that you can push the horse's neck out in front of you by emphatically tucking your seat bones. The horse may start taking longer steps in response, at which point you'll know you're on the right track. Sometimes, if your pelvis is blocked in walk, freedom can be facilitated by temporarily exaggerating seat movement. Once you connect, reduce seat movement to blend appropriately with the walk, and let the horse lead you.

Significance of the Shoulders

When walking on foot, your limbs inherently move in diagonal pairs. To understand this consciously, take a walk off the horse and study your movement. You'll discover that your left shoulder draws back when you step forward with your left foot; your right shoulder draws back when you step right. Now try walking in place, holding imaginary reins. Are your shoulders still alternating, or have they become rigid due to your hand and arm position? If your shoulders are tense, resume walking and allow your arms to swing loosely. When you take up imaginary reins, work slowly with awareness until you can sustain your natural shoulder movement in walk while keeping your hands in position.

Shoulder movement must carry over into your riding for you to effectively follow the horse. While the movement will be subtler on horseback, your shoulders continue to move laterally, each one drawn back as you step forward with the corresponding seat bone. I sometimes call the shoulders a rider's "final frontier," particularly if much time has been spent developing a *following pelvis*, but shoulder movement has yet to be explored.

Shoulder tension is an extremely common obstacle that most every modern rider brings to the horse, to some degree. If your shoulders feel tight, they can be suppled with Shoulder Rolls and Arm Circles (see pp. 127 and 137). You may benefit from momentarily exaggerating shoulder movement to inspire more rhythmical participation in this part of your body, as long as this does not disturb your horse. Once loosened, train your shoulders to follow inconspicuously in walk.

Rhythmical Rider Movement Chart

THE "FOLLOWING" SEAT: WALK

WALK	**LEFT** **1** **3**	**RIGHT** **2** **4**	**RIDER NOTES**
RIDER	L hip drops L seat bone bears more weight L side of pelvis tucks under L leg contacted by horse's barrel L shoulder gently drawn back	R hip drops R seat bone bears more weight R side of pelvis tucks under R leg contacted by horse's barrel R shoulder gently drawn back	Your weight alternates from the left to the right seat bones, which feel like they "glide" from the back of saddle to the front as each side of pelvis "tucks" under you. Stabilize your torso; remain upright. Allow lateral shoulder movement. If your body feels "stuck" and unmoving, exaggerate then refine movement.
HORSE	L hind followed by L fore L side of back dips down L barrel swings into rider's L leg L shoulder glides back	R hind followed by R fore R side of back dips down R barrel swings into rider's R leg R shoulder glides back	In the time it takes the horse to take two steps, you take just one "seat bone step." Breathe and count your own "steps": 1-2-3-4. Close your eyes to increase awareness of how the horse's back alternately "dips," and how each side of your seat must move independently to follow the horse.
LONGEUR'S ROLE	Watch horse's L foreleg hit ground Call out, "LEFT" Prompt rider to tuck L seat bone under and gently push L side of seat forward when the horse's barrel moves into the rider's L leg Encourage natural movement of shoulders in walk, as on foot	Watch horse's R foreleg hit ground Call out, "RIGHT" Prompt rider to tuck R seat bone under and gently push R side of seat forward when the horse's barrel moves into the rider's R leg Encourage natural movement of shoulders in walk, as on foot	Count as the horse's foreleg hits the ground or his barrel moves into the rider's leg, or as the rider's seat moves, and call out, "1-2-3-4," or "Left-right-left-right," to help the rider synchronize her seat rhythm with the horse's movement. If the rider is not supple enough to "follow," address flexibility of hip joints and pelvis.

Fig. 9.2 *Learning to move with the horse by consciously participating in the gait: the rider's body will naturally respond to the movement of the horse's walk as described above if the rider is supple, sits in balance, and "allows" the movement to happen.*

With freedom of movement in pelvis *and* shoulders, you can more naturally follow the horse. Allowing him to move you in regular, fluid walk steps can be very relaxing.

Walk Music

This musical chart depicts our seat movement in walk and relates it to the horse's movement—you are like two musicians playing different instruments, performing the same song. While you mark out beats with your left and right seat bones, the horse's hoofbeats strike the ground individually, creating a *four-beat* gait. In the time it takes you to perform *four* "steps" of walk on your seat bones, the horse has completed *two* full strides (or *eight* horse steps). Focusing on your own steps improves awareness and familiarity of the gait. By participating consciously, you more readily connect with the walk and learn to orchestrate your different movement with the horse (fig. 9.3).

> **TIP**
>
> When you realize that your participation has become less *analytical* and more *intuitive*, riding often feels like a walking meditation.

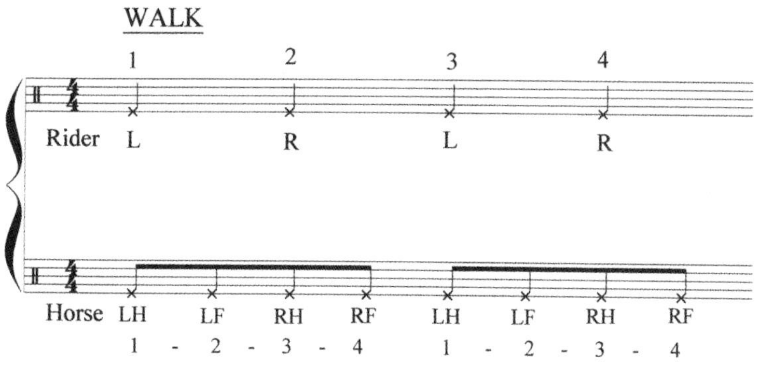

Fig. 9.3 *In the time it takes us to perform four "steps" of walk on our seat bones, the horse has completed two full strides.*

The rider's seat conveys the "music" of the horse's body to the rider.

CHARLES HARRIS

Centering Breath in Walk

Once you have learned to regulate seat movement in walk as shown on fig. 9.3, the next step is to integrate your breath. This will enhance your participation in the gait and help keep you rhythmical and focused. Strive to match the length of inhalation with exhalation, as each phase of your breath corresponds to four steps of walk on your seat bones. (Remember, *four* steps of "seat-bone walking" corresponds to *two* full horse strides) Count to a higher or lower number if necessary—the idea is to consciously connect breathing with movement. With practice, this will feel natural and become an influential rider skill.

HOW-TO

Step 1 While walking in basic seat, focus on your seat bone movements and count *four* seat bone steps aloud: left-right-left-right or 1-2-3-4, then repeat. Continue until you establish regularity (fig. 9.4).

Step 2 Now with hands around your center—outside in front, inside behind—count seat bone steps silently and focus on your breath. Inhale through your nose into the space between your hands for a count of four, taking an equal number of steps. Exhale through your mouth with an abdominal lift (see p. 87), while taking another four steps. Listen to the sound of your breath and maintain seat rhythm.

Step 3 Continue as long as you and the horse are comfortable, removing your hands if desired. Use this conscious breath as often as possible in all your walk work.

TIP

Notice if and how the horse changes under your seat as you regulate abdominal breathing and seat movement in walk. Remain aware of your center and ensure that your front hand does not move higher on your body.

Fig. 9.4 *Steps 1 & 2: Inhale through your nose for four "seat-bone steps," then exhale for four "seat-bone steps," and repeat.*

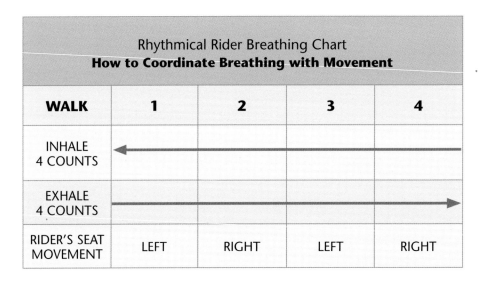

Rhythmical Rider Breathing Chart
How to Coordinate Breathing with Movement

WALK	**1**	**2**	**3**	**4**
INHALE 4 COUNTS				
EXHALE 4 COUNTS				
RIDER'S SEAT MOVEMENT	LEFT	RIGHT	LEFT	RIGHT

Longeing Exercises in Walk

1 Once you are regulating abdominal breathing with rhythmical seat movement in walk, you can add a variety of hand positions and arm exercises for more challenge. (I'll be discussing trot and canter later in this chapter.) Arm movements should blend with seat and breath to ensure synchronization with the gait. Frequently reward the horse using your free hand(s) to stroke withers, neck, and haunches. For increased balance and strengthening, practice arm exercises in two-point position.

2 Expand your longeing repertoire with the suppling exercises recommended for walk (see p. 178). Try combining compatible arm and leg exercises to improve coordination, such as a lower body exercise like Scissor Stretch with an upper-body one like Arm Raise (pp. 103 and 128), or Legs Away with Symmetry (pp. 108 and 134). Be creative! (See fig. 9.5.)

Fig. 9.5 *Practicing Arm Circles (p. 137) in walk while rhythmically breathing and "stepping" on your seat bones is a test of mind-body coordination.*

3 Work with stirrups to instill confidence. Then practice dropping one stirrup, walking for several moments with one imaginary stirrup, and eventually placing your foot back in without looking. Repeat on the opposite side, and then with both sides simultaneously.

4 Practice riding upward and downward halt-to-walk transitions. Have the longeur request transitions at various points on the circle so the horse does not anticipate. Continue breathing and counting, even in halt, when halt transitions are part of your work.

5 Alternate between the basic seat and two-point position in walk, with and without stirrups. Experiment with moving smoothly between these two postures—count eight steps in one seat, then switch to the other for another eight steps, and so on. Add arm exercises and decrease the count for more challenge.

6 Learn about transitions within the walk by shortening and lengthening strides. Notice how your seat movement is reduced when the horse takes shorter steps, and how it moves more when the horse takes longer strides.

7 Have the longeur set up ground poles on the circle to vary your walk work and introduce obstacles.

8 Vault-off in walk. Remember to breathe, look forward, and land on the ground facing forward, in step with horse.

Recommended Suppling Exercises for Work in Walk

Midsection/Center

Guided Relaxation *(sitting)*	p. 72
Release Legs to Gravity *(sitting)*	p. 84
Centering (Abdominal) Breath *(all postures)*	p. 87
Advanced Centering Breath *(all postures)*	p. 88
Complete Breath *(all postures)*	p. 89
Centered Pelvis *(postural adjustments)*	p. 91
Four Corners *(weight shifts)*	p. 95
Slow Pendulum *(sitting)*	p. 96

Lower Body

Scissor Stretch *(sitting)*	p. 103
Frog *(sitting)*	p. 104
Modified Frog *(sitting)*	p. 106
Dancer *(sitting)*	p. 107
Legs Away *(sitting and two-point)*	p. 108
Ankle Suppling *(sitting)*	p. 109
Thigh Rotation *(sitting)*	p. 111
Standing in Stirrups *(heels down and up)*	p. 113
Two-Point Position	p. 115
Chin to the Mane *(two-point)*	p. 117
Toe Touch *(all variations/sitting/two-point)*	p. 118
Gentle Back Bend	p. 120
Around the World	p. 121

Upper Body (all sitting)

Head & Neck Stretches	p. 125
Bent Willow	p. 126
Shoulder Rolls	p. 127
Arm Raise with Breath	p. 128
Crescent	p. 129
Chest Expansion	p. 130
Big Horse Hug	p. 132
Easy Twist	p. 133
Symmetry	p. 134
Symmetry Twist	p. 135
Side Stretch	p. 136
Arm Circles & Windmill	p. 137
Elbows Opened/Closed	p. 139
Hands Opened/Closed	p. 140
Pass the Glove	p. 141
Double Whips	p. 142
Carrying Cups	p. 143

*Note: In parentheses, I have qualified each exercise with terms that indicate how/when the exercise should be practiced. *Sitting* means you should be in your basic seat; *all postures* means the exercise can be combined with all suppling exercises and seat work; *postural adjustments* indicates the exercise consists of evaluating and fine-tuning your seat and position within the gait; you will learn to execute *weight shifts* in motion where noted; some exercises are recommended for practice in the forward seat or *two-point position*, which will add variety; *slow sitting* means the gait should be regulated and the tempo reduced to build confidence and feel in your basic seat; and *all variations* means you can practice each phase of that particular exercise in the recommended gait.

"Following" the Trot

Basic Seat Sitting

Like the walk, your seat bones move separately in trot, although at a quicker tempo. As weight shifts laterally from left to right, your seat is challenged by the trot's vertical (up/down) movement, which lifts each hip then drops it down. There is also more momentum, generated by the horse's thrust. This increases longitudinal (forward/back) movement in your pelvis as the horse's hind legs alternately push your seat bones underneath more energetically than in walk.

Although the trot presents increased movement to absorb, if unobstructed, you can learn to follow in the basic seat without grip, relying on abdominal strength for postural stability and holding on with your hands as necessary. It is when your muscles are clenched and joints blocked that the trot is difficult to sit. The key to following the trot is to identify and release tension, then learn to consciously move your seat in time with the horse.

While the trot's vertical movement *seems* more prominent, by riding with a soft seat, supple lower back, and flexible hip joints you can more readily feel the alternating left-right pulsations. Keeping the trot *slow* limits forward momentum so you can focus on lateral weight shifts and identify your seat bone "steps." Even if you haven't quite grasped the feeling of alternating seat bones in trot, you can help yourself by calling (aloud or silently) "left-right, left-right," or the familiar cadence, "*left, left, left-right, left*" until your seat responds.

Establishing a four-beat count in trot sounds like: "1-and-2-and-3-and-4-and" with the "ands" silent. I have found this much more effective than counting a "1-2, 1-2" cadence based on the horse's two-beat stride, as that *sounds* hurried, and a rider's tempo can *become* hurried as a result. If your seat speeds up, it can accelerate the horse, so to more effectively regulate the speed at which you trot, learn to regulate your seat "steps" first (fig. 9.6).

While counting, feel your hips lift and drop alternately, as weight shifts from one seat bone to the other. Move subtly and avoid pushing your pelvis to the side or tipping your upper body. Stretch up through your spine, keeping your head balanced. As feel improves, you'll notice that each side of your body—from shoulder, elbow, hip, knee, and heel—releases alternately in sitting trot. For example, as the inside hip drops, that entire side of your body yields to gravity and sinks, immediately followed by the outside. This sensation helps deepen your seat and anchor you to the horse.

It also helps prepare you for rising trot—each time your weight shifts to the outside, say "down," then each time it shifts to the inside, say "up." This will enable you to pick up the correct posting diagonal by *feel*, as you become synchronized with the horse. Once vertical and lateral motion are familiar in slow sitting

Rhythmical Rider Movement Chart

THE "FOLLOWING" SEAT: TROT

TROT	**LEFT** **1** **2** **3** **4**	**RIGHT** **and** **and** **and** **and**	**RIDER NOTES**
RIDER **Sitting Trot**	L hip drops L seat bone bears more weight and presses forward L side of body sinks into horse L shoulder gently drawn back	R hip drops R seat bone bears more weight and presses forward R side of body sinks into horse R shoulder gently drawn back	Keep your torso upright, back muscles soft, and allow a subtle lateral sway of shoulders in time with your hips. Say out loud: "Left, left, left-right, left," to establish rhythm, or count, "1-and-2-and-3-and-4-and," (with the "ands" silent). Use your abdominals for stability; do not grip with your legs.
RIDER **Posting Trot**	Count the "up" beat to emphasize posting and establish rhythm Left rein: synchronize rising and sitting with the right (outside) foreleg ↑ and ↑ and ↑ and ↑ and 1 2 3 4	Count the "down" beat to emphasize a deeper seat and connection Right rein: synchronize rising and sitting with the left (outside) foreleg ↓ and ↓ and ↓ and ↓ and 1 2 3 4	From the saddle, glance down to watch the horse's outside shoulder move forward and back in order to determine the correct "diagonal." When it comes back, sit. When it goes forward, rise. If you have difficulty determining this, attach a strip of masking tape vertically on the outside shoulder and watch it move. Count each time you rise, or each time you sit to establish and maintain four-count rhythm.
HORSE	One diagonal pair of legs moves: L foreleg and R hind L forefoot on the ground L side of back dips	The other diagonal pair of legs moves: R foreleg and L hind R forefoot on the ground R side of back dips	The horse moves one diagonal pair of legs with every "step" you take with your seat bones. In the time it takes you to move two seat bone steps, he has taken one full, two-beat stride of trot. The horse should maintain a regular rhythm. Count your steps aloud for audible rhythmic focus. Slower speeds will cultivate your relaxation and feel.
LONGEUR'S ROLE	Watch L forefoot hit the ground and use it to count beats Prompt rider to drop L hip and release L side of body to gravity when foreleg hits Encourage natural lateral sway of the rider's shoulders	Watch R forefoot hit the ground and use it to count beats Prompt rider to drop R hip and release R side of body to gravity when foreleg hits Encourage natural lateral sway of the rider's shoulders	Choose one foreleg and count it, calling, "Left, left, left-right, left," or "1-and-2-and-3-and-4-and," (the "ands" are silent), to help the rider establish rhythm. Use the same count for posting, or call, "UP," or "DOWN"—but try to avoid the hurried sound of calling out both. Keep the horse slow until the rider is secure and ready to increase the tempo.

Fig. 9.6 *Learning to move with the horse by consciously participating in the gait: the rider's body will naturally respond to the movement of the horse's trot as described above if the rider sits in balance and can absorb all movements—left, right, up, down, and forward.*

trot, move the trot up to tempo to experience increased impulsion in the working gait, which is preferable for rising trot.

Working in sitting trot can be very relaxing and another chance to experience a moving meditation on horseback. However, if your seat is stiff, practice suppling and awareness exercises such as relaxation techniques—exaggerated bouncing to unlock your seat is inadvisable and disturbs the horse. A great way to understand your participation in trot is to jog in place on foot! First, take small steps; get a rhythm going. You might even press fingertips into your seat bones to feel them lift and lower, as they do on horseback. To learn how tension interferes, clench your buttocks muscles. Notice how this restricts hip joints, tightens lower back and thighs, and limits knee flexion. Release, and feel freedom return. To increase movement, lift your knees higher. Clench again, noticing how difficult it becomes to sustain more activity; then release.

Continue jogging in place now with imaginary reins, and pay attention to shoulder and arm movements. If unrestricted, shoulders naturally sway left and right in jog, as in walk. Because of the prominent vertical bounce, when relaxed in jog, shoulders also "shrug" up and down in rhythm with our lower body. Intentionally tighten shoulders, upper back, and clench your arms to see how tension disconnects your upper body from the movement. Then relax and allow shoulders to move naturally, as your arms soften and remain in position. If you routinely walk or jog for fitness, use those unmounted activities to scan and release unnecessary clenching to improve freedom of movement on and off the horse. Strive to remember how your body feels in its own version of walk and jog when relaxed. Then take what you have learned on foot and apply it to your riding—what have you discovered?

Basic Seat Rising

Posting or rising gives us another option to absorb the trot. Because slow trot does not provide much "lift" for posting, it's best to practice in working trot to take advantage of the horse's suspension. However, it helps to make a dry run in slow trot or walk, to review or introduce the rising mechanism. Your initial challenge is to lift up out of the saddle while maintaining balance and alignment. To accomplish this, simply stand upright, let weight sink into thighs and stirrups, and lead the movement with your center (lower abdomen).

When longeing in rising trot, it's best to start *with* stirrups. In fact a good preparatory exercise is Standing in Stirrups (p. 113), which ensures legs are lined up underneath your center as heels stretch down for a secure balance. Counting beats in rising trot is the same as sitting trot: 1-and-2-and-3-and-4-and (with the "ands" silent). Instead of experiencing lateral weight shifts on the seat bones, stand and sit alternately. Standing is your "up beat." Returning to the saddle is your "down beat." You can select either beat as a focus for counting.

For example, counting the "up beat" works well to establish a posting rhythm if you're just learning, or if you need to emphasize the standing phase. However, if you lose your alignment and slip into a chair seat, you might resort to excessive hip thrust in the up beat, pushing your pelvis from the back of the saddle over the pommel. This exaggerated movement can have a "chasing" effect on the horse, driving him out from underneath. A solution is offered by your other counting option—focusing on the "down beat." Whenever you exhibit too much "air time" in the up beat, you can emphasize the sitting phase to improve seat connection and prevent posting too high.

Trot Music

This musical chart depicts your rhythmic pattern in trot and compares it with the horse's rhythm (fig. 9.7). As in walk, you mark out beats with left and right seat bones when sitting. When rising count either the up or down beat depending on emphasis. The horse's hooves strike the ground in diagonal pairs in trot, creating a two-beat gait. Your rhythms are similar—in the time it takes you to take four full strides of trot, the horse has also taken four strides: one rider stride (left/right, or up/down) = one stride of trot. Focusing on your movement enables you to more mindfully participate, which leads to your ability to identify the horse's footfall patterns by feel.

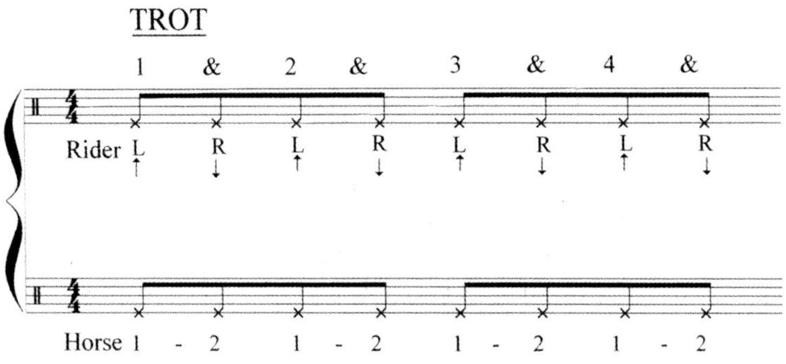

Fig. 9.7 *In trot, the horse and rider's rhythms are similar—in the time it takes you to take four full strides of trot, the horse has also taken four strides. One rider stride (left/right or up/down) equals one stride of trot.*

Centering Breath in Trot

Once you have learned to regulate your movement in trot, the next step is coordinating your breath. Match the length of each inhalation and exhalation to correspond with two beats of trot. Count to a higher or lower number if necessary—the goal is to consciously connect breath with movement. Use hands-on bodywork to help maintain a low center of gravity and increase awareness. This breath work can be practiced in sitting and rising trot, in two-point (where you will feel weight shift from left to right legs), with and without stirrups, eyes opened or closed (fig. 9.8).

HOW-TO

Step 1 While trotting in basic seat, focus on lateral seat movements or posting, and count aloud: 1-and-2-and-3-and-4-and (with the "ands" silent), then repeat. Continue long enough to establish regularity.

Step 2 Now count silently and become aware of your breath. Inhale for a count of two as you take two full-seated strides (1-and-2-and), or as you post twice. Then exhale for a count of two as you sit two more strides (3-and-4-and), or post twice more.

Step 3 Continue breathing and trotting as long as you and the horse are comfortable, matching a two-beat inhalation with a two-beat exhalation. Use this conscious breath as often as possible in all your trot work.

TIP

The longeur can call out: "*In-hale-2-and-Ex-hale-2*" to help you keep your beat while practicing Centering Breath in trot. Notice any changes in the horse, as you integrate your breathing and body movement with his trot.

Rhythmical Rider Breathing Chart
How to Coordinate Breathing with Movement

TROT	**1**	**and**	**2**	**and**	**3**	**and**	**4**	**and**
INHALE 2 COUNTS	←	←	←	←				
EXHALE 2 COUNTS					→	→	→	→
SITTING TROT	**LEFT**	RIGHT	**LEFT**	RIGHT	**LEFT**	RIGHT	**LEFT**	RIGHT
RISING TROT ACCENT ON UP-BEAT	**UP**	DOWN	**UP**	DOWN	**UP**	DOWN	**UP**	DOWN
RISING TROT ACCENT ON DOWN-BEAT	**SIT**	STAND	**SIT**	STAND	**SIT**	STAND	**SIT**	STAND

Fig. 9.8 *Step 2: Inhale for a count of two as you sit two full-seated strides (1-and-2-and), or as you post twice. Then exhale for a count of two as you sit two more strides (3-and-4-and), or post twice more.*

Longeing Exercises in Trot

1 Choose from a variety of free-hand positions and arm exercises to include with trot while sitting, rising, and in two-point position. Keep arm movements slow, controlled, and synchronized with the rhythm of your seat, breathing pattern, and the horse's movements (fig. 9.9).

2 Practice the various suppling exercises recommended for trot (see Sidebar).

3 Trot with and without stirrups while sitting, rising, and in two-point.

4 Drop one stirrup and, with that leg, take up an imaginary stirrup. Continue trotting with toes up; then take stirrup back without looking. Repeat on opposite side. Then drop

Recommended Suppling Exercises for Work in Trot

*Note: In parentheses, I have qualified each exercise with terms that indicate how/when the exercise should be practiced. *Sitting* means you should be in your basic seat; *all postures* means the exercise can be combined with all suppling exercises and seat work; *postural adjustments* indicates the exercise consists of evaluating and fine-tuning your seat and position within the gait; you will learn to execute *weight shifts* in motion where noted; some exercises are recommended for practice in the forward seat or *two-point position*, which will add variety; *slow sitting* means the gait should be regulated and the tempo reduced to build confidence and feel in your basic seat; and *all variations* means you can practice each phase of that particular exercise in the recommended gait.

both stirrups, ride with imaginary stirrups for several strides, and then take them back. Strive to maintain the same tempo in the horse whether you have stirrups or not.

Fig. 9.9 *Being longed over ground poles at the sitting trot without stirrups challenges your seat balance and ability to follow the horse's more emphasized, often loftier, trot strides.*

5 Alternate between sitting and rising trot in basic seat with stirrups. For example, count eight strides sitting, then eight strides rising, while rhythmically breathing. Reduce the number of strides for more challenge, or experiment with various combinations (sit for two strides, post for four, etc.) The goal is to not disturb the horse or cause him to change tempo.

6 When alternating between sitting and rising *without* stirrups, take imaginary stirrups when rising. Then return to sitting trot, release legs to gravity, and let them dangle. Sitting trot may feel like a "rest position" after posting without stirrups!

7 Shorten stirrups for trot work in two-point. When rising, slightly incline torso forward from hip joints. Alternate between two-point, sitting, and rising for an adjustable seat.

8 Have the longeur vary the horse's tempo and stride by practicing transitions within the trot (slow/working/slow, or shortening/lengthening) while sitting, rising, and in two-point.

9 In rising trot, experiment with various posting combinations. For example, sit for two beats (1-and-2-and) then stand up for two (3-and-4-and). Or sit for three, and stand for four. Mix it up.

10 Work on upward and downward transitions between gaits based on the horse's level of training and your own (e.g. walk/trot/walk, or trot/halt/trot/walk, etc.) Have the longeur request transitions at different points on the circle so the horse does not anticipate. Keep counting in halt when halt transitions are part of the exercise.

11 Work over ground poles, cavalletti, or low jumps on the longe to vary trot work and promote your ability to follow the horse over obstacles.

12 Vault-off in trot. Remember: land facing forward, in step with the horse.

Fig. 9.10 *Learning to move with the horse by consciously participating in the gait: follow the canter by tucking your tailbone and "scooping" with your pelvis with each stride. Counting aloud will keep you focused on your own rhythmical movement.*

"Following" the Canter

In canter, the seat seems to "scoop" with each stride as the horse creates a rocking sensation. Your seat bones do not "brush" the saddle or slide from back to front. Rather, when following canter, seat bones remain in the deepest part of the saddle as your pelvis tucks then tilts alternately. This causes your lower back to flatten then hollow, as you roll from the back edges to the front edges of your seat bones every stride (fig. 9.10).

The horse's canter stride is described as a "jump" as he pushes off the ground for a moment of suspension, in which all hooves

Rhythmical Rider Movement Chart
THE "FOLLOWING" SEAT: CANTER

CANTER	**LEFT LEAD** **1** **2** **3** **4**	**RIGHT LEAD** **1** **2** **3** **4**	**RIDER NOTES**
RIDER	Pelvis "scoops," tailbone tucks L hip drops L seat bone bears more weight L inside shoulder gently drawn back	Pelvis "scoops," tailbone tucks R hip drops R seat bone bears more weight R inside shoulder gently drawn back	Lift up through the front of your torso as your back muscles sink. Use your abdominals for stability; do not grip excessively with your legs. Lift through the crown of your head, remaining upright. Keep your hip joints moveable.
HORSE	L foreleg reaches further forward than R foreleg L side of back dips down before moment of suspension or "jump"	R foreleg reaches further forward than L foreleg R side of back dips down before moment of suspension or "jump"	Each of the horse's three-beat strides equals one "scoop" of your pelvis. Count four "scoops," then repeat. The horse should be balanced, round, and maintain a steady tempo.
LONGEUR'S ROLE	Watch the rider's pelvis "scoop" with each stride and call out, "1-2-3-4" Prompt the rider to place more weight on the back edge of the inside L seat bone to maintain seat balance on the circle Ensure the front axis of the rider's torso is rotated toward the direction of travel: outside R shoulder forward, inside L shoulder back	Watch the rider's pelvis "scoop" with each stride and call out, "1-2-3-4" Prompt the rider to place more weight on the back edge of the inside R seat bone to maintain seat balance on the circle Ensure the front axis of the rider's torso is rotated toward the direction of travel: outside L shoulder forward, inside R shoulder back	Have the rider count strides aloud with you to establish rhythmical movement and assist the horse in maintaining the canter. Monitor the rider's alignment and regulate a steady canter beat and tempo in horse. Excessive speed will increase rider anxiety and difficulty in developing canter feel.

are briefly airborne. To follow and adhere to this movement, abdominal strength is instrumental. Your abdominal muscles offer stability to seat and torso, and prevent you from tipping forward and back.

To follow the canter, strive to remain upright and centered, while isolating pelvic movements. Avoid tipping in any of the four directions. Let weight spread across your seat and into the backs of your thighs; scan for excessive grip. Widen your straddle and strive to release legs to gravity as you focus on breathing and moving your seat rhythmically with the horse.

The longe circle size will increase in canter due to the speed and energy of this faster pace. To prepare, be sure you are accomplished in working trot sitting and rising without stirrups before introducing the canter. Your position changes slightly in canter when you draw your outside leg and hip back behind the girth, which will make your inside hip seem further ahead. It also lightens your outside seat bone, placing more weight on the inside. This weight shift is crucial for lateral seat balance and is sustained throughout the canter.

Canter Music

This musical chart depicts your rhythmic pattern in canter and compares it with the horse's rhythm (fig. 9.11). Unlike walk and trot, you mark out canter beats with one "scoop" of your pelvis. Each time your tailbone tucks, it feels like your seat scoops. Give this movement one beat. Count to four, and then repeat. To count steps, count strides: one stride = one beat = one scoop of your seat. In the time it takes you to make one scoop, the horse has taken a three-beat canter stride beginning with the outside hind, followed by a diagonal pair (inside hind/outside fore), and then the leading inside foreleg. Rather than counting "1-2-3, 1-2-3, 1-2-3," which again, sounds hurried, count "1 – 2 – 3 – 4 –" which corresponds to four strides of canter.

TIP

Novices preparing for canter work may wish to begin in two-point position, then introduce the full seat once a feel of the gait has been established.

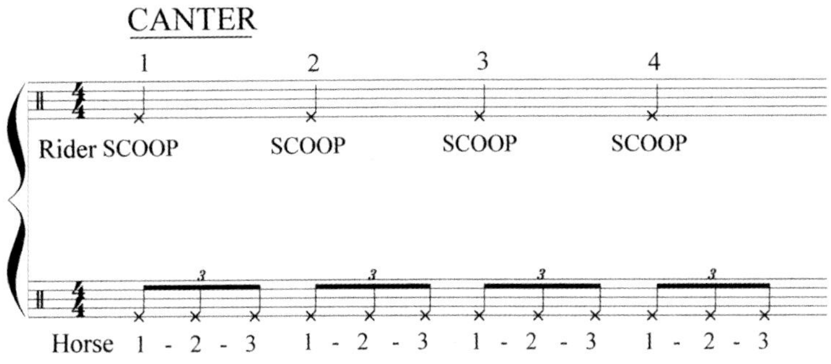

Fig. 9.11 *In the time it takes you to make one "scoop" of your pelvis, the horse has taken a three-beat canter stride beginning with the outside hind, followed by a diagonal pair (inside hind/ outside fore), and then the leading inside foreleg.*

Centering Breath in Canter

Once you are regulating seat movement in canter, the next step is to blend rhythmical abdominal breathing. Match the length of inhalation and exhalation to correspond with two "scoops" of your seat. Adjust your count as necessary—the point is to consciously connect breath with movement. Practice in basic seat and two-point, with and without stirrups, eyes opened or closed, with or without hands-on bodywork (fig. 9.12).

HOW-TO

Step 1 While cantering in basic seat, focus on your seat's "scooping" movements, counting aloud for each four horse strides: "1-2-3-4," and repeat. Continue long enough to establish regularity.

Step 2 Now count silently and become aware of your breath. Inhale through your nose for a count of two, as your seat scoops twice. Exhale through your mouth for a count of two as you scoop for two more strides.

Step 3 Continue breathing and cantering, matching a two-beat inhalation with exhalation as long as you and the horse are comfortable. For best results, use this fundamental technique in all canter work to help secure your seat balance and safety.

TIP

Counting aloud helps ensure you are breathing and combats anxiety-based breathing habits, which can quickly cause a loss of balance in this fast pace.

Rhythmical Rider Breathing Chart
How to Coordinate Breathing with Movement

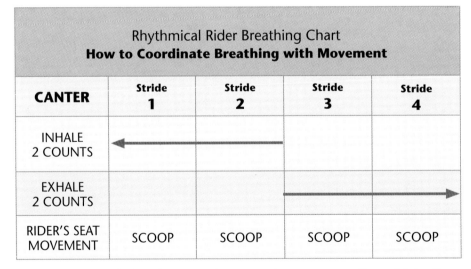

CANTER	**Stride 1**	**Stride 2**	**Stride 3**	**Stride 4**
INHALE 2 COUNTS	←	←		
EXHALE 2 COUNTS			→	→
RIDER'S SEAT MOVEMENT	SCOOP	SCOOP	SCOOP	SCOOP

Fig. 9.12 *Step 2: Inhale through your nose for a count of two, as your seat "scoops" twice, then exhale through your mouth for a count of two as you "scoop" for two more strides.*

Longeing Exercises in Canter

Fig. 9.13 *Jenny is regulating her breath and seat movement by counting out loud in canter. This helps you focus and more consciously participate in this faster pace.*

1 Choose from a variety of free-hand positions and arm exercises to add to canter work in basic seat or two-point position. Keep arm movements slow, controlled, and synchronized with the rhythm of your seat, breathing pattern, and the horse's strides (fig. 9.13).

2 Practice the various suppling exercises recommended for canter (see p. 190).

3 Canter with and without stirrups, sitting and in two-point.

4 Practice dropping the inside stirrup and picking it up without looking. Repeat with the outside, then with both. When you drop your irons, assume an imaginary stirrup position.

5 Alternate between basic seat and two-point. For example, count four strides sitting, then four strides in two-point, while continuing to integrate your breath. Your goal is to not disturb the horse or cause him to change tempo as you change positions.

6 In basic seat and two-point have the longeur request tempo changes from slow to working canter; alternate shortening and lengthening strides.

7 Based on the horse's level of training and your own, practice transitions between gaits: canter/trot, canter/walk, canter/halt, canter/trot/walk/halt, etc. Continue keeping time in halt, when halt transitions are part of your work.

8 Have the longeur arrange ground poles, cavalletti, or low jumps on the circle to vary the canter work and promote your ability to follow the horse over obstacles in canter.

9 Vault-off in canter. Remember: land facing forward and in step with horse.

Recommended Suppling Exercises for Work in Canter

Midsection/Center

Release Legs to Gravity *(sitting)*	p. 84
Advanced Centering Breath *(all postures)*	p. 88
Centered Pelvis *(postural adjustments)*	p. 91

Lower Body

Modified Frog *(sitting)*	p. 106
Legs Away *(sitting/two-point)*	p. 108
Ankle Suppling *(sitting)*	p. 109
Standing in Stirrups *(with heels down)*	p. 113
Two-Point Position	p. 115
Chin to the Mane *(two-point)*	p. 117

Upper Body (all sitting)

Head & Neck Stretches	p. 125
Shoulder Rolls	p. 127
Arm Raise with Breath	p. 128
Easy Twist	p. 133
Symmetry	p. 134
Symmetry Twist	p. 135
Arm Circles & Windmill	p. 137
Elbows Opened/Closed	p. 139
Hands Opened/Closed	p. 140

*Note: In parentheses, I have qualified each exercise with terms that indicate how/when the exercise should be practiced. *Sitting* means you should be in your basic seat; *all postures* means the exercise can be combined with all suppling exercises and seat work; *postural adjustments* indicates the exercise consists of evaluating and fine-tuning your seat and position within the gait; you will learn to execute *weight shifts* in motion where noted; some exercises are recommended for practice in the forward seat or *two-point position*, which will add variety; *slow sitting* means the gait should be regulated and the tempo reduced to build confidence and feel in your basic seat; and *all variations* means you can practice each phase of that particular exercise in the recommended gait.

CHAPTER 10

"Leading" the Horse's Gaits

When I went to train in Germany I had already been competing at Intermediaire I level but nevertheless I was put on the lunge for half an hour at least twice a week. It really works. In this way I was trained not only in passive sitting but also in active sitting. For example, I had to learn how to use my seat to slow the horse down and even stop him without reins.

KYRA KYRKLUND

Phase Three: The Active Seat

After learning to participate in the gaits by following and "listening" passively to the horse in Phase Two: The "Following" Seat, the next step in Riding Without Reins is to develop an *active* seat and learn to communicate with the horse, that is, influence his movement by using the body language of your seat, weight, legs, and eventually hands.

Phase Three: The Active Seat guides you to ride correctly from seat to hand, and just as you learned to *follow* the horse from walk to canter, an *active* seat likewise evolves gradually. In fact, you may start to take on an active role inconspicuously as your instructor or longeur asks you to execute upward transitions on your own. It is when you start *leading* the horse equally well in all three gaits and can consistently communicate both upward and downward transitions, while setting the rhythm, tempo, and length of stride—initially without reins—that you become effective in Phase Three and are ready to take your reins.

Then, if desired, you can proceed to Phase Four: The Educated Seat, during which you learn to train the horse.

Rider "Leads," Horse Follows

This phase of seat development introduces another, albeit intangible, rider quality. Utilizing the same basic skills, and moving in the same rhythmical patterns in all gaits, what sets an *active seat* apart from a *following seat* (discussed in chapter 9) may be difficult for others to observe. However, it manifests in the horse's performance... and you'll feel it. What changes is your relationship with the horse—you evolve into a leadership role.

Although no longer just *following,* you'll continue to absorb the gaits as you begin to *conduct* them. Now that you know how the horse moves, and how *your body moves* on horseback, you focus on developing the tools for actively communicating—developing your equitation by blending "listening" with an expanding vocabulary of "talking" skills. You learn about aiding (delivering aids to the horse) and how to function in a "managerial" capacity by directing gaits, establishing rhythm and tempo, and requesting transitions.

As the longeur starts to turn over these tasks, you'll become aware that one of your most important responsibilities is to establish and maintain a steady rhythm through sustained movement pulsations in your seat. Essentially you become a "rhythm keeper." When your seat slows, so the horse slows. When it becomes more active, the horse follows. When it stops altogether, the horse stops with you. To learn this, you benefit by longeing on a well-trained riding horse that is sensitive to the seat. Through his response or lack of response, the horse provides you with an immediate confirmation of accomplishments and mistakes.

Without reins, your focus is not yet on the horse's head and neck position—

Phase Three: The Active Seat—Rider "Leads," Horse Follows

Sample Longe Session

1 After an unmounted warm-up and routine equipment check, start by Mounting with Breath (p. 67). From the saddle, reassess your tension level. If necessary, perform a Guided Relaxation in Halt (p. 72). Proceed with a halt warm-up and include centering and breathing exercises, such as Release Legs to Gravity (p. 84), Centering Breath/Advanced Centering Breath (p. 88), Complete Breath (p. 89), Centered Pelvis (p. 91), Four Corners (p. 95), Slow Pendulum (p. 96), and a selection of lower and upper body suppling exercises (see chapters 6 and 7).

2 In preparation for walk, take a deep breath, and as you exhale ask the horse to walk forward using active aids. Immediately begin practicing Centering Breath in Walk (p. 176) as you coordinate your movement in a steady rhythm. Using seat, weight, and leg regulate the horse's walk (in the working or medium gait for dressage riders) as you set and maintain the tempo. Refer to "Leading" the Walk (p. 196).

3 Next, practice your personalized walk warm-up that includes a sequence of lower body and upper body suppling exercises based on the obstacles you still need to address, and the specific results you desire (see list on p. 150). Remember to "work within," cultivating the Eight Basic Objectives in each walk exercise, and "circle" back (on your circular path) to your centering work as needed.

4 Once you have centered and suppled and are effectively regulating the horse's walk, practice transitions "with breath" (halt/walk/halt) using your seat, weight, and leg to communicate. Voice aids from the saddle can also help until your equitation becomes clear to the horse.

5 Practice shortening and lengthening the horse's walk stride, using seat, weight, and leg. The instructor or longeur can continue to support your efforts, as needed.

6 Maintain seat and position while striving to keep the horse's gait consistent and at the same time challenging yourself: for example, drop and pick up stirrups; let go with one or both hands while practicing various arm positions; or move from basic seat to two-point position. For list of walk exercises, see p. 178.

7 When you are ready to work actively in trot, repeat Steps 2 through 6, and refer to "Leading" the Trot (p. 198). Challenge yourself with trot suppling exercises (p. 184) while striving to keep the gait consistent.

8 When you are ready to work actively in canter, repeat Steps 2 through 6, and refer to "Leading" the Canter (p. 200). Challenge yourself with canter suppling exercises (p. 190) while striving to keep the gait consistent.

9 In progressive stages, you will demonstrate your readiness to take up the reins and establish contact with the bit. Start this practice first in walk, then trot, and finally canter. With your instructor's guidance, practice seat work in all three gaits with the addition of your reins.

10 You will eventually demonstrate your readiness to ride off the longe line with your reins. Before you do, first learn to longe a horse from the ground. Take on the role of longeur, and direct the horse using longe rein, longe whip, voice, and ground-based body language.

his carrying posture is still facilitated by the longeur and the side reins. However, you can learn to improve his posture even without reins, by moving energy *"from back to front"* with your seat and leg while being longed. Using your seat to maintain rhythm, and applying driving aids to engage the haunches and direct energy forward, you learn how to "invite" the horse to lift his back and stretch his neck forward and down. Influencing the horse like this without reins is one of the most valuable lessons you can ever learn on the longe, particularly if you aspire to train or ride dressage horses. Many new riders with reins in their hands become *hand*-oriented, not *seat*-oriented. This is unfortunate, as with insufficient focus on seat development, they can hardly prevent themselves from riding "front to back," as using hands for balance and security is in our nature!

This is precisely why being longed is so indispensable. On the longe, you are able to engage in the most logical training method ever invented for educating a rider—one that teaches you to ride *from seat to hand*, not hand to seat.

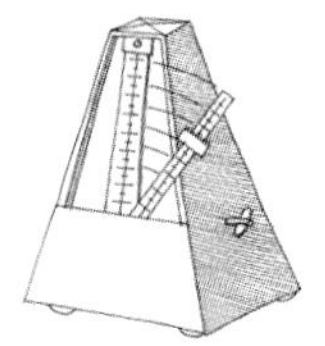

Fig. 10.1 *A controlled, active seat functions like a metronome—an instrument that maintains a steady tempo by delivering a consistent beat—and imparts a sense of rhythmic authority to the horse.*

Authority in the Seat

An active seat imperceptibly becomes an instrument for regulating the gaits. When you were developing a *following* seat, the horse kept the beat and taught you how the gaits felt. You learned to follow *his* rhythms, which might have fluctuated due to your initial awkwardness or lack of control. To learn to participate in each gait, you identified your seat movements and attached an audible focus, by counting your seat bone "steps" aloud. Next, you developed a rhythmical cadence by integrating breathing with seat movement. This helped you internalize the rhythm of each gait.

Through experience and an ever-increasing familiarity in the gaits, you can learn to develop a metronome-like quality in your seat. This will allow you to use your seat to communicate *rhythm* and *tempo* to the horse. So, rather than following, you become a rhythm-keeper—a leader of the dance. The horse now follows your rhythms. While your leg drives as necessary, your seat functions like "cruise control," maintaining a steady speed in your body and horse.

This metronome-like quality imparts an "authority" in your seat that most horses notice and respond to readily (fig. 10.1). A well-trained riding horse will connect to an "authoritative" seat, both mentally and physically, displaying greater attentiveness and remaining "on the ready" for additional instructions. As you become able to elicit a cadenced performance from the horse, your seat will blend so well with the movement that it brings no attention to itself. Yet, within your steady-movement pulse, you'll continue to exchange subtle communications, moment by moment.

Despite my reference to cars, your seat is anything but mechanical. To maintain the horse's trust, an authoritative seat must sensitively balance *talking* with *listening*, *softness* with *firmness*, *work* with *rest*. It should remain *feeling* and communicative, able to respond deftly to the horse to keep him comfortable in his work.

Educating the Leg to the Active Seat

Educating your leg for riding involves a combination of form, function, and *feel*. You've been cultivating leg position and feel all along—thighs hanging from flexible hip joints, a deep softly bent knee, ankles supple and flexed, heels lower than the toe (fig. 10.2). In *following seat*, you even brought the lower legs into a passive contact with the barrel. Now, with an *active seat*, you learn to maintain a consistent position with or without stirrups in preparation for using active leg aids.

Many times I have asked students to drop their stirrups, only to watch as their leg position fell apart, and balance was instantly lost. It is important to realize that stirrups are not responsible for keeping your heels down, knees bent, or for maintaining contact—an educated leg learns to do all those things independently, and considers a stirrup merely a place to rest the foot. Nor is the saddle responsible—thigh blocks, knee rolls, and repositioned stirrup bars do not educate the leg—and the sticky substance some riders use to adhere their leg to the saddle is preposterous!

Fig. 10.2 *Your lower body contact continues to evolve as you (rather than the longeur) begin to more actively give aids with your seat and leg. Educating your leg involves "tempering" the rhythmical driving influence of the lower leg with an appropriate amount of passivity in the upper leg, ensuring the horse has "room to move" as he fulfills your requests.*

By first allowing passivity to develop, you eventually reach the stage where active aids and position become a priority. Do not rush this process. If you still struggle with releasing grip and feeling the movement, attempts to establish the correct form and function will be premature. Many riders are tempted to force the matter, which is unproductive. We cannot compel flesh and bone into a posture simply because we want to, or because someone orders us to—an educated leg must evolve. Positioning the legs without *feel* requires more effort (or tack) to hold stiff legs in place... and the cycle of grip and disconnection unfortunately continues.

"Leading" Transitions

You learned to integrate breath when *following* transitions. Now, to *lead* transitions with an active seat, use your breath in the same manner while applying seat, weight, and leg aids. Continue to prepare with an inhalation, and execute all transitions with an exhalation. Engaging the abdominals helps stabilize seat and position during each gait change.

To request upward transitions, your active leg aids will drive the horse. From a halt, especially if the horse has just spent several moments standing during your warm-up, he may have "grown a root," so give him time to refocus and get into gear. For sensitive horses, a light touch may be all that's required. If a horse appears lethargic, an emphatic bump with the heels may be useful initially. Start by applying light aids, increasing pressure if needed. Your intention is to develop aids that are less coarse. Learn to read the horse and communicate tactfully.

To support seat balance in upward transitions, bring your torso back slightly, tuck in your tailbone, and shift weight to the rear edges of your seat bones. Not only does this stabilize your seat, but also indicates to the horse that you are about to drive the haunches. Then, with an exhalation, abdominal lift, and the appropriate touch of your legs, you should find yourself in the faster gait and in balance. Immediately begin regulating the rhythm with your seat and set the appropriate tempo, using your legs actively if more impulsion is needed.

Downward transitions are requested by alleviating the driving aids and engaging the abdominals during exhalation (see Centering Breath p. 87) to cease or stop seat movements. For stability, keep your legs in contact as you come back to center, bringing pelvis and torso upright, and allowing your back muscles to hang off your skeleton and feel heavy, from shoulders to seat. Your transition can even be counted down (e.g. from walk to halt: 4-3-2-1-halt) to help you coordinate your aids. As you become more skilled and request advanced transitions, such as canter-walk, your inner thigh muscles may be engaged as long as grip is not prolonged, nor joint mobility compromised.

Horses with "body armor" may not readily "hear" seat communications (see p. 59). However, with patience (and sometimes including voice aids), numb horses start to listen, regain sensitivity, and eventually respond. Most trained horses of average sensitivity, even if not usually ridden from the seat, will respond to seat aids naturally, as the message is simple and makes sense—an active seat essentially tells the horse, "I move, you move. I stop, you stop."

"Leading" the Walk

In walk, the horse's barrel swings left to right, and alternately touches your lower legs. The contact it makes offers the opportune time to deliver driving aids with your *calves*. While it is easy to get caught up in

Fig. 10.3 *When you, rather than the longeur, become the horse's "leader" in walk, and you transition in/out/ within the gait without reins, it involves an appropriate blend of active/passive aids and rhythmical control of your legs and seat.*

the swing of the horse's pendulous belly, which pushes your legs away when leg contact is passive, as you develop awareness and coordination your active legs can learn to meet the barrel halfway (fig. 10.3).

Sustaining the Walk

Wrap your legs around the barrel and call "left-right" as you feel it swing. Have the longeur confirm when you correctly identify the movement. Continue calling, and realize that you are cueing yourself for the driving aids. For example, as the barrel presses your left leg, press the barrel with an isometric squeeze of the left calf. This encourages the left hind leg, which is just about to leave the ground, to push off with more thrust. Immediately afterward, release your left calf, and then apply the right calf. The release of lower leg pressure is as important as the active aid itself, as incessant muscular contractions make aids indistinguishable and your legs could tire, or the horse grow numb. The release of an active lower leg aid does not mean you must remove your calves from the horse—just stop squeezing.

However, squeezing calves may cause your thighs to squeeze, as well. Until you develop isolation between lower and upper legs, try a more "percussive" aid, meeting the barrel with a light "bump" of your heel or ankle. This may cause your lower legs to move on and off the horse, and while it certainly isn't a "finished product," it will at least teach you to alternate lower leg aids and prevent unnecessary grip. With continued lessons on the longe, you can develop a leg that hugs the horse, and delivers aids through isometric squeezes, not obvious bumps with the heel.

Lengthen and Shorten the Walk

To coordinate leg aids with seat movements: as your left seat bone tucks, your left leg aids simultaneously; ditto on the right. To lengthen the stride, use stronger leg aids and take longer walk "steps" with your seat (see p. 172). To shorten, use less leg and shorter steps. Counting silently or aloud will aid you in managing seat, legs, and of course shoulders that continue to follow the movement. Rhythmical aiding, stepping, and breathing will inspire the horse to move rhythmically under you, producing a walk that is cadenced and relaxed

"Leading" the Trot

We are increasingly challenged in trot with vertical, horizontal, and lateral movements to manage, along with more momentum. To begin leading the gait, request an upward transition on an exhalation, while wrapping your legs around the barrel and squeezing both calves simultaneously (fig. 10.4).

Sustaining the Trot

To sustain the gait, establish an appropriate leg contact and count your seat bone "steps" to set a steady rhythm and regulate speed (see p. 179). If the trot needs more impulsion, increase the isometric pulsations of your calves—pressing them inward and upward in rhythm with the trot. On the circle, you may need to drive more with your inside leg for bend, outside leg for thrust. Be sure to release your calf muscles (not your leg position) after any increased activity, returning to a "maintenance-level" leg contact.

In rising trot, the driving aids are best delivered during the sitting phase, as your seat will be more stable and aids will correspond with the inside hind. Apply driving aids in rhythm and release them as you rise up. When your lower legs inspire a livelier trot, your seat responds by immediately regulating the new tempo and absorbing the increased activity of the gait.

If the horse lags behind, *maintain seat tempo* as your legs act promptly, with your tailbone tucked, to bring the horse back to speed. Or, if the horse gets ahead and moves faster than you, do not "follow" him, but *emphasize the original tempo* in your seat as you center your pelvis and reduce or eliminate driving aids to bring him back. When you develop authority in your seat, you can lead the horse by slowing down or speeding up the pace, even without reins.

Slow the Trot

If you have ever been instructed to "post slower" to reduce a horse's speed, this is accomplished by emphasizing the "down

Fig. 10.4 *With determination, your self-control evolves in trot and you will become more confident, letting go with your hands one by one, while taking a "leadership" role.*

beat" and sinking into the saddle fully, rather than brushing the seat and popping up again. To post more slowly, think of lingering in the saddle a fraction of a second longer to slow the horse. If there is no response, "scan" your seat for clenched muscles. With a "hard" seat, any efforts to slow the horse can backfire, and you may actually push him away faster. Try reciting this affirmation: *The softer my seat, the slower my horse.* The more you invite the horse to stay under you, the more you prevent him from running away.

To lead the gait, your seat should be saying, "*Stay here, under me.*" When your instructor talks about the horse being "in front of your leg," it is his *energy* you want to feel surging forward and out in front of your legs, but his body must remain underneath, his center of gravity aligned with yours, neither falling behind nor running ahead.

Lengthen the Trot

To *lengthen* the trot, tuck your tailbone and ask for more thrust with stronger legs aids. Ensure your seat can accommodate more movement by remaining supple in the hip joints and lower back, and taking longer seat bone "steps" when sitting (see p. 179), or posting more emphatically in rising trot.

Shorten the Trot

To shorten the stride, reduce leg aids (close thighs as a restraining aid, if necessary), remain centered and soft, engage your abdominals while reducing seat movement.

"Leading" the Canter

Leading the horse in canter relies on the rhythmical "scooping" of your seat (see p. 186), with even more weight carried on the inside seat bone, combined with isometric pulsations from your inside leg to encourage engagement and flexion. It also involves your outside leg placed a few inches back on the barrel to assist with alignment and thrust (fig. 10.5).

Because each canter stride involves a significant "jump," there is another leg function that can help the horse create a more balanced carrying posture. It makes use of a longer rider leg position in basic seat (with the appropriate flexion in knees and ankles) to influence the horse's abdominal muscles. As your legs reach down and around the barrel, with the appropriate contact and use of your calves, which pulse inward and upward, you can coax the horse to contract his abdominals. This supports his posture, much like abdominal lifting supports your own. Asking the horse to engage his abdominals also encourages him to tuck his pelvis, engage his hind legs, and lift his back muscles under your seat. This posture is desirable for weight bearing and is what it means when the horse is "on the bit."

Lengthen and Shorten the Canter

To lead the horse in canter even without reins, strive to regulate the tempo of your seat. When you move emphatically, you can stretch out the stride. When your seat

Fig. 10.5 *For advanced riders with sufficient self-control, "leading" the horse in canter while being longed may be facilitated by taking the reins as necessary to help maintain a rhythmical, balanced gait.*

movement is more consolidated, you can shorten the canter. Each time your pelvis scoops, stretch up through the front of your body, lift abdominals, and let your back muscles sink. These combined sensations help elevate the horse's forehand and engage his haunches, making the canter more balanced.

Conclusion

Once you have this solid set of rider basics, and the horse accepts your leadership with accurate and willing responses to your seat, you are ready to take the reins (fig. 10.6). This opens a new realm of opportunity, with additional skills to develop as you learn to influence the horse with the addition of your hands. To be given the reins while being longed, you'll continue to benefit from the longeur's assistance and a controlled environment.

Whether a novice rider, one who has previous riding experience but needs retraining, or one who is aware that continuing education is the way to go, by progressing through your seat development and the Riding Without Reins program—transitioning from *passenger* to *follower* then to *leader* you earn the right to take the reins again once you've acquired the ability to use your seat completely independently of your limbs.

Holding the reins is a privilege reserved for those entitled to be called "riders" because they have demonstrated total control over their own body.

CHARLES DE KUNFFY

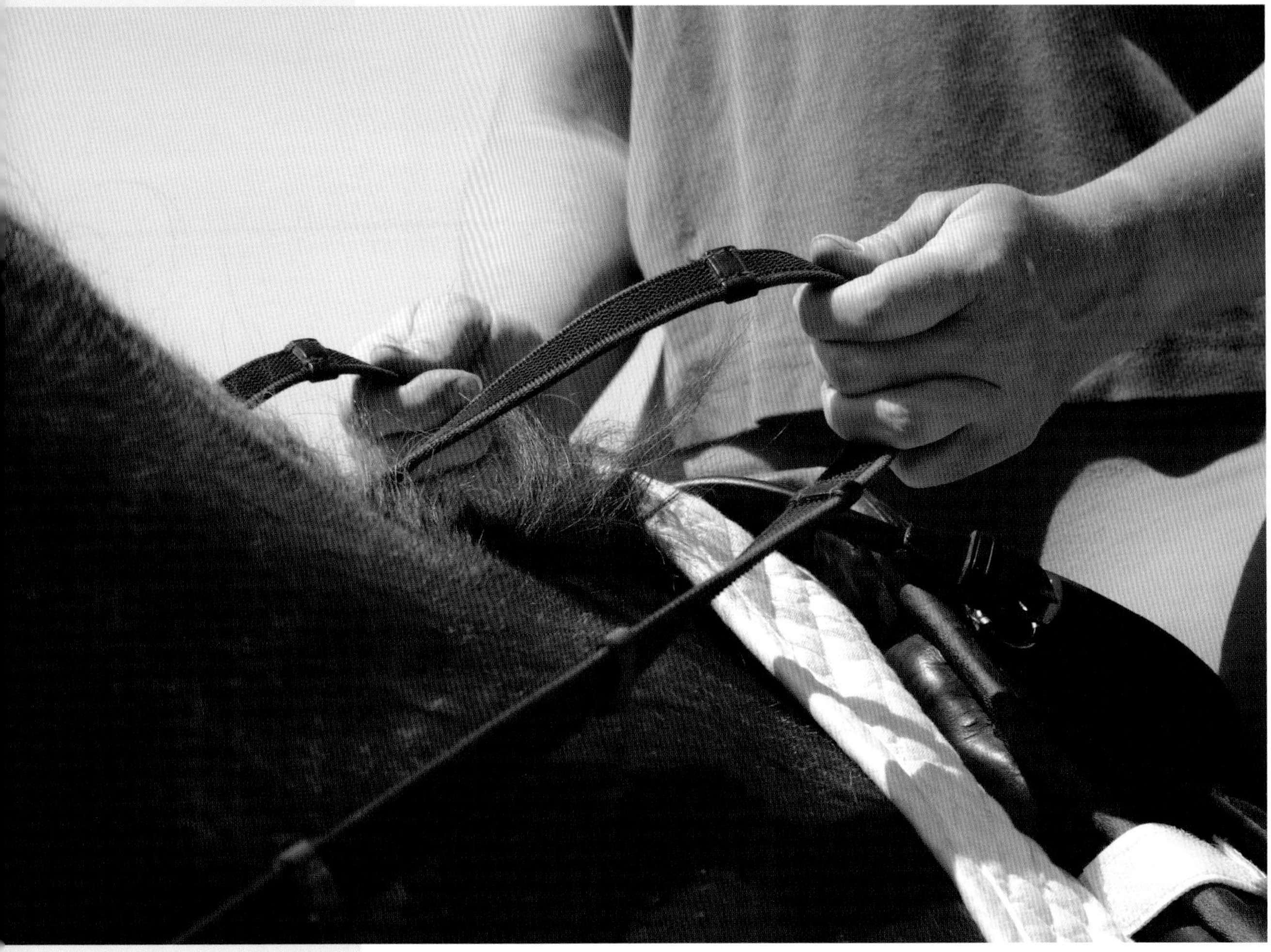

Fig. 10.6 *Once you have a solid set of rider basics, and the horse accepts your leadership with accurate and willing responses to your seat, you are ready to take the reins.*

The directing of the horse, all halts and half-halts and collecting aids continue to be undertaken by the body and independently of the reins. Ultimately, the reins are used only to perfect the overall picture; they are used solely through the most subtle "impulses," to provide the final polish to the complete harmony of two beings.

KLAUS FERDINAND HEMPFLING

CHAPTER 11

The Rider as Trainer

Finally, the rider must gain the insight that it is the journey, and the journey alone, that is the goal. A rider who understands this will develop into a person with whom the horse will work in unison. In this sense, rein contact resulting from an independent and balanced seat is essential to developing trust and agreement between horse and rider, and a practical concern for the welfare of the animal is manifested in gentle and empathetic communication through the reins.

GERHARD KAPITZKE

From Leader to Trainer

There is yet another stage of seat development, if you wish to progress higher on your circular path and aspire to train horses and increase their athletic potential for pleasure or sport. For riders interested in dressage or horse training, I cannot overemphasize the importance of working conscientiously through Phases One through Three before segueing into Phase Four: The Educated Seat. Once you are effectively communicating with reins, you may opt to begin a new journey as a trainer, learning to use your ever-evolving riding skills to improve the horse.

However, it is unrealistic to think that you could educate a horse and improve his frame and performance before acquiring a solid foundation of basics and an advanced level of self-control. Even as your seat becomes authoritative, your skills more accomplished, an ongoing program of being longed is necessary to help keep obstacles at bay and allow you to monitor basics and equitation, as these must be honed throughout your training career.

When developing a dressage seat, longeing reinforces the skills acquired in Phase Two and Three. It may amaze you to learn that it is possible to achieve *even deeper levels of relaxation* over time, to "blend" more closely with the horse than you ever thought possible. The magic of creating union with the horse really is about letting go of tension, and that is an ongoing challenge and a primary reason for rider longeing.

With the horse as your partner (yet as always, your teacher), you enter into a progressive system organized into levels that are recognized nationwide (and with slightly different terminology, worldwide). From Intro to Training Level, First through Fourth Level, and up to the internationally-recognized levels of FEI performance culminating in Grand Prix, there is a long way to go—even with all you have accomplished so far in riding.

Despite your rider basics, equitation skills, the ability to both absorb and lead the horse, in becoming a trainer you may start once again at the beginning, using your knowledge to progress a less experienced equine partner up the levels. And as you become a trainer, you continue to learn lessons from each horse on what is an infinite path of knowledge.

Phase Four: The Educated Seat—Rider as Trainer

Sample Longe Session

1 Warm up off the horse *and* in the saddle at halt and walk. Be sure to include centering exercises and suppling exercises that address both lower and upper body.

2 Practice Centering Breath (p. 87) and seat work in the *basic seat* progressively—in all three gaits—to confirm your *feel* of both passive and active sitting. Work with and without stirrups.

3 Once you have established a steady cadence in the horse, challenge your ability to maintain this, as well as the integrity of your seat and position, by practicing a variety of suppling exercises recommended for trot and canter.

4 When being longed for a dressage seat, work with an experienced trainer who can teach you to put the horse into a working frame and "on the bit" in all three gaits by riding from back to front, *seat to hand*. Do this first without reins, and then with. Your trainer should instruct you on the body language necessary and the appropriate blend of active and passive aids as you learn to engage the horse's hindquarters and abdominals, as he lifts his back into the correct carrying posture.

5 On the longe, strive to improve the horse's performance by using seat, weight, leg, and rein aids to cultivate mental and physical relaxation in the horse and develop rhythm and impulsion in the gaits. The longeur can support your efforts by aiding from the ground as necessary. The goal is to reinforce the *feel* and communication that you accomplished on the longe line, and transfer these desirable training skills to riding off the longe.

PART V

APPENDICES

Teaching the rider on the longe is, first, a science, which progresses as an art. From a balanced posture/seat the rider refines his applications, which develop aesthetic qualities.

CHARLES HARRIS

APPENDIX 1

Vaulting for Riders

The various unique and ingenious vaulting exercises are all designed to be fun and challenging while encouraging harmony and partnership with the horse and rider. Each vaulting movement can easily be adapted to fit the needs and abilities of any level of student. This rapidly builds success, skill and poise which transfers to many other aspects of their life. Since the horse is under the command of the instructor the vaulter is free to focus on his or her own balance, form and control, allowing them to learn faster and more effectively.

NANCY STEVENS-BROWN (AMERICAN VAULTING ASSOCIATION PRESIDENT)

Another Type of Longeing

There is a unique type of group riding lesson that supports the development of rider basics and includes longeing, while at the same time cultivating a lively team spirit: *vaulting*—the practice of gymnastics on horseback (fig. 12.1). Vaulters learn to follow the horse's movements while performing a variety of mounted postures, from the most basic to the incredible, such as splits, backbends, and handstands performed at the canter.

Fig. 12.1 *More experienced vaulters participate in the training of other students as well as the longe horses—a reflection of the camaraderie and teamwork encouraged at vaulting clubs.*

While you may think vaulting is just for kids and wonder what it possibly has to do with your riding, I enthusiastically agree with the American Vaulting Association's assertion that, "Equestrian vaulting is for everyone."[1] Vaulting is the safest equestrian discipline[2] (I discuss this further on p. 211) and *vaulting for riders* (i.e. longeing bareback using a surcingle with large handles—see fig. 12.4) is an ideal riding prerequisite as it provides the opportunity to more rapidly achieve a basic seat and the ability to follow the horse's movements in walk, trot, and canter. For many, particularly those interested in dressage, it can also present the opportunity to ride a more collected horse. Seasoned vaulting horses work with a higher degree of engagement and uphill balance than most conventional lesson horses, and recreational vaulting can contribute to a budding dressage rider's feel and understanding of this equine posture.

Even if you try vaulting as an adult (as I did at forty-something!), it may be the most fun you will ever have on horseback *and* it will improve your seat and balance *without fail*!

Background

The origins of vaulting date back thousands of years on the European continent. Recognized as an FEI (Féderation Equestre Internationale) discipline in 1983, the modern sport of equestrian vaulting developed in post-war Germany and was only first introduced to the U.S. in 1956 when Elizabeth Searle brought a film of German vaulters to California for her Pony Club. A decade later in 1966, she co-founded the American Vaulting Association.

1 American Vaulting Association (AVA), 2005, URL: http://www.americanvaulting.org/faqs.html.

2 AVA, URL: http://www.americanvaulting.org/safety.

American vaulting took root on the West coast and since then has spread across the country due to increased exposure and enthusiasm. "Vaulting for riders" is a relatively new learning opportunity as, in recent years, competitive vaulting has expanded to include all types of non-competitive equestrians—adults, children, and handicapped riders.

Fig. 12.2 *Riding without reins on an experienced longe horse is the most direct way to achieve a correctly balanced basic seat and position.*

Accelerated Learning and Increased Safety

It is worth noting that, while a typical rider strives to master one or two riding positions with stirrups and reins (the basic seat and/or the forward seat), which can take *years*, a rider that vaults is introduced to a *collection* of mounted postures without stirrups or reins, including the basic seat, and often learns them in a matter of weeks (fig. 12.2). Vaulting professionals report that it is the *norm* for students to quickly learn the basic seat *and more* when longeing on a vaulting horse. In fact, the U.S. Pony Club Vaulting Handbook states, "Using vaulting techniques, the time required in learning to ride safely can be cut in half."[3]

"With a lower incidence of injury than dressage, most vaulting injuries are comparable to those seen in gymnastics and are generally composed of sprains."[4] As the safest of all equestrian activities, vaulting offers a controlled longeing environment. With *horse control* in the hands of the longeur, students can focus on *self-control* by learning to maintain the correct alignment and move rhythmically with the horse.

Vaulting also addresses safety training, something most other riding programs fail to provide. Riders learn safe dismounts and landings first off a stationary

I have found that as a method of teaching, using the roller (surcingle) reduces the time taken to learn to ride safely; you will quickly be able to progress to the faster paces because of the confidence the roller gives you. Instant success is the norm rather than the exception, as competence in the basic exercises can be achieved in a matter of weeks: learning to ride with saddle and bridle can, and often does, take months if not years.

ANN SAGAR

3 Handbook and Rules for United States Pony Club, Vaulting Handbook (Lexington, KY: USPC, 1999, p.1).

4 AVA, URL: http://www.americanvaulting.org/safety.

Figs. 12.3 A & B *The vaulting barrel is used as a training aid in teaching the basics of position (A) as well as for practicing more difficult balanced postures or group freestyle programs (B—Photo courtesy of Valley View Vaulters).*

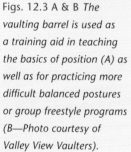

barrel, then a moving horse. Vaulting horses are longed in an enclosed arena with slightly deeper, springy footing for softer landings. For these reasons, vaulting for riders helps decrease a rider's chances of falling, as well as the *fear* of falling.

Francie Dougherty, trainer and longeur for Great Falls Vaulters in Maryland believes that "Vaulters never fall off a horse—they make unplanned dismounts." She says, "Vaulters are taught how to fall. On the mats, they're constantly doing tumbling exercises to increase their ability to land and roll and each of them know five or six different ways to get off a horse. One of the first lessons they're taught is how to dismount using the surcingle, then they're taught how to swing out away from the horse so they don't end up underneath—they learn on the barrel first—and are taught what to do if things go wrong before they're even taught how to do it right. Vaulters always land facing forward, going with the horse, that's the key. And they land with their knees bent and running—they literally hit the ground running."

Vaulting Equipment and Attire

Vaulting Barrel

Vaulting barrels may be constructed of wood, or more commonly, metal oil drums with welded handles and legs that can be adjusted for height. The drum is covered with thick padding and a durable cover.

These barrels, or "surrogate horses," serve as training aids for vaulters. They are used to introduce basics and for both compulsory and kür practice (figs. 12.3 A & B). Mastering exercises on a stationary barrel builds confidence and prepares vaulters for practice on a moving horse.

In a group lesson, barrels offer a means for vaulters to continue practicing while others are on the vaulting horse, or while the horse is warming up or resting. Barrel use helps prevent overly fatiguing the vaulting horse. A barrel can also be used for indoor practice during inclement weather, or when a vaulting horse cannot be worked. In short, the barrel is a vaulting essential. (For information on how to build your own vaulting barrel or purchase one, contact the American Vaulting Association at www.americanvaulting.org.)

Vaulting Surcingle

The vaulting surcingle or "roller" is a specially designed strap that buckles around the horse (fig. 12.4). While some models have a built-in girth, others have a detachable girth, which allows one surcingle to be used on a variety of horses. The surcingle must be securely fitted and fastened in a way that does not chafe the horse.

When selecting a surcingle, the needs and safety of both the vaulter and the horse must be considered. For example, a vaulter relies on the surcingle's stability, using the two sturdy "grips" as handholds. Grips come in various shapes or "bends," heights, and thicknesses to suit a vaulter's preference (it is important to note that while some surcingles are built for serious and rigorous use, others are intended only for light use). The gullet comes in a choice of heights (low, medium, or high) that can influence a vaulter's performance and the horse's comfort at the withers. Gullet padding can be thin, medium, or thick and also plays a role in how the surcingle fits the horse.

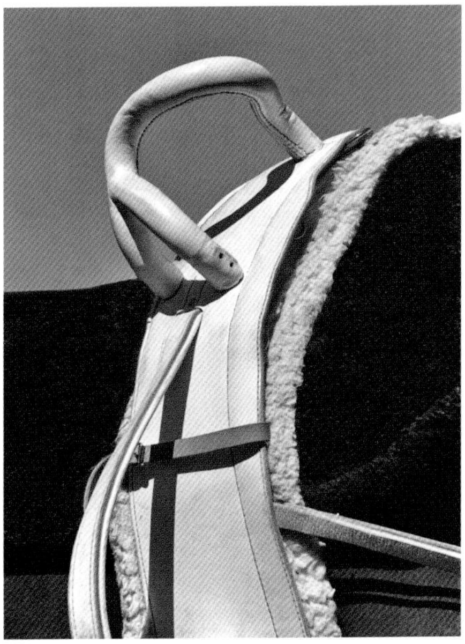

Fig. 12.4 *The vaulting surcingle is specially designed to offer the vaulter security and stability while fitting the horse comfortably and correctly.*

Surcingles may have additional loops called "Cossack straps," which are foot straps that enable a vaulter to stand from the side of the horse, as often seen in freestyles. These, too, come in different widths. (With such a wide range of features and prices, buying a quality vaulting surcingle is similar to buying a quality saddle!)

There is something very reassuring about grasping the large handles or "grips" of a vaulting surcingle while astride a horse. Perhaps it is because our hands are able to do what they do best when we feel unsteady—hold on! Even without reins, stirrups, or a saddle, the surcingle can enable us to feel secure on horseback almost immediately. And, with only a two-inch foam pad beneath our seat, we

Fig. 12.5 *Helmets are considered hazardous in equestrian vaulting as they potentially interfere with balance, particularly when pressing the head against the horse's body, as in this shoulder stand.*

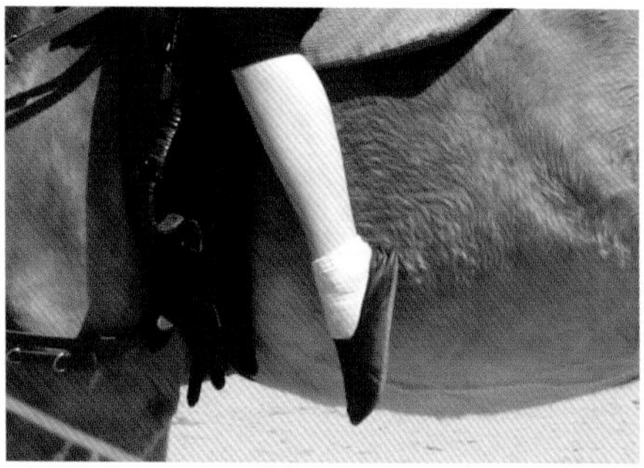

Fig. 12.6 *Slip-on vaulting shoes like these promote balance and feel. Sneakers or athletic shoes are a fine substitute for beginner vaulters.*

readily absorb the horse's movement and develop balance.

Helmets

Helmets are considered unsafe in vaulting as they potentially interfere with balance, particularly in advanced positions where the vaulter's head is pressed against the horse[5] or another vaulter (fig. 12.5).

Footwear

Riding boots with low heels, while perfect for balancing feet in stirrups, are unsuitable for vaulting. Rather, soft slip-on vaulting shoes promote balance and feel (fig. 12.6). Riders that wish to try vaulting can usually start with soft-soled tennis or athletic shoes.

Other Clothing

Riders trying vaulting should dress comfortably in sweatpants, breeches, or riding tights. (Note: full-seat breeches restrict movement and are not advisable for vaulting or yoga practice.) Riding gloves are unnecessary, as there are no reins to hold.

The Vaulting Horse

While fun and educational for riders, vaulting (and longeing in general) can be very soothing for horses. As in any longeing environment, the person astride is not responsible for directing or steering the horse—this is the longeur's role. It is never a vaulter's intention to influence the horse from his back, although the horse greatly influences the vaulter.

Like the vaulters themselves, vaulting horses must be supple, strong, and balanced, with an unwavering focus and sense of calm (fig. 12.7). The horse should develop consistent gaits and a tolerance for unusual movements on and around

5 Faulkner, MD, Robert, "Vaulting Safety and the Use of Protective Headgear," American Medical Equestrian Association News, (May 1996, Vol. VI, Number 2), URL: http://tarlton.law.utexas.edu/dawson/amea/may96nws.htm

his body. From vaulters running in motion alongside as they prepare to mount (fig. 12.8), to a variety of sitting, kneeling, or standing positions (fig. 12.9), to dismounts ranging from gently dropping to the ground to dramatically flipping off the haunches, the horse must keep a constant, rhythmical beat.

Some riders may be concerned that the repetitive nature of longeing may result in injury to their horse, or cause the horse to become bored or sour, but in truth there are many positive effects of long-term longeing seen in vaulting horses—and they undergo far more longe-line training than the average riding horse (fig. 12.10).

Vaulting coach and trainer Rick Hawthorne and his wife Virginia founded Valley View Vaulters over 25 years ago with a team of seven vaulters and one horse. They now have a collection of vaulting horses, two locations in Southern California, and are currently the largest vaulting club in the United States. Many horses are donated to this non-profit organization and often arrive with tendon, shoeing, or attitude problems. The training these animals receive includes a great deal of longeing as well as top-notch attention and care, and it transforms them...always for the better.

Regarding their horses' longevity and absence of injury in the face of long-term, frequent longeing, Rick reports, "Many of our vaulting horses have lasted 15 to 20 years after they've been trained. As long as they are shod properly, taken care of and

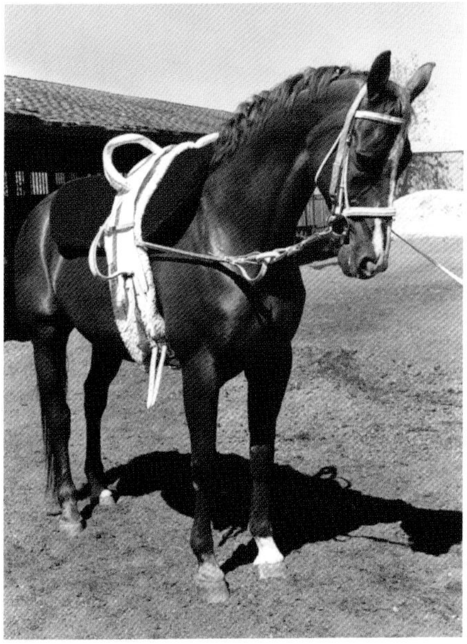

Fig. 12.7 *"Waldmeister" is a former dressage horse with an "uphill" frame, collected gaits, and an even, rhythmic tempo. Here he is correctly outfitted for vaulting practice.*

Fig. 12.8 *The vaulting horse needs to tolerate unusual movements on and around his body. Here, Gerardo runs alongside Waldmeister as he prepares to mount.*

Fig. 12.9 *Experienced vaulting horses learn to accept multiple vaulters in a variety of positions and movements on their back—as seen here as a vaulting group practices their advanced routine. Photo courtesy of Valley View Vaulters.*

Fig. 12.10 *Despite their extensive training that involves frequent longeing, vaulting horses enjoy their work, experience great longevity, and are rarely injured on the job.*

trained properly—longed both directions to keep them evened out, with pre-longeing exercises to train them to bend correctly, and with time limits on the longe line—it has been our experience that there are no more leg problems in a vaulting horse than there are with any other discipline for whatever reason; many vaulting horses last for many years. Our horses never have back injuries, either. We go the extra mile to take care of them."

Virginia adds, "We're seeing that the vaulting horses tend to live longer and perform longer. Our first horse died at 32 of cancer! He was still working up until the very end, and that's not an exception. The horses are walked in between vaulters, they get treats, they love the attention they get and will do whatever they can to perform correctly. All vaulting horses need to do is trust you and know what is going on around them. They don't have to deal with someone on their back telling them to do something differently all of a sudden. That's why the vaulting horses love vaulting."

Generally speaking, correct longeing can have a sedative, mellowing effect on a horse as a result of the low stress involved. "That's why I've said that problem horses make awesome vaulting horses," Rick says, "because they don't have to think; they just do the circles. Problem or troubled horses are made, not born—undesirable characteristics and attitudes can be changed. Training is a process, and if you go at it slowly, you'll always get a good horse."

Vaulting Basics

Learning to vault begins with compulsory exercises and, for those who wish to advance, progresses into freestyle (kür) movements, performed by individuals or teams with up to three vaulters on a horse at once. Freestyles include gymnastic and dance moves, even yoga postures!

A typical group vaulting lesson begins with groundwork and warm-up exercises (a practice that riders from all disciplines would be wise to adopt). Positions are introduced off the horse and practiced on the "vaulting barrel," where students simulate a mounted position and are taught to align properly. After vaulting on, barrel work includes practicing the basic seat (see p. 14) and other compulsory exercises, and concludes with vaulting off (fig. 12.11).

The student then moves to a live horse on the longe line, where acquiring rider basics is the main course (fig. 12.12). Work is done at the halt, walk, trot, and canter, based on ability.

Compulsory Exercises

The basic sitting position in vaulting is identical to the basic riding seat (see p. 14)

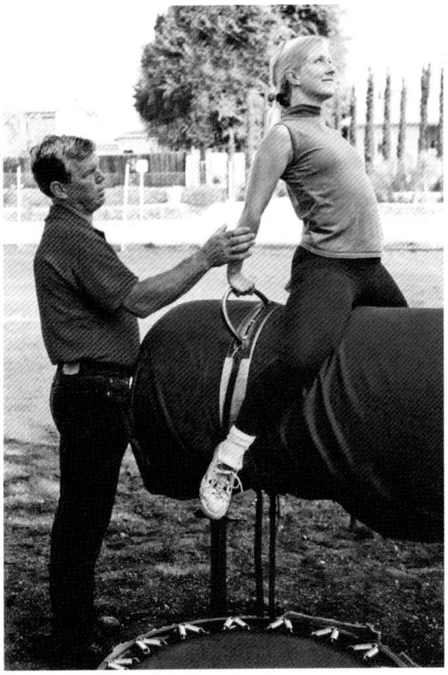

Fig. 12.11 *The vaulting barrel is the ideal venue to practice bodywork, sculpt the rider's position, establish seat balance, and learn new mounts, safe dismounts, and compulsory exercises.*

Fig. 12.12 *Once the rider has practiced a movement on the vaulting barrel, he moves to the live horse, where the handles on the surcingle offer security as he gains confidence and establishes his seat at the halt, walk, trot, and canter.*

"I learned early on that vaulting would help my riding. One of the first things I started doing in vaulting was working on my seat at the sitting trot. Vaulting increased my flexibility and I learned to sit the trot without the pain I once felt due to tightness in my hips. This increased flexibility has given me more confidence, a greater comfort level with various positions on a horse, and more options if I feel I might come off. But most importantly, these things give me more ways to NOT come off. I have been vaulting for about five years and it is fun, which is one of the main reasons I continue. The best thing about vaulting is a sense of pure joy. When you do something you never imagined you could do before, there is a sense of great joy and freedom, and the feeling that you can do anything."

Sheryl North, 47-year-old radiologist and novice-level eventer

Fig. 12.13 *Here, Elizabeth demonstrates the ideal vertical alignment: ear, shoulder, hip, and heel lined up, pelvis centered, legs lightly wrapped around the horse's barrel, torso upright, head poised upon neck, chin level with the ground. Her hands and arms are relaxed, and positioned as if she was holding the reins.*

Fig. 12.14 *"Basic Seat" with arms extended.*

with the exception of the toes, which point down, not up. The ideal vertical alignment has the vaulter's ear, shoulder, hip, and heel lined up, pelvis centered, legs lightly wrapped around the horse's barrel, torso upright, head poised upon neck, and chin level with the ground (fig. 12.13). The vaulter's hands on the grips are often in a position comparable to holding the reins, and as in riding, hands and arms should be relaxed, not clenching. This basic posture should be familiar to riders, as it is what we all aspire to achieve in the saddle.

Besides vaulting on while the horse is in motion, compulsory exercises include:

- "Basic Seat" with arms extended (fig. 12.14).
- "Flag," a posture that includes kneeling on the horse and extending the inside arm and outside leg (fig. 12.15).
- "Mill," which involves making a complete 360-degree turn, momentarily sitting facing in each of the four directions (fig. 12.16).
- "Scissors," a two-part flight movement that first involves swinging the legs above the horse's back and then crossing one over the other to land sitting backward on the horse (fig. 12.17). The sequence is repeated to return to sitting astride.
- "Stand," which begins by kneeling, then hopping up onto both feet with arms extended (fig. 12.18).
- "Flank," another two-part flight movement that begins with swinging the legs above the horse's back and concludes with dismounting to the outside of the vaulting circle (fig. 12.19). This is somewhat similar to a rider's emergency dismount, see p. 69.

Riders may have difficulty believing such positions are feasible, but that is the amazing thing—once you try vaulting, you may very well achieve what you never thought possible and far exceed the challenges of the basic riding seat, which suddenly seems easier. As confidence grows, you'll feel comfortable letting go of the grips and maintaining seat balance in all three gaits. With such rapid success, you may wish to explore more exciting postures on horseback and take advantage of what vaulting has to offer (figs. 12.20 A & B).

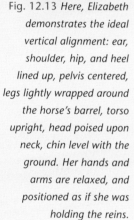

Fig. 12.15 *"Flag."*

Fig. 12.16 *The "Mill," which is similar to the rider exercise Around the World (see p. 121).*

Fig. 12.17 *"Scissors."*

Fig. 12.18 *"Stand." Photo courtesy of Valley View Vaulters.*

Fig. 12.19 *"Flank."*

Figs. 12.20 A & B
Advanced vaulters achieve sophisticated levels of balance, strength, and self-control. Vaulting for riders can help you transfer the same confidence, ability, and seat independence to your work in the saddle.

So, Where Do I Sign Up?

As I mentioned at the beginning of this chapter, vaulting in a group setting is an excellent prerequisite for conventional riding lessons, regardless of age. "Vaulting for riders" classes, clinics, and private lessons are available for adults as well as children. In addition to refining basic riding skills safely and directly, these classes impart an array of intangible benefits, such as courage and confidence. I encourage riders and instructors to explore the resources available at vaulting clubs nationwide: superb longe horses, experienced longeurs, and instructors well versed in longe lessons and seat development.

For example, Rick and Virginia Hawthorne of Valley View Vaulters in California offer two-hour classes during which a group of up to ten equestrians at the same skill level shares one horse, each individual receiving up to three practices on the longe horse. These affordable group lessons include groundwork, barrel work, longeing, and offer a direct route to achieving rider basics, with the added bonus of working with a very experienced longeing team.

Similar learning environments are becoming more readily available as vaulting clubs multiply across the nation. However, "vaulting for riders" may still be scarce in some parts of the country. Over that, I share Francie Dougherty's musings, "I'm wondering why there isn't a vaulting barrel, vaulting tack, and at least one vaulting horse at every training barn. Especially those places that teach beginner riders!"

Virginia Hawthorne adds, "In Europe, riders often learn to vault before they learn to ride. It's basics: how to be good to yourself, how to be good to your horse. And we should adopt that here—every stable that teaches riding should have vaulting, or know where to get it. Vaulting for riders...I would say that's as important as helmets for riders."

"When vaulting was suggested as a supplement to riding lessons, my first reaction was, 'At my age!?' I envisioned back flips, human pyramids, and gymnastics on horseback...but the more I learned about it, the more it made perfect sense. As a novice rider, I found that trying to achieve balance while learning to control the horse at the same time led to a cycle of miscommunication and frustration as horses responded to every one of my unintentional aids. Vaulting separates the tasks of controlling the horse from developing my seat, taking me out of my head and into my body. It increases awareness, teaches me to concentrate on flexibility, release tension, and understand how I affect the horse. I've also done my share of gymnastics—backward roll dismounts, trotting on knees, even standing in walk—things I never expected to do! It's all part of the fun and challenge that keeps me coming back. As I gain more balance and confidence with vaulting, I am amazed at how quickly this transfers into my riding lessons."

Janine Pizano, 46-year-old software engineer and recreational rider

Conclusion

As I pointed out in the early pages of this chapter, a vaulter can accomplish the basic seat and more within weeks, and this begs the question: what are we missing as riders when we struggle to accomplish our basic seat, sometimes for years, on a riding horse? The answer is: *longeing*. Simply put, with more opportunities to longe, we can achieve our basic seat in far less time.

APPENDIX 2

Old Ways in a New World: Longeing's History and Modern Renaissance

The Italian Riding Masters of the Renaissance have left written descriptions of the preparation and suppling of their horses by unmounted work with the lunge, the long-reins, the pillars, the whip and the long cane. It is very likely that these methods were not new at the time, and that these Riding Masters had been taught them by their own masters who were themselves heirs to a long tradition. The lunge, with the whip, and with or without the cavesson is still in use almost everywhere.

GENERAL DECARPENTRY

The Cavalry's Influence

An old world tradition, longeing originated in Europe as a method of training war horses and soldiers. Over the centuries, the art of longeing was passed down orally from riding master to student, and throughout the world cavalry training often included this foundation.

Although military officers on both sides of the Atlantic did debate how best to teach equitation to their cavalrymen (some advocated high school methods as practiced by the Spanish Riding School—see p. 226—while others favored a lesser degree of collection), longeing was frequently employed as a judicious training method. A first-hand account of how longeing was used in one particular military setting is offered by Captain Roy Elderkin, former Chief Equitation Instructor for the Grey's Scouts in Rhodesia (1975–1982), possibly the last known mounted infantry unit in history (fig. 13.1). Elderkin reveals that training the recruits involved a condensed program—three weeks of longeing, two hours per day. During the first week riders were longed *with* stirrups to build confidence, and over the next two weeks they longed *without* stirrups to hone seat skills. This system demanded mental concentration and physical effort, but expeditiously produced riders with supple, balanced seats and effective equitation. And living up to their high standards of training, the Grey's Scouts instructors were themselves longed monthly to prevent bad riding habits.

Fig. 13.1 *Captain Roy Elderkin, a former dressage judge, used longeing to expedite the training of the Rhodesian Grey's Scouts and develop riders with balanced seats and effective aids. Photo courtesy of Roy Elderkin.*

Modern Battles

The horse world changed dramatically when mounted armies were outmoded and military riding academies ceased to exist. In 1971, several decades after this transition, a conference of international riding instructors took place for the first time, attended by representatives from most European countries, the U.K., Russia, and the U.S. Its purpose is best described in this excerpt from the opening speech by the President of the British Equestrian Federation (BEF), Colonel Sir Michael Ansell:

> *I believe that throughout the world there is almost an explosive growth in the number of persons wishing to ride. It is difficult to assess why this has come about. Perhaps it may be that with shorter working days there is consequently more leisure. Perhaps it may be the desire to take part in some form of "risk" sport.*
>
> *I am confident that we all agree that riding and the care of horses and ponies can do nothing but good for the building of character. But any sport or activity of this kind is costly, and the normal person does not like to waste his money and, therefore, in order to get the best out of it one should try to do it correctly. Whether it be tennis, golf or riding one must learn the best way to take part, and so get the maximum pleasure. The better one rides, the more fun it is.*

In the pre-war years we were fortunate, as much instruction was provided by officers and non-commissioned officers from "mounted" regiments of the services. However, with the disappearance of the horse from the services, this source of supply has gradually dried up. There can be little doubt that there is now a world shortage of top instructors and the object of this three-day convention is to find out how each of us in our various countries gets over this problem—how the many riders are being provided with instruction and how the instructors are trained.

Several decades have passed and this situation has not been resolved. Even though we no longer ride into battle, many of us still "battle" as riders—fighting our horses, fighting ourselves, and blocking our own efforts, often without understanding why—which can make riding a real struggle. Many modern riders perceive riding as a series of cues and maneuvers, and building a secure foundation in basics takes a lower priority than excitement, entertainment, risk-taking, and competition. In addition, instructors often allow students to "run before they can walk," focusing more on riding mechanics or developing arena navigational skills than on crafting a rider's seat and position—and thus putting the safety and well-being of both horse and rider at risk.

The truth is longeing has been overlooked as a rider-training tool. Riders who "train overseas" are often envied by their peers, but many an experienced rider has, once there, suddenly found himself at the end of a longe line under the scrutiny of a European trainer intent on filling in educational gaps and correcting faulty equitation. Riders should not have to travel abroad for seat development and a full repertoire of basic skills, nor does the average equestrian have the means to do so. A sensible solution is to revive longeing in our riding schools and stables, and therefore enhance our instructional systems for developing competent riders in every discipline.

Equestrians need not subscribe to any particular philosophy to profit from longeing. Even the most casual, recreational riders can benefit from this tradition that more directly imparts balance and *feel* for safe, enjoyable riding. And though there are novices, amateurs, children, and parents of child riders, even instructors who think they are "beyond" longe lessons, longeing is *not* for beginners only. This belief is limiting and reveals a lack of knowledge.

And then there are the innumerable benefits horses gain from rider longeing. The concept of being attuned to the nature and welfare of the horse was first documented by General Xenophon, a master of horsemanship in Ancient Greece, whose expertise on riding and training war horses nearly 2,500 years ago is still referenced today. As a direct opportunity for seat development, longeing upholds Xenophon's teachings—on the longe line, we can avoid making mistakes while preserv-

Many of our riders are coming up through their riding educations without a firm training in the basic balanced position, resulting all too often in disastrous results for both horses and riders.

JILL HASSLER-SCOOP AND KATHY KELLY

ing the well-being of the horse, as it is he who suffers most under an ineffective seat.

The Renaissance

Although the standards and discipline once cultivated in military settings is fading from modern equestrian culture, the Spanish Riding School (SRS) survives, as it has for over 400 years, offering a thriving link to our classical past. In fact, it may have helped inspire a renaissance, as evidenced by the excitement generated by present-day Spanish Riding School clinicians offering longe lessons to riders all over the world. In June 2005, *Dressage Today* magazine reported on the teachings of Andreas Hausberger, a member of the SRS since 1984. "Hausberger says American riders in his clinics are waking up to the value of longe lessons," writes Jec Ballou. "He says many clinic participants are excited to be put on the longe line at his suggestion...an occasional longe lesson is invaluable for all riders...it allows them to work on their athleticism, which is the crux of a good riding position and influence over the horse. It gives them a way to isolate exercises that improve coordination, agility and balance—necessary tools for all riders."

The old ways will always be with us-every time we mount and dismount from the left, or ride with our feet in the stirrups and a bit in our horse's mouth, we are keeping with tradition. Longeing can be of great service to horsemen and horsewomen today, and we must only put this technique into a context we understand for it to be "new" again.

All the great masters have gone through all the mistakes, and would like so much to help others avoid them. If they thought that beginners should make these mistakes, or that there was some benefit to them, they would not so uniformly and vehemently plead to others to avoid them.

WALTER ZETTL

Recommended Resources

Developing Rider Basics

BOOKS & DVDS

Benedik, Linda and Veronica Wirth. *Yoga for Equestrians: A New Path for Achieving Union with the Horse* (Book—US: Trafalgar Square Books, UK: Kenilworth Press)

Benedik, Linda. *Yoga & Riding Techniques for Equestrians* (VHS/DVD—Trafalgar Square Books)

Benson, Herbert. *The Relaxation Response* (Book—HarperCollins Publishers)

Davis, Ph.D., Martha, Elizabeth Robbins Eshelman, MSW, Matthew McKay, Ph.D. *The Relaxation & Stress Reduction Workbook* (Book—New Harbinger Publications)

Farhi, Donna. *The Breathing Book: Good Health and Vitality Through Essential Breath Work* (Book—Owl Books/Henry Holt and Company, LLC)

Hassler-Scoop, Jill K. and Kathy Kelly Ph.D, et al. (*including a chapter by Linda Benedik*). *The Riding Experience & Beyond: Personal Development for Riders* (Book—Goals Unlimited Press)

Hölzel, Petra and Wolfgang. *Learn to Ride Using Sports Psychology* (Book—US: Trafalgar Square Books, UK: Kenilworth Press)

Lasater, Ph. D., P.T., Judith. *Relax and Renew: Restful Yoga for Stressful Times* (Book—Rodmell Press)

McKay Ph.D., Matthew. *The Daily Relaxer: Relax Your Body, Calm Your Mind, & Refresh Your Spirit* (Book—New Harbinger Publications)

Novak, Janice. *Posture, Get It Straight! Look Ten Years Younger and Ten Pounds Thinner and Feel Better than Ever!* (Book—Expert Publishing ; DVD—Janice Novak Health Education Services, http://www.improveyourposture.com)

Rentz, Kristen. *YogaNap: Restorative Poses for Deep Relaxation* (Book—Marlowe & Company)

Schinke, Robert J. and Beverly Schinke. *Focused Riding* (Book—Compass Equestrian Limited)

Vilga, Edward. *Yoga In Bed: 20 Asanas to do in Pajamas* (Book/DVD—Running Press Book Publishers)

Von Dietz, Susanne. *Balance in Movement: The Seat of the Rider* (Book/DVD—US: Trafalgar Square Books, UK: JA Allen & Co.)

WEB SITES

Linda Benedik. http://www.harmonywithhorses.com.

Yoga Journal. http://www.yogajournal.com.

Desktop Yoga. http://www.mydailyyoga.com.

American Society for the Alexander Technique. http://www.alexandertech.org.

American Vaulting Association. http://www.americanvaulting.org.

AUDIO/CDS: GUIDED RELAXATION

Guided audio programs soothe mind-body and induce a deep relaxed state, often sleep. Audio resources can help prepare you for riding, however, *do not* listen to guided relaxations behind the wheel of a car. If you are looking for sounds to relax while driving, choose ambient music, with or without subliminal programming, such as *Effortless Relaxation* (Inner Peace Music) or *Music for Healing & Unwinding: A Musical Prescription for Balance and Harmony*, both featuring recording artist Steven Halpern, a pioneer in the field of sound healing (The Relaxation Company). Or, try self-hypnosis programs such as: *Improving Athletic Performance, Dropping Fear and Anxiety, Stress Reduction,* and more, available from Leigh Martin, M.S., Director of the Santa Susanna Center for Hypnosis and Education (http://www.susannacenter.com).

When you can dedicate yourself to stress release in a quiet environment, try these guided audio programs:

Lite, Lori. *Indigo Dreams: Adult Relaxation: Real Techniques for Real People Feeling Real Stress and Anxiety* (Lite Books, http://www.litebooks.net)

McManus, PT, MA, MS, Carolyn with Stella Benson, Harpist. *Relaxation Body Scan & Guided Imagery for Well-Being* (Carolyn McManus, http://www.carolynmcmanus.com)

Miller, M.D., Emmett and Steven Halpern. *Letting Go of Stress: Four Effective Techniques for Relaxation and Stress Reduction* (Inner Peace Music)

Pitkoff, M.S., Barry. *The Gift of Relaxation - Stress Relief, Sleep, Wellness* (Center for Human Potential, http://www.center4hp.com)

Longeing the Horse

BOOKS & DVDS

Fielder, Paul. *All About Lungeing* – Allen Photographic Guide No. 20 (Book—US: Trafalgar Square Books, UK: J.A. Allen & Co.)

German National Federation. *Lungeing – The German Riding and Driving System: Book 6*, The Official Instruction Handbook of the German National Federation (Book—US: Half Halt Press, UK: Kenilworth Press)

Harris, Susan. *Horse Gaits, Balance and Movement* (Book—Howell Book House)

Harris, Susan. *The USPC Guide to Longeing and Ground Training* (Book—Howell Book House)

Hempfling, Klaus Ferdinand. *Dancing with Horses: The Art of Body Language* (Book/DVD—US: Trafalgar Square Books, UK: J.A. Allen & Co.)

Hill, Cherry. *Longeing & Long Lining the English & Western Horse* (Book—Howell Book House)

Hill, Cherry. *101 Longeing & Long Lining Exercises* (Book—Howell Book House)

Kapitzke, Gerhard. *The Bit and the Reins* (Book—US: Trafalgar Square Books, UK: J.A. Allen & Co.)

Klimke: Ingrid and Reiner. *The New Basic Training of the Young Horse* (Book—US: Trafalgar Square Books, UK: J.A. Allen & Co.)

Politz, Gerhard, ed. *USDF Lungeing Manual* (Book—http://www.usdf.org)

Stainer, Sylvia. *The Art of Lungeing* (Book—US: Trafalgar Square Books, UK: J.A. Allen & Co.)

United States Pony Club, Inc. *USPC Guide to Longeing* (DVD—http://www.ponyclub.org/)

Bibliography

American Medical Equestrian Association - Safe Riders Foundation. "Helmet Safety." 2006. URL: http://www.ameaonline.org/helmet_safety.html

Ballou, Jec A. "Longeing at the Spanish Riding School." *Dressage Today*. June 2005, p. 67–72.

Belasik, Paul. *Dressage for the 21st Century*. North Pomfret, VT: Trafalgar Square Books, 2001.

Benedik, Linda and Veronica Wirth. *Yoga for Equestrians*. North Pomfret, VT: Trafalgar Square Books, 2000.

The British Horse Society and The Pony Club. *The Instructor's Handbook*. Pony Club, 1985.

Bundesministerium für Land- und Forstwirtschaft. *The Spanish Riding School*. 1966.

de Kunffy, Charles. *Dressage Principles Illuminated*. North Pomfret, VT: Trafalgar Square Books, 2002.

de Kunffy, Charles. *Dressage Questions Answered*. New York: Arco Publishing, 1984.

Decarpentry, General. *Academic Equitation*. North Pomfret, VT: Trafalgar Square Books, 2001.

Diggle, Martin. *Teaching the Mature Rider*. London: J.A. Allen, 1993.

Elkins, Elizabeth. "U.S. Dressage: Staking a Claim at Home and Abroad." *Dressage Today*. September 2004, p. 35–39.

Faulkner, MD, Robert. "Vaulting Safety and the Use of Protective Headgear." *American Medical Equestrian Association News*. May 1996. Volume VI, Number 2. URL: http://tarlton.law.utexas.edu/dawson/amea/may96nws.htm

Fielder, Paul. *All About Lungeing*. London: J.A. Allen, 1999.

German National Equestrian Federation. *Lungeing, The German Riding and Driving System: Book 6*. Addington, Buckingham: Kenilworth Press, 1990.

German National Equestrian Federation. *The Principles of Riding*. Addington, Buckingham: Kenilworth Press, 1997.

German National Equestrian Federation. *Vaulting, The German Riding and Driving System: Book 3*. Addington, Buckingham: Kenilworth Press, 1992.

Harris, Charles. *Fundamentals of Riding: Theory & Practice, The Official Manual of Association of British Riding Schools*. London: J.A. Allen, 1996.

Harris, Susan. *Horse Gaits, Balance and Movement*. New York: Howell Book House, 1993.

Harris, Susan. *The USPC Guide to Longeing and Ground Training*. New York: Wiley Publishing, 1997.

Hassler-Scoop, Jill and Kathy Kelly, Ph.D. *Equestrian Education: Professional Development for Instructors*. Huson, MT: Goals Unlimited Press, 2002.

Hassler-Scoop, Jill and Kathy Kelly, Ph.D. *The Riding Experience & Beyond: Personal Development for Riders*. Huson, MT: Goals Unlimited Press, 2002.

Hempfling, Klaus Ferdinand. *Dancing with Horses: The Art of Body Language*. North Pomfret, VT: Trafalgar Square Books, 2001.

Henriques, Pegotty. *Balanced Riding: A Way to Find the Correct Seat*. Addington, Buckingham: Kenilworth Press, 2000.

Hill, Cherry. *Longeing and Long Lining the English and Western Horse: A Total Program*. New York: Howell Book House, 1999.

Hillsdon, Penny. *Pathfinder Dressage: The Philosophy and Training Techniques of the World's Top Trainers*. London: J.A. Allen, 2000.

Hölzel, Petra and Wolfgang. *Learn to Ride Using Sports Psychology*. North Pomfret, VT: Trafalgar Square Books, 1996.

Inderwick, Sheila. *Lungeing the Horse & Rider.* Newton Abbot, Devon: David & Charles, 1977.

Kapitzke, Gerhard. *The Bit and the Reins.* North Pomfret, VT: Trafalgar Square Books, 2004.

Kottas, Arthur. *The Art of Classical Dressage, Part I: Basics – Lungeing the Horse.* C.H.S.Video Productions.

Knowles, Josephine. *Teaching Riding.* London: J.A. Allen, 1999.

Kyrklund, Kyra and Jytte Lemkow. *Dressage with Kyra: The Kyra Kyrklund Training Method.* North Pomfret, VT: Trafalgar Square Books, 1998.

Langworst, Rebecca. "Longeing for Suppleness." *Dressage Today.* March 1997, p. 44–49.

Lewis, Anne. *Teaching Basic Riding.* London: J.A. Allen, 1988.

Loch, Sylvia. *The Classical Seat: A Guide for the Everyday Rider.* Haslemere, Surry: Horse & Rider Magazine, D.J. Murphy Ltd., 1988.

Marczak, Julian & Karen Bush. *The Principles of Teaching Riding: The Official Manual of the Association of British Riding Schools.* Newton Abbot, Devon: David & Charles, 2001.

Meyners, Eckart. *Fit for Riding, Exercises for Riders and Vaulters.* Middletown, MD: Half Halt Press, 1992.

Ottevaere, James A. *American Military Horsemanship.* Bloomington, IN: AuthorHouse, 2005.

Podhajsky, Alois. *The Complete Training of Horse and Rider in the Principles of Classical Horsemanship.* North Hollywood: Wilshire Book Co., 1967.

Podhajsky, Alois. *The Riding Teacher.* North Pomfret, VT: Trafalgar Square Books, 1993.

Politz, Gerhard (editor). *USDF Lungeing Manual.* United States Dressage Federation, 1996.

Richter, Judy. *The Longeing Book.* New York: Prentice Hall Press, 1986.

Sagar, Ann. *Vaulting: Develop Your Riding and Gymnastic Skills.* London: B.T. Batsford Ltd., 1993.

Schaefer, Ruth Sabine. *Feeling Dressage: How to Achieve Harmony with Your Horse.* Lexington, KY: The Blood Horse, 2003.

Schmelzer, Angelika. *Lungeing – Be safe and proficient.* Brunsbek: Cadmos Verlag, 2004.

Schut-Kery, Sabine with Louisa Zai. "Take Charge of Your Dressage Education." *Dressage Today.* August 2005, p. 43–46.

Serber, Ellen. "Yoga and the Stress Response." 2006. URL: http://www.mydailyyoga.com/yoga/yoga_and_stress.html

Sivewright, Molly. *Lessons on the Lunge for Horse and Rider.* London: Ward Lock, 1996.

Society of the Military Horse. "Public Forum – General Topics and Archives." 2006.URL: http://www.militaryhorse.org.

Stanier, Sylvia. *The Art of Lungeing.* London: J.A. Allen, 1993.

Stedwell, Paki. *Vaulting: Gymnastics on Horseback.* New York: Julian Messner, 1980.United States Pony Club. *Vaulting Handbook.* Lexington, KY: USPC, Inc., 1999.

von Dietze, Susanne. *Balance in Movement: How to Achieve the Perfect Seat.* North Pomfret, VT: Trafalgar Square Books, 2005.

Williams, Dorian. *Great Riding Schools of the World.* New York: Macmillan, 1975.

Williams, Moyra. *Understanding Nervousness in Horse and Rider.* London: J.A. Allen, 1990.

Windisch-Graetz, Mathilde. *The Spanish Riding School.* New York: A.S. Barnes and Co., 1966.

Wood, Perry. *Real Riding: How to Ride in Harmony with Horses.* Addington, Buckingham: Kenilworth Press, 2002.

Xenophon. *The Art of Horsemanship.* London: J.A. Allen, 1962.

Zettl, Walter. *Dressage in Harmony.* Boonsboro, MD: Half Halt Press, 1998.

Acknowledgments

I'd like to recognize my early teachers: Thanks to Steve Benedek of Camp Olympic in Maryland for the disciplined riding, adventurous cross-country, and a command that will ring in my ears forever: "*SIT on that horse*!" To Debbie Johnson for introducing me to dressage as a teenager, deepening my seat, and providing mounted exercises I continue to pass on to students. To Patricia Shipley for the many apprentice, internship, and clinic opportunities. To Lake Erie College for my academic equestrian education, to instructors Gretchen Singleton, Sylvia Wilson, and Lynn Klisavage who was my coach in the dressage Prix de Villes and whose commitment and style were a great influence.

Thanks also to all my riding students, for enabling me to hone my craft. And, to my trainers, the masters whose legacy remains an inspiration, and all my equine teachers, I am forever grateful.

Many played a role in creating this book—with much appreciation, I thank Trafalgar Square Books for the opportunity to present this program, and to Caroline Robbins, Martha Cook, and Rebecca Didier for working to streamline and clarify my ideas. A world of thanks to Mary Markoff of Calleva Equestrian Education Program in Maryland for her generous support, encouragement, and optimism; and to her staff, particularly instructors Jenny Cordrey and Christa Mobley for "modeling" in multiple photo shoots and Megan Draheim for her generous photographic contributions, to working students Sarah Dolson for helping "behind the scenes," Samantha Albotra and Mikell McDonald for taking part in the photos, and to rider and photographer Kathy Andrle for her artistic eye.

Many thanks to Rick and Virginia Hawthorne of Valley View Vaulters in California for their enthusiasm and assistance, to Sheryl North for introducing me to "vaulting for riders," to Janine Pizano for sharing her vaulting experiences and helping with photos. Thanks to Francie Dougherty for her passion and insights, and to the Great Falls Vaulters in Maryland for the photo opportunity.

Much appreciation to my associates at The Society of the Military Horse, especially Mounted Police and Military Equitation Instructor Ron Smith for his support and knowledge, historical and contemporary. To Captain Roy Elderkin for generously revealing his experiences and expertise on longeing, to Joe Sullivan for his hospitality, and to author Jim Ottevaere for kindly providing insights on longeing.

Family members and friends also generously contributed to this project—thanks to my sister Sharon and nieces Sierra and Marissa Mondin for helping with the photo shoot, to Greg Mondin for his technical line drawings, to my brother Vince, Gerri, and Allie Benedik for affording a private "writing studio," to Valerie Helfrich and Uncle Bob Benedik for transportation assistance, and to my brother Steve (Boss) Benedik for helping with the horses. To friend, artist, and rider Rebecca Burke for her interpretive illustrations, to my musical accomplice David Kaufman for the walk/trot/canter charts, and to A.K., Julia Bruns, and Deirdre Lewis for their contributions to the photos. To my "cousin," author and rider Holiday Reinhorn for helping with things too many to mention…and for inspiring the phoenix to rise again. To all who have supported my work, thank you!

Y como siempre, muchas gracias y mucho amor para mi esposo, Gerardo Espitia.

Index

Page numbers in *italic* indicate illustrations or photographs.